COFFEE AND COMMUNITY

MAYA FARMERS
AND FAIR-TRADE MARKETS

SARAH LYON

UNIVERSITY PRESS OF COLORADO

© 2011 by the University Press of Colorado

Published by the University Press of Colorado
5589 Arapahoe Avenue, Suite 206C
Boulder, Colorado 80303

The University Press of Colorado is a proud member of
the Association of American University Presses.

The University Press of Colorado is a cooperative publishing enterprise supported, in part,
by Adams State College, Colorado State University, Fort Lewis College, Mesa State College,
Metropolitan State College of Denver, University of Colorado, University of Northern
Colorado, and Western State College of Colorado.

∞ The paper used in this publication meets the minimum requirements of the American
National Standard for Information Sciences—Permanence of Paper for Printed Library
Materials. ANSI Z39.48-1992

Library of Congress Cataloging-in-Publication Data

Lyon, Sarah.
  Coffee and community : Maya farmers and fair-trade markets / Sarah Lyon.
     p. cm.
  Includes bibliographical references and index.
  ISBN 978-1-60732-056-2 (cloth : alk. paper) — ISBN 978-1-60732-057-9 (pbk. : alk. paper)
— ISBN 978-1-60732-058-6 (e-book) 1. Coffee industry—Guatemala. 2. Coffee—Social
aspects—Guatemala. 3. Competition, Unfair—Guatemala. I. Title.
  HD9199.G82L96 2010
  338.1'7373097281—dc22
                              2010042218
Design by Daniel Pratt

20   19   18   17   16   15   14   13   12   11   10 9 8 7 6 5 4 3 2 1

Contents

Acknowledgments

In fall 2005, several months after completing my Ph.D., I attended a Wenner-Gren conference for young researchers at which the foundation's president, Leslie Aiello, sagely reminded us in attendance that our research is not complete until it is published. I have often repeated those words to myself over the past five years as I struggled to balance the seemingly endless demands of work and life. I have come to realize that my research was incomplete: I owed a large debt to the many people who selflessly offered me their time and shared their invaluable thoughts with me over the course of interviews and informal conversations conducted between 2000 and 2006 in Guatemala, Seattle, and Vermont. More than anything, this book represents a follow through on the promise I made to them. Out of respect for their confidentiality I do not name them in the text; however, it is my greatest hope that they know how thankful I am for their contributions. I am especially grateful to the people of San Juan La Laguna and the members of La Voz who so graciously welcomed me into their community, cooperative, and homes. They taught me more than the practicalities of organic coffee production—from them I learned the importance of coupling a strong work ethic with a generosity of spirit and the enduring significance of an agrarian lifestyle in an increasingly complex and urban world.

In addition, this research would not have been possible without the assistance and support of a variety of individuals in various organizations. A sincere thank you to Rick Peyser and the many employees at Green Mountain Coffee Roasters who opened their office doors to me during the course of my two research trips to Vermont. I especially thank Steve Sabol and Chuck Jones for allowing me to tag along on several employee coffee tours in 2002 and 2003. A special thanks as well to Karen and Francisco at Elan Organic Coffees. Prior to his becoming the Guatemalan Minister of Agriculture, I was lucky enough to meet Edin Barrientos at the Guatemala City USAID office. He generously shared with me his knowledge of the Small Coffee Farmer Improvement Program and provided critical support at the earliest stages of this research by first introducing me to La Voz. In addition, I thank the many Anacafé employees who agreed to interviews in both Guatemala City and San Pedro and the countless NGO employees and members of the boards of directors at cooperatives across the highlands who sat down with me and shared their knowledge and understanding of fair trade and coffee. Genuine thanks to the extended Richardson family for providing lodging, advice, and company during the months of research in Seattle. This research would not have been possible without the interest and support of the members of the Northwest Sustainable Coffee Campaign, including the many coffee roasters, small and large, who consented to interviews and the employees and volunteers at Seattle Audubon, the Songbird Foundation, the Church Council of Greater Seattle, TransFair, and Global Exchange.

Special thanks to Eric Lindland, Matt Dudgeon, and especially Jenna Waites for helping to keep me sane during the trials and tribulations of fourteen months of dissertation fieldwork. Peggy Barlett continues to provide unrelenting support to this day, and without her early interest and strong commitment to social and economic justice this project would have not been possible. Thanks also to Carla Freeman, Rick Dolan, Silke von Essenwein, and Faidra Papasaviliou at Emory University and Laura Raynolds at Colorado State. I consider myself lucky to have landed at the University of Kentucky, surrounded by such interesting colleagues who appreciate the ongoing importance of research on livelihoods in a changing world. Special thanks to Erin Koch (for the reading and free babysitting),

Cristina Alcalde, Tad Mutersbaugh, Lisa Cliggett, Peter Little, Sue Roberts, Lucinda Romberg, Srimati Basu, and Emily Burril for providing reading labor and advice over the years. I am ever grateful to Walter Little for his close read of the manuscript and the many valuable suggestions he made for improvement. Thanks also to Ted Fischer and the anonymous reviewers for their suggestions. Finally, thanks to Darrin Pratt and the staff at the University Press of Colorado.

Without the ongoing support of my extended family this research would not have been possible. Thanks to Olivia, who is always ready to take a walk when it is time to step away from work. Thanks to Ruth Anne for funding that first trip to Guatemala way back when and all the support, financial and otherwise, over the years. Thanks to Chris for starting my lifelong love affair with books and for convincing me there were already enough lawyers in the world. To Marcel and Stephanie, without your unending help I would have abandoned this book and current research projects long ago to the constant distractions of working motherhood. To Mike and Harper I am eternally grateful for all those distractions—this would all be meaningless without you.

COFFEE AND COMMUNITY

1

Introduction

Fair trade is a form of alternative trade that seeks to improve the position of disempowered small-scale farmers through trade as a means of development. The movement, which promotes labeling, certification, and consumer action, rejects the narrow view of third-world producers as victims and instead emphasizes the role that northern consumption can play in their economic empowerment and well-being. Its supporters argue that it contests the conventional agro-food system and the exploitative relations of production characterizing it. The growing popularity of fair-trade coffee reflects our own cultural assumptions and anxieties surrounding free trade, corporate globalization, economic injustices, and the politicization of everyday consumption practices. In recent years, the United States has emerged as the world's largest fair-trade market. In 2008 over 87 million pounds of fair-trade-certified coffee were imported into the United States from more than 250 producer organizations around the world. TransFair USA estimates that in 2008 alone sales of fair-trade-certified coffee in the United States generated more than $32 million in additional income for coffee farmers (TransFair 2009). Although overall coffee sales are stagnant, specialty coffee sales have grown at 13 percent per year over the past decade, and certified coffees, such as fair trade, account for close to 4 percent of the world market (Giovannucci and Villalobos 2007). Fair-trade products on the whole still represent a minor share of the world market, currently about US$4 billion; however, the worldwide retail value of fair-trade sales increased 22 percent in 2008 (FLO 2009).

In 1977, long before the fair-trade coffee market began its rapid expansion, a small group of Tz'utujil Maya coffee farmers met under the shade of a ceiba tree in the center of their Guatemalan village, San Juan La Laguna, located on the shores of Lake Atitlan. They formed a cooperative that day, La Voz Que Clama en el Desierto ("A Voice Crying Out in the Wilderness"), which today sells more than eight containers of fair-trade and organic-certified coffee to the second-largest specialty coffee roaster in the United States, Green Mountain Coffee Roasters. In turn, Green Mountain retails the members' coffee to consumers like you and me. They sell the coffee online and in offices, supermarkets, and McDonald's outlets. The growing market share of fair-trade and organic products in U.S. retail outlets indicates that as consumers we increasingly accept the notion that our individual shopping habits can radically alter the conditions of production in distant locations. We are told that simply by sipping our morning cup of organic fair-trade coffee we are encouraging environmentally friendly agricultural methods, community development, fair prices, and shortened commodity chains. The pictures of smiling, dark-skinned farmers adorning coffee bags and decorating corner coffee shops readily convince us that, in the words of Green Mountain Coffee Roasters, we can "Taste a Different World."

The central goal of this book is to explore this "different" world by employing fair-trade coffee as an entry point for analyzing what it means for producers, consumers, and intermediaries alike to have an identity that is simultaneously embedded in local circumstances *and* shaped by a growing role in global spheres of exchange and commodity flows. As the privileged consumers of fair-trade coffee, it is easy to imagine that we are the primary actors in this commodity circuit, for without our interest and disposable income, the market would not exist. However, the members of La Voz, whose lives seem so distant from our own, work together with coffee roasters, importers, and certifiers in the United States to construct coffee's meaning and the ways that it is marketed and consumed in coffee shops and homes across the country. *Coffee and Community* critically evaluates the collective action

and combined efforts of fair-trade network participants to construct a new
economic reality, demonstrating that while fair-trade confers many positive Thesis
benefits to small farmer communities, there are also significant drawbacks
to their participation in this transnational commodity circuit.

SO, COFFEE GROWS ON TREES?

Before beginning this research on coffee in 2000, my knowledge of coffee
production and trade was limited to a vague notion that Colombia's coffee
was high quality (like most Americans my age, I had been bombarded with
advertisements of Juan Valdez and his cute burro since childhood) and that
the owners of Central America's vast coffee plantations were somehow responsible for the violent civil wars that region experienced during my youth.
I smugly patted myself on the back for being a sophisticated consumer who
shunned the cans of Folgers and Maxwell House that sat in my parents'
kitchen cabinets in favor of the colorful (and significantly more expensive)
bags on the shelves of the local natural-foods store. I always bought my
coffee on the go from the "gourmet" shops, such as Starbucks and Caribou,
adjacent to campus—I would never deign to show up in class carrying a generic cup of coffee from the cafeteria. More recently I have listened to many
coffee consumers share their firm conviction with me that Ethiopian coffee
is the highest quality, that Jamaican Blue Mountain and Hawaiian Kona coffee must be superior because they certainly cost more, or that they *would*
buy fair-trade or organic coffee but it simply does not taste as good. Like me,
very few of them knew that coffee grows on trees, in very specific locations,
and that quality has much more to do with altitude and processing than it
does with sleek advertising campaigns and high prices. As with so many
commodities, we consumers are largely ignorant of the complex web of
ecology, capitalism, and human relationships that delivers these dark beans
to our kitchens and favorite neighborhood coffee shops.

The ecology of the coffee plant makes it a tropical commodity. For
example, *Arabica*, the variety of coffee marketed as specialty or gourmet
(and produced by the members of La Voz), requires between seventeen and
twenty-five degrees Celsius and a minimum of 1200 to 1500 millimeters of
annual rainfall with an approximately three-month-long dry season (Talbot
2004:31). When planted at lower altitudes in the tropics, *Arabica* is suscep-
tible to disease and fails to produce the desirable "hard bean" found in the
colder climates, which encourage a slower-maturing fruit. On the other
hand, *Robusta* coffee, commonly used in conventional coffee blends, can be
grown at much lower altitudes (e.g., in Brazil and Vietnam). The certified-

Process

coffee commodity network, which is the subject of this study, begins in San Juan's patchwork of small coffee fields and ends in the cups of U.S. consumers. Producing high-quality, certified coffee requires almost daily attention. In San Juan, as in many Latin American coffee communities, this labor primarily falls to the male heads of households and, depending on the size of the family's holdings, their sons. However, during the coffee harvest between December and March, wives, younger children, and, if necessary, hired *mozos* (day laborers), work together to pick the cherries by hand as they ripen and carry them on their own backs, using a tumpline, or on their horses each afternoon to the *beneficio* (wet mill), where it is weighed and emptied into the washing tanks. Because coffee cherries quickly begin to ferment, they must be washed within several hours of being picked. After washing, the pulp of the coffee cherries is removed by machine, releasing the two coffee beans inside. Under the supervision of the four beneficio employees and regular rotating overnight shifts of cooperative members, the beans then ferment in water for twenty-four to forty-eight hours. After fermentation, the remaining pulp is washed off and the beans are spread on a patio to dry, which can take up to three days because of San Juan's high altitude (approximately 1,500 meters). The coffee is then bagged and shipped to a mill in Guatemala City, where the final parchment skin is removed during dry processing. It is then shipped to Green Mountain Coffee Roasters in Vermont, where it is roasted and marketed to consumers. The Guatemalan highlands produce some of the highest quality and distinctively flavored coffees in the world. The members of La Voz grow *Typica*, *Bourbon*, and *Caturra* varieties of fair-trade and organic-certified coffee. Nurtured in fertile, volcanic soils under a diverse shade canopy, these coffee beans have a good balance of acidity and body that is spiced with a hint of winey ferment and fruit flavors.

Coffee's introduction to Latin America during the second half of the nineteenth century intensified existing transnational flows and affected diverse individuals and landscapes. Historically, Latin America dominated coffee production, and at one point in the nineteenth and twentieth centuries coffee was the leading export of nearly half the countries of the Americas and an important secondary crop in others. Today it remains a major export in many Latin American countries. In Guatemala, coffee cultivation and the exploitative political and social structures that supported it did indeed contribute to the civil unrest that resulted in the nation's civil war and continues to shape the political, economic, and cultural reality (Williams 1994; Paige 1997). Despite this history, however, it became increasingly attractive to smallholders beginning in the 1970s, because coffee is easy to store and

FIGURE 1.1. *Washing and depulping freshly picked coffee cherries in the cooperative's wet mill.*

handle, its value has historically surpassed that of comparable agricultural products, it can be grown on steep slopes, and can be fairly easily rejuvenated even if neglected for a time (Sick 1999). People in San Juan called

FIGURE 1.2. *Bagging dried coffee for storage.*

the introduction of coffee "the bomb" that exploded in the community, bringing income that enabled families to end their seasonal migration to lowland plantations, build cement-block houses, and educate their children. This trend toward small-scale coffee production was replicated around the world during the twentieth century as it became clear that the idea of "bigger is better" was an illusion in coffee cultivation. Access to land was not a key ingredient for coffee production. Instead, capital and labor were the scarce factors of production: small producers could rely on self-provisioning and family labor, and compared with large landowners, smallholders usually returned higher yields per hectare, per unit of capital, and per laborer, all other things being equal (Topik and Clarence-Smith 2003a:389).

Within San Juan and across Guatemala, rural communities of smallholders struggle to diversify their economic livelihoods as it becomes increasingly difficult to sustain a family solely through agriculture. Juaneros strive to educate their children to save them the backbreaking labor and daily toil that they say characterize their own lives as *campesinos* (small-scale farmers). For example, since I first visited San Juan in 2000, community members have invested heavily in tourism and other small businesses. San Juan sits on the shores of one of the most beautiful lakes in the world, and although Juaneros have been slow to capitalize on the flows of foreigners that visit this popular destination every year, they are now trying to catch up

[handwritten margin note: benefits of coffee in this community]

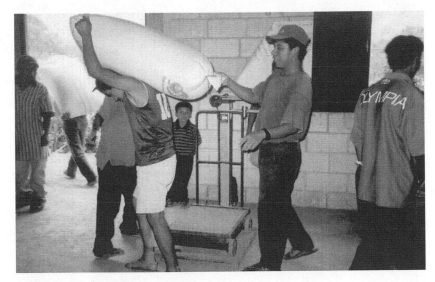

FIGURE 1.3. *Weighing dried coffee before shipment to Guatemala City for final processing.*

to their neighbors, such as the residents of San Pedro and Santiago Atitlan, who have long welcomed tourists. Despite this economic diversification, coffee remains central to both Guatemalan and Juanero economic identity, although it is not the financial powerhouse it once was. In the past, coffee farming brought great rewards to Juaneros, and they are reluctant to abandon the crop now even though many years they struggle to earn a decent living. Their options for agricultural diversification are limited by the small size of their landholdings. Furthermore, coffee is a perennial tree crop that requires a significant initial investment. Members of La Voz often referred to their coffee trees as their "children" who they had lovingly tended for decades—children they were understandably reluctant to rip out now.

Guatemala claims seven distinct coffee-producing regions and exported nearly 7 million pounds of fair-trade certified green coffee into the United States in 2008 (TransFair 2009), making it the seventh-largest supplier to the market. Approximately 31 percent, or 700,000, of Guatemala's rural laborers are employed in the coffee industry (Varangis 2003:8; Lewin, Giovannucci, and Varangis 2004). Forty-five percent of Guatemala's coffee is classified as strictly hard bean (SHB: grown above 1,200 meters) and 19 percent as hard bean (HB: grown between 800 and 1,200 meters), meaning it commands a higher price in the international coffee commodity market. Latin America

7

in general is the leading source of specialty coffees, and several countries, such as Colombia and Guatemala, have historically focused on coffee quality and the establishment of infrastructure and institutional mechanisms to foster consistency (Lewin, Giovannucci, and Varangis 2004:115).

Today, between 20 and 25 million small farmers produce coffee in more than fifty countries around the world, most being very small-scale family farmers or those with fewer than five hectares (Nicholls and Opal 2005:81) who are especially vulnerable to market fluctuations. In general, the undifferentiated nature of bulk commodities (such as wheat, soya, coffee, cocoa, and sugar) meant historically that it was easier for small-scale farms to participate. However, bulk commodity markets are characterized by instabil-

FIGURE 1.4. *The view of Lake Atitlan and surrounding volcanoes from San Juan.*

ity, structural oversupply, stiff global competition, historic downward price trends, and declining terms of trade for producing countries and regions (Fox and Vorley 2006:164). The volatility of the international coffee market has increased since 1989, when the International Coffee Agreement (ICA), which set quotas and helped stabilize prices, was not renewed. During the years when I conducted the bulk of my research (2001–2003), international coffee prices established on the New York Coffee, Sugar and Cocoa Exchange and the London International Futures Exchange declined to a hundred-year low when adjusted for inflation (Lewin, Giovannucci, and Varangis 2004). The unprecedented low that the international price for green coffee reached in 2001 was primarily the result of two transformations in addition to the demise of the ICA in 1989. First, roasters and international traders consolidated their market shares, contributing to oligopolistic market conditions. Second, producing countries lost their ability to control export flows and stocks as a result of market liberalization (Daviron and Ponte 2005:113, 121). Additionally, the percentage of coffee's value returned to the producer has declined significantly over the past decades. Today the International Coffee Organization estimates that 12 percent of the average supermarket price and less than 3 percent of the price of brewed coffee purchased out of home is paid to the grower (Giovannucci and Koekoek 2003:32).

Many people publicly blamed the rapid growth of Vietnam's coffee production in recent years for the coffee crisis. Between 1990 and 2000, Vietnam boasted a 1,400 percent increase in coffee production, and by 2000–2001 it was the second-largest producer in the world with an annual production of 14.7 million bags (Giovannucci 2002; Talbot 2004). Although Vietnam may have been the most visible contributor to overproduction, it was not the only one. For example, Brazil produced a bumper crop in 1998–1999 of 38 million bags from 3.4 billion trees. According to Giovannucci (2002), estimates suggest that during the coffee crisis there were 4.4 billion Brazilian coffee trees in production with another 1.5 billion developing. Similarly, during the 1990s, production increased in India and Uganda by more than 30 percent, in Guatemala by 20 percent, and in Ethiopia by 25 percent (Talbot 2004:128). The Vietnamese coffee expansion began before 1994, when the World Bank resumed lending there. Giovannucci (2002) contends that the credit extended to small farmers through the 1996 Rural Finance Project financed less than 5 percent of Vietnam's coffee expansion. Nonetheless, Don Mitchell, a World Bank economist, stated that "Vietnam has become a successful producer . . . In general, we consider it to be a huge success" (quoted in Collier 2001). At the 2002 Anacafé conference, Panos Varangis of the World Bank gave a presentation titled "Perspectivas del café a Nivel Mundial." Even though Varangis argued that Guatemalan producers must continue to increase their coffee quality, the audience became clearly unsettled. One Guatemalan attendee interrupted him by standing up and saying,

> It seems illogical to me that we, who produce quality coffee, have to be socially and environmentally responsible and Brazil and Vietnam don't. It's hypocritical. Migration to the United States grows every year and our governments are losing a source of revenue that could be used to pay off the loans we have with institutions such as this one. Why does the World Bank continue to give money to these producers and doesn't help the producers of truly quality coffee, our countries depend on the taxes of coffee to pay our loans with you!

Varangis answered, "We don't support certain crops, only rural development in general." Even though Varangis was not technically booed off the stage, there was little point in him continuing his presentation after this interchange, and Anacafé officials stepped in and presented him with his celebratory book, promptly ending the session.

The coffee crisis had a significant impact on Guatemala's economy. During the 1999–2000 harvest, coffee represented 21 percent, or $600 million, of Guatemala's total exports. However, by 2001 this fell to 12 percent ($320 million) (Varangis 2003; Lewin, Giovannucci, and Varangis 2004) and rural unemployment soared to an estimated 40 percent (Collier 2001). Eduardo Weymann, finance minister at the time, reportedly warned that "the government will be paralyzed" if new revenues are not found (Collier 2001). In response to the coffee crisis, the Guatemalan congress authorized a trust fund to finance agricultural diversification, agro-processing, marketing, and debt-restructuring programs for producers. The fund was authorized to raise $100 million through bonds offered in the domestic market at an interest rate of 8.5 percent and administered by the Bank of Rural Development, or BANRURAL. Forty million dollars was earmarked for small producers and 60 million for medium and large coffee producers (Varangis 2003:18). Although coffee prices have since rebounded, it is logical to expect that there will be another devastating coffee crisis in the near future because market conditions have not fundamentally changed in recent years.

The most obvious solutions to the coffee market's instability and periodic crises are to reduce drastically the current levels of coffee production and to diversify agricultural production. However, coffee is a tree crop that does not produce until at least three years after planting, so supply responds slowly to price, which tends to produce recurring tree-crop price cycles, triggering the Polanyian double movement, or inevitable movement for social protection resulting from the extension of the self-regulating market (Talbot 2004:36). The market volatility is particularly threatening to the millions of small-scale coffee producers around the world who often lack sufficient capital to weather market downturns, such as the members of La Voz. Small-scale coffee producers are especially vulnerable to market fluctuations as they often do not have formal lending institutions or alternative livelihood options, and the long-term investment required for coffee production makes them reluctant to plant other crops (Sick 1997).

Coffee certification systems, such as fair trade, may help sustain the livelihoods of a portion of small-scale producers. Certification is particularly useful for smallholders because it allows for consistency of characteristics, improves market transparency, provides marketplace credibility, and captures the demand and price incentives of niche markets (Lewin, Giovannucci, and Varangis 2004:109). According to some estimates, up to 30 percent of the world's small-scale coffee producers are now linked to fair-trade networks (Conroy 2001:20, in Murray, Raynolds, and Taylor 2006:182) and a high percentage of those also produce organic-certified coffee. However, the market for fair-trade coffee, currently the largest among certified commodities, remains insufficient: the Fairtrade Labelling Organization International (FLO) estimates that the capacity of producers worldwide who could meet certification standards is roughly seven times the current volume exported via fair-trade channels (Murray, Raynolds, and Taylor 2006). This raises the obvious question of whether fair-trade certification and other similar models will provide sufficient protection to small-scale coffee producers when they inevitably face the next devastating price crisis.

FAIR-TRADE COFFEE

Fair trade's roots reach back more than half a century into U.S. and European history. In 1942, a group of British Quakers founded Oxfam with the intention of raising funds for wartime relief. Similarly, the Mennonite and Brethren in Christ churches in North America founded the fair-trade handicraft retail outlet Ten Thousand Villages in 1946. Beginning in the 1950s, secular alternative trade organizations emerged in European nations, such as Twin Trading in Britain, Fair Trade Organisatie in The Netherlands, and SOS Wereldhandel in West Germany. The growing number of organizations first imported handicrafts and later agricultural products, such as honey, coffee, and tea, from marginalized, less-developed countries. In turn, they sold the products through social groups, in churches, and in World Shops, which now number nearly 2,700 (Giovannucci and Koekoek 2003:39). Although they did not handle large volumes, these organizations did accumulate marketing experience and fostered educational consciousness-raising (Vander Hoff Boersma 2002). In Guatemala the fair-trade movement began in the mid-1970s when SOS Holland began commercializing Guatemalan coffee internationally via Federation of Agricultural Coffee Producing Cooperatives of Guatemala (FEDECOCAGUA) under the trademark Indio Kaffee (Johnson 2006:58, cited in Arce 2009). In 1988, The Netherlands became the first country to launch a fair-trade consumer label, Max Havelaar. With the help of the Dutch priest Franz Vander Hoff, the label was created through a partnership between the Mexican coffee cooperative Union of the Indigenous Communities of the Isthmus Region (UCIRI) and the Dutch development organization Solidaridad. The Max Havelaar label marked a distinct departure from the 100 percent fair-trade emphasis of previously existing alternative trade organizations because it enabled mainstream coffee roasters to trade a fraction of their total coffee volume on fair-trade terms. It also enabled mainstream retail outlets, such as large supermarkets, to place one or two niche-market fair-trade products on their shelves. The Max Havelaar label was copied in other countries, such as Belgium (1991), Switzerland (1992), Germany (1993), France (1993), and the United Kingdom and Australia (1994) (Giovannucci and Koekoek 2003:39). In 1989, an international group of alternative trade organizations formed the International Fair Trade Association (IFAT). Similarly, in 1989, handicraft-oriented organizations in the United States formed the Fair Trade Federation (FTF). In 1997, Fairtrade Labelling Organization International (FLO) formed to systematize fair-trade national labeling and certification standards. The organization currently monitors labels in seventeen member countries, including the United States, through TransFair USA, which was founded in 1998.

There are three contemporary components of fair trade. First, there are alternative trading organizations that operate independent trading circuits and assume the character of social networks; in this way they can underwrite fair-trade claims without formal guarantees, such as FLO certification. Second, there is the social movement–based promotion of fair trade ranging from specific initiatives for the adoption of fair trade to political campaigns to change the rules of conventional trade (Wilkinson 2006:4). Third, there is the FLO-registered formal certification system. Coffee, the first and most developed fair-trade commodity, represents the backbone of the formal certification system, and it is this third component that this book is focused on. Fair trade is one of many certification systems and voluntary corporate codes of conduct that emerged in the 1990s as a result of the convergence of several factors, including the accelerated globalization of economic activity; the retreat of the state, especially from its role in regulating business behavior; the increased significance of brands and corporate reputation, which made companies vulnerable to bad publicity; the growth of international communications, which facilitated the dissemination of information about working conditions and environmental concerns; and the growth of nongovernmental organizations (NGOs) campaigning around issues of human and labor rights (Jenkins 2002:27).

The increasing popularity of fair trade and the expansion of certified products and producer groups necessitated FLO International's internal split in 2003 into two legal entities: FLO Certification Ltd. is responsible for certification, inspection, and trade auditing (following ISO 65 Standards for Certification Bodies) and the charitable side of FLO regulates all other activities. FLO-Certification Ltd. is one of the largest international social-economic certification bodies, inspecting organizations in the fifty-eight countries currently covered by FLO certification (FLO 2007a). Initially, FLO did not charge coffee-producer organizations a certification fee because the organization's operational and marketing expenses were covered by the five-cents-per-pound licensing fee paid by roasters. However, in 2003 the board of directors introduced an initial certification fee (for cooperatives with fewer than 500 members, such as La Voz, the fee is US$2,500) and an annual renewal fee (US$637 base) to help the organization "provide high quality certification and trade auditing services" (FLO 2007a).

There are five widely cited criteria for fair-trade certification:

1. Small farmers must be organized into democratically run cooperatives.

2. Buyers must guarantee a floor price (currently US$1.35 + $0.20 organic differential).

3. Buyers must offer farmers credit to help cover harvest costs, up to 60 percent of contracted value.

4. Importers and farmer cooperatives must develop long-term trading relationships.

5. Farmers must pursue ecological goals.

As defined by FLO, small-scale farmers cultivate fewer than three hectares of coffee, harvest between 1,000 and 3,000 pounds of green coffee a year, are not dependent on hired labor, and manage their farms with their own and their families' labor. Despite the decided emphasis on family farms, FLO prohibits both the employment of children under the age of fifteen and work conditions that may "jeopardize schooling or the social, moral or physical development of the young person" (FLO 2007a). During the research period (2001–2006), the coffee cooperative earned $1.41 per pound for its fair-trade and organic-certified coffee ($1.21 fair-trade minimum + $0.05 social premium + $0.15 organic differential). Despite the fact that producers have widely disparate production and living costs and that many nations' economies have been ravaged by inflation, from 1988 to 2007 this price was raised only once (by $0.06 per pound) (Rice and McLean 1999:57). In 2007, the FLO board voted to increase the base price, social premium, and organic differential with the result that today La Voz is paid $1.55 per pound ($1.25 fair-trade minimum + $0.10 social premium + $0.20 organic differential) for their washed Arabica coffee (FLO 2009). Although fair trade offers small-scale coffee producers a significant buffer from sharp market downturns, the terms of exchange for fair-trade certified coffee have deteriorated over the past decade. The recent increase in the base price represents only a 3 percent increase over twenty years. Simply to maintain its value in constant dollars, the price paid to producers for a pound of green coffee should now be more than two dollars a pound. And as is explained in subsequent chapters, although the fair-trade price paid to producers has stagnated, the demands of the fair-trade market have grown more challenging for producers to meet.

Recent years have witnessed a move toward market-friendly approaches to international development, such as fair trade, as poverty is increasingly viewed as the simple result of a lack of effective integration into the market economy. By the end of the 1990s calls for market-friendly, poverty-reducing growth were the mantra of the donor community, with a wave of policies and programs developed to harness the forces of globalization to benefit the poor (Dolan 2005a:414). This growing focus on market-based poverty reduction has led some aid organizations to direct their efforts toward more functionally oriented peasant groups, such as commodity-specific producer associations like La Voz. Fair trade shares similar attributes with a variety of certification schemes emerging in response to the failure of nation-states to meet the demands made of them in a globalizing economy, including organic, sweat-free, and forest-stewardship labels. Such initiatives date to the mid-1970s, when international organizations like the Organization for Economic Cooperation and Development (OECD) and the International Labor Organization (ILO) developed codes of conduct for multinational corporations, partly in response to corporate involvement in political upheavals in Latin America. The early to mid-1980s witnessed a wave of code activity in response to several major scandals and catastrophes, including Nestle's marketing of breast-milk substitutes in Latin America (Bartley 2005:220).

By facilitating the incorporation of "marginal" populations into market economies, the shifting development focus, of which fair trade is a key component, may indirectly serve neoliberal state goals. For example, fair trade has experienced a high degree of success recently, in the form of rapid sales expansion and its adoption by institutions like the World Bank and conventional corporations, because of its neoliberal conception of the market that emphasizes exchange relations over social relations (Fridell 2007). Similarly, national governments and international development agencies have directly and indirectly contributed to the rise of fair trade mostly through financing services. However, the goals of these support efforts have not been entirely consistent with those of fair trade as they are often focused on generating short-term development (frequently tied to longer-term debt, as in the case of La Voz) and less on a vision of social justice (Murray, Raynolds, and Taylor 2006). The market-based poverty solutions increasingly pursued by development agencies and NGOs have been criticized for subtly disempowering those they seek to aid.[1] Although they are presented as alternatives to development, certification initiatives such as fair trade reflect the larger trend toward market-based solutions for poverty reduction. However, this points to one of today's most pressing political issues: if trade is the route for growth and poverty reduction, what rules should govern international

FT is compatible with neoliberalism

trading practices and the formation of international trade agreements and organizations? Many argue that in recent years the international fair-trade movement has shied away from this critical issue, instead focusing on growing markets and working within the capitalist system.

LINKING PRODUCERS AND CONSUMERS

Anthropologist William Roseberry (1996) named coffee the beverage of postmodernism, not to suggest that coffee exists in a unique relationship with capitalism but that it provides a window through which we can view a range of relationships and social transformations. This includes the critical links between the consumption habits of northern consumers and the promotion of economic and social justice in countries that consistently threaten individual freedoms, such as Guatemala. The cooperative's name, translated as "A Voice Crying Out in the Wilderness," honors Saint John the Baptist, the village's patron saint, who is said to have preached in the desert, baptizing converts in the river Jordan. Agricultural cooperatives were specifically targeted for violent reprisals by the Guatemalan military throughout the civil war, and more than three decades after its founding, the cooperative's name evokes the resiliency of this group and the strength of its communal practices in the face of persecution. Although these internal characteristics set the stage for the group's long-term success, without the secure export market the cooperative has maintained since first shipping its certified organic and fair-trade coffee to northern consumers in 1991, it is doubtful whether it would continue to enjoy the member loyalty that it does today.

Despite the benefits that fair trade brings to the members of La Voz, a critical evaluation of the fair-trade coffee network reveals that it does not in fact fundamentally challenge the contemporary neoliberal organization of the international market. Instead, in its current guise fair trade provides small farmers a "shaped advantage" by assisting their participation in the global economy (Fridell 2007). However, fair trade's contradictory emphasis on the transformation of conventional markets from within differentiates it from development programs that are not rooted in explicit social and economic justice goals. Analyses of commodities, such as fair-trade coffee, and the circuits they travel are powerful tools for reconnecting producers and consumers with the goal of reducing structural inequities in a globalizing world. Analytically linking the members of La Voz to the consumers of fair-trade coffee in the North illustrates the ways in which fair trade can potentially challenge the logic of the expanding free market by promoting a critical consumer culture that challenges the individualizing culture of capitalism. A renewed emphasis on cooperation and solidarity, through attempts to build collaborative networks across national, economic, and cultural borders by nurturing relationships between southern producers and northern consumers, can help reorient the focus of fair trade away from a myopic focus on market expansion and selective advantage toward broad calls for new forms of international market regulation and truly just trade policies.

Despite fair trade's emphasis on transnational relationships, the construction of local places is an absolutely critical component of the contemporary certified coffee market as regional variations and place-based appellation systems are employed as marketing tools in an increasingly differentiated market landscape. In fact, this is so commonplace that it is difficult to imagine how a roaster might advertise La Voz's coffee without referencing the rich volcanic soils and highland climate of the Atitlan region. Furthermore, the growing importance of both the particularity of place and certification within the market means that gradually the characteristics of the producers themselves, such as their indigeneity, are used to distinguish coffees and subtly capitalize on consumers' romantic images of hardworking small-scale farmers dedicated to producing high-quality products. When cooperative members discuss what it means to be Juanero today, they routinely reference their ties to the land, their common language (and colloquiums that are distinct from their nearby neighbors), and a collective history. Even when they leave in search of work, they remain tied to their natal community through their ongoing relationships with their family members who regularly draw them back for Holy Week and patron-saint festivities.

The case of La Voz dramatizes the continued salience of community-based identities and it also reveals the power relations shaping collaboration and solidarity within the cooperative and transnational fair-trade networks in which it participates. For example, the daily process of cooperation itself is fraught with tension as members and management continuously negotiate complex decisions, such as whether to sell the land of a cooperative member who refuses to pay his loans or to fire an employee who "borrowed" funds without permission. Similarly, the relations between the cooperative members and outside certifiers, roasters, and agencies, such as Anacafé and United States Agency for International Development (USAID), demonstrate both the promises and perils of fair trade's attempts to forge meaningful connections across space and sharp class divisions. Their very connections with these outside forces are reshaping their own locality as they relinquish some of the control over production practices they have long enjoyed as

17

self-employed small producers to meet the high quality demands of competitive international markets.

My goal is not to follow the coffee as it circulates through the network but instead to examine how this product is embedded in diverse economic and social strategies across space. This exploration of the connectivity fostered by fair-trade networks challenges popular understandings of the global experience, which uncritically celebrate mobility and flows. A more accurate understanding of globalization for most people, including coffee consumers like ourselves and producers such as the members of La Voz, is that of staying in one place but experiencing the ruptures and dislocations, both positive and negative, that globalization brings to us. The connectivity engendered through fair-trade networks does not shorten the distance between these shaded coffee plots in rural Guatemala and the urban coffee shops we hurriedly rush through in search of a quick pick-me-up. Although the physical distance remains, we, meaning both the coffee consumers and the members of La Voz, experience the distance in different ways. When we purchase Green Mountain Coffee Roasters coffee at our supermarket, those distant coffee fields become more accessible to us through the representative stories decorating the promotional materials and the company's website. Similarly, when members of La Voz debate just how much U.S. consumers pay for their coffee and question why they receive so little money in exchange, they demonstrate that those distant worlds are becoming more fathomable to them. This leads them to challenge their own lack of power in this global market by, for example, publicly calling on USAID to lower the interest rates on their loans or applying for their own export license, actions that would have been unthinkable only a few years earlier.

Following a commodity such as coffee along its transnational pathways helps us to reveal the social relationships that are obscured in an international marketplace marked by a firm separation of production and consumption. This creates a sharp lens through which we can better understand, and make sense of, the integration of local contexts, such as the offices of Seattle coffee roasters and the small plots of coffee tended by Maya producers, into the world system. In short, although the lives of small-scale actors, such as the members of La Voz, may be shaped by transnational economic processes and export commodity production, they are not necessarily determined by these external forces, and these actors themselves help shape global flows and Guatemala's participation in the world economy.

For this reason, even though I conducted research in Seattle, Vermont, and Guatemala among the many participants in the fair-trade coffee network, the stories in this book are primarily told from the point of view of the members of La Voz. While I conducted my research, I quickly realized that following the certified coffee as it moved through the many nodes of the commodity network would lead me away from the unique perspective on power and collaboration that an exploration of the "wake of things" (Walsh 2004:226) provides. As an economic anthropologist who takes for granted that exchange is vested in social relations and inequities, I found that I was most interested in how power is exercised within the emerging relationships constituting fair-trade networks; I wanted to examine who was gaining and who was losing and question who has a voice. These are not new questions; they are simply older dilemmas of social justice returning to us in new forms (Collins 2003). These questions were best answered by rooting the analysis among the most vulnerable participants in the certified coffee market, the producers. However, the producers' story cannot be adequately told without fully analyzing the convergence of their daily practices with the motivating forces and dreams of certified coffee advocates in the North, such as the members of Seattle Audubon, who spoke of their passion for shade-grown coffee. Furthermore, it is impossible to truly reveal the power relations structuring certified coffee markets without fully understanding the complex ways in which the economic goals of coffee roasters and importers are embedded in their own social relations and cultural identities.

ORGANIZATION OF THE BOOK

Chapter 2, "The Historical Convergence of Local Livelihoods, the Global Economy, and International Politics," uses the voices of community elders and historical research to demonstrate that San Juan has a long-term and dynamic history of involvement in regional, national, and transnational economic and political processes. Resistance to colonialism and world market forces as well as integration within these systems of power form an underlying tension throughout Guatemalan history. This chapter sets the stage for a more dialectical understanding of the interaction among global and local forces, material conditions, and ideology, especially in relation to the international coffee economy.

Chapter 3, "'Trade Not Aid': Assessing Fair Trade's Economic Impact on Cooperative Members and Their Families," critically evaluates one of fair trade's hallmark slogans, "Trade Not Aid," by exploring two commonly cited economic benefits of fair trade, higher prices and access to credit. It demonstrates that cooperative members do benefit from both; however, the advantages may be less significant than northern consumers believe. The chapter also highlights the conflict that emerged within the cooperative over the increasing numbers of insolvent members, ultimately arguing that the conversations sparked by the disagreement strengthened the group's long-term prospects.

Chapter 4, "Obligatory Burdens: Collaboration and Discord within the Cooperative," analyzes both the meaning and practice of cooperation within the group and assesses the organizational capacity of the cooperative. It begins with an examination of a particularly contentious cooperative meeting in which a member emphatically reminded his companions that "We are cooperative members or we are nothing!" The chapter closely examines internal relations, the flow of information, and the sharing of decision-making power among the management, the board, and the general assembly to question the extent to which cooperation, and by extension fair trade, promotes democracy and transparency within local spheres. The chapter closely examines the emerging tensions between the membership and the increasingly powerful cooperative management and the ways in which cooperative members actively work to check administrative power through often repeated rumors of managerial corruption. It argues that cooperation is an ongoing process of negotiation and conflict resolution rather than an intrinsic and static value of indigenous communities. In addition, the chapter foregrounds the story of Juana, a cooperative founder, to shed light on the failure of fair-trade coffee networks to adequately protect and promote gender equity within producer groups.

Chapter 5, "The Political Economy of Organic and Shade-Grown Coffee Certification, Local Livelihoods, and Identities," tracks between the motivations and dreams of the Seattle birders who are shade-grown, organic coffee advocates and the reality of certification and production practices in the members' fields. It explores three key contradictions within the shade-grown, organic-certified coffee markets. First, there is a tension between a regional history of organic production as liberatory practice and the contemporary reality of organic certification, which contributes to the transformation of organic agriculture into a form of eco-colonialism rooted in global class differentiations. Second, there is a tension between the pride generated by the cooperative members' perceptions of quality and the strict quality standards required for participation in the specialty-coffee market. The imposition of externally derived certification requirements necessitates internal surveillance mechanisms that reshape social relations and practices among members. Third, there is a conflict with northern conceptions of the producer "other" as these are expressed in certification standards imposed in the name of tropical conservation on the one hand and in the ways that people's understandings of their landscape, place, and community are shaped by their livelihoods on the other. Essentially, this chapter asks the same question posed by the cooperative member questioning certification standards: What good will two more shade trees do?

Chapter 6, "Managing the Maya: Power in the Fair-Trade Market," demonstrates that although in theory fair-trade coffee networks are marked by mutual dependence, cooperation, and trust, in practice the members of La Voz are subjected to a high level of governance and external surveillance as a result of their hierarchical relationships with northern buyers and certifying agencies. The power inequities are most evident within two realms: first, in the fair-trade certification process, which is marked by a low degree of producer understanding and low levels of producer participation in the collective establishment of standards and movement goals; and second, in the processes of quality control, which entail surveillance of production and processing. The analysis reveals that fair-trade coffee networks fail to nurture truly equitable relationships among participants, begging the question of why cooperative members willingly submit to the external governance. The chapter demonstrates that the benefits, such as market information, product improvement, and economic security in the face of market uncertainties, gleaned through fair-trade market participation outweigh the costs.

Chapter 7, "Marketing the Maya: Fair Trade's Producer/Consumer Relationships," explores fair-trade coffee marketing materials to demonstrate that the producer/consumer relationship in fair-trade coffee networks is heavily mediated by advertising and the intermediaries who celebrate symbolic quality attributes and shape consumer preferences. Existing scholarly attempts to understand fair-trade producer/consumer relationships fail to fully capture the complexity of producers' relationships with northern consumers. They cannot explain what it means to be Maya in the world market (versus in the cooperative and the community). Nor do they explore how fair-trade market relationships are informed by the reinforcement of differences and northern impressions of "community," small-scale farmer poverty, and in some cases indigeneity. This chapter delves into these complex questions to demonstrate that producers and consumers are united in an imaginary community sustained through advertising, media, and roaster/retailer intermediaries rather than embedded economic relationships.

2

The Historical Convergence of Local Livelihoods, the Global Economy, and International Politics

A robust understanding of the cultural politics of fair-trade coffee and its attendant economic, social, and environmental processes is best gained through long-term ethnographic research among the principal actors. However, like all social phenomena, fair trade is by its very nature historical and the relationships among the individuals and events in our particular moment cannot be fully abstracted from their past and future settings (Mintz 1985). The reality of contemporary fair-trade coffee exchange is contingent upon the historical trajectory of coffee production and the centuries-long interplay of local livelihoods, global economic forces, and international politics. Therefore, a thorough analysis of this complex market is by necessity spatially specific and must emerge from a situated examination of the fields of power through which this commodity moves. This chapter presents a brief overview of Guatemalan history from the perspective of the Juaneros, highlighting key themes that emerged during interviews with cooperative members and elders in the community. It selectively examines the history of coffee in Guatemala, the complex relationship between the state and agrarian communities, seasonal labor migration, military service, mid-twentieth-century attempts at agrarian reform, the local introduction of coffee and chemical fertilizers, and finally the civil war and its aftermath.

Although San Juan may appear to be an "out of the way place" (Tsing 1993) populated by a "people without history" (Wolf 1982) who have only recently begun participating in global markets, it in fact has a long-term and dynamic history of involvement in regional, national, and transnational economic and political processes. Furthermore, far from remaining a passive bystander in the face of external agency, the community and its individual inhabitants have actively shaped (and continue to do so) these larger processes. Resistance to colonialism and world market forces as well as integration within these systems of power form an underlying tension throughout Guatemalan history. This chapter is intended to provide a corrective to the historical anthropological approach to smaller communities, which failed to allow for the possibility of resistance and interplay with the global capitalist system. Instead, it builds on the important historical work of scholars such as Smith (1978, 1984, 1990), Carey (2001, 2006), and Little (2004, 2008) to present a more nuanced understanding of the interaction among global and local factors, material conditions, and ideology in recognition of the fact that rather than "containers for Maya identity and 'stuff,'" Maya communities are in fact crossroads of transnational economic and political relationships (Adams 2001).

Many students of Guatemalan history tend to code Mayas as victims and Ladinos as villains, hesitating to examine the complex relations that bind the Maya to their communities as well as to Ladino society (Watanabe 1995; Stoll 1999; Grandin 2000). Watanabe argues that this trend emerges from an academic tradition of "othering" in which the two modalities of Maya anthropology—the romantic and the tragic—compete (1995:33). Stoll goes a step further to argue that the preoccupation with victimhood is rooted in political correctness and identity politics, noting that because all individuals have multiple identities and can be viewed as privileged in regard to others who are less fortunate, dilemmas arise—such as how do we define victims, why are they victims, and what should be done next (Stoll 1999:244). Rather than viewing the Maya through the lens of a timeless culture or, conversely, a self-perpetuating insular culture, Watanabe urges us to uncover the combination of continuities and transformations, resistance and oppression, cultural forms and historical realities shaping Maya realities. As he eloquently states, being Maya is predicated on the ongoing activities and iterations of particular individuals in specific places, or in other words, "Maya is what Maya do as long as other Maya acknowledge it as such" (Watanabe 1995:35). In my own struggles to understand the history of San Juan and, more broadly, the intersecting history of coffee production and Maya communities in Guatemala, I slowly realized that simplistic explanations rooted in Maya victimization failed to fully account for the factors motivating local cultural change at specific junctures in time. They also discounted the agency of Juaneros, who actively shaped not only their own history but the nation's as well.

Coffee has been a major traded commodity since the sixteenth century and it remains one of the most valuable internationally traded agricultural commodities in world history. Its introduction to Latin America intensified existing transnational flows and impacted both individuals and landscapes. By the late 1800s, coffee had become Guatemala's primary export, the foundation of wealth, the determinant of social status, and the arbiter of political power among the nation's elite. In later years, coffee cultivation, and the exploitative political and social structures that supported it, contributed to the unrest that resulted in the nation's civil war and continues to shape its political, economic, and cultural reality into the present (Cambranes 1985; Woodward 1990; Williams 1994; Paige 1997). Coffee production played the critical role in the transformation of Guatemala's division of labor into one more aligned with a capitalist mode of production (Smith 1978; McCreery 1994) as the growing demand for coffee in the North required strenuous work in the South. However, "the office workers taking their coffee breaks in the U.S. and Europe gave scant thought to the black slaves or Mayan Indians who labored in the coffee fields . . . to provide their drinks" (Topik, Marichal, and Frank 2006). The contemporary fair-trade coffee market attempts to rectify this by educating northern consumers about the conditions of production behind their daily cups of coffee.

THE COFFEE CENTURY

Roseberry describes the nineteenth century (1830–1930) as *the* coffee century in Latin America (1995:3), and Guatemala is no exception to this. According to the Anacafé-sanctioned *The History of Coffee in Guatemala*, coffee cultivation began in the latter half of the nineteenth century in the Antigua gardens of Jesuit monks (Wagner 2001:32). However, academic historians provide an alternative and decidedly less idyllic version of coffee's introduction. The first phase of commercial coffee growing in Guatemala (1840–1871) began when wealthy merchant-landowners learned of the commercial successes of the crop in Costa Rica and commissioned the *licenciado* (lawyer) Manuel Aguilar in 1845 to write a practical manual on how to plant, cultivate, harvest, and process coffee based on his Costa Rican experiences (Handy 1984:59; Williams 1994:53). By 1855 coffee *fincas* were springing up around Coban, Antigua, and Amatitlan, and coffee replaced nopal-cochineal cultivation in the last two areas. The value of coffee among all Guatemalan exports rose from 1 percent of total exports in 1860 to 44 percent in 1870, when it became the largest single export commodity, a position it has held ever since (Woodward 1999:150).

During the 1850s and 1860s, coffee growers began to dominate department governments in coffee zones and increasingly influenced the policies of the national government. By 1866, coffee constituted 23 percent of Guatemala's exports. However, President Rafael Carrera was unable or unwilling to institute the legal changes demanded by the increasingly powerful coffee planters (Handy 1984:60). Led by General Justo Rufino Barrios (who served as president from 1873 to 1885), coffee rebels from the western highlands took state power in 1871 and enacted exploitative land and labor measures intended to promote coffee cultivation and exportation among non-Maya Guatemalans (Grandin 2000:110). The liberals saw themselves as scientific realists, believing that order and progress were the two goals worthy of greatest emphasis (Woodward 1999:156). At the heart of the liberal state was a desire for rapid economic growth through expansion of agro-exports (Woodward 1990:60). Their goal was to redirect Guatemala's agricultural export economy toward coffee production and away from cochineal, which was traditionally grown by small-scale peasant producers. Unlike the production of cochineal, coffee production required significant capital investments in technology, such as tanks and drying facilities. These capital demands, coupled with the processing requirements, favored medium and large estates over smaller family farms (McCreery 2003:192). The emergence of Guatemala as a coffee state corresponds to the moment when coffee exports exceeded combined exports of Guatemala's original agricultural export crops, including cochineal (Paige 1997:14).

Beginning in the first half of the nineteenth century with the production of cochineal and intensifying in the second half of the nineteenth century with the introduction of coffee and later sugarcane, bananas, cotton, and other products, Guatemala became one immense plantation (Cambranes 1985:30). Nineteenth-century Guatemala is a prime example of the process of primitive accumulation, defined by Marx as "the process by which the factors of production that are necessary to a capitalist economy . . . are freed from the restrictions typically placed upon them in and by noncapitalist forms of production so that they can become market commodities" (McCreery 1994:2). Although coffee cultivation did not "implant" capitalism in rural Guatemala, it did transmit the secondary effects of the expanding world economy to large areas of the countryside that previously had little or no part in export agriculture (McCreery 1994:174). The coffee state worked assiduously to liberalize both labor and land in its relentless pursuit of agro-export development. Even though liberal reforms theoretically favored Indians by granting them equality before the law and access to more land and opportunity, in practice, Guatemala's indigenous majority gained little from the liberals, who rejected the paternalism of the conservatives while using the impoverished masses as the manpower to provide the material advances of their regimes (Woodward 1999:174).

Coffee is a labor-intensive crop. Coffee person-days per acre cultivated are relatively high: approximately fifty-five in comparison to sugar (forty) and beans (twenty) (Williams 1994:106). Early planters demanded forced Indian labor to plant, tend, and harvest the coffee in ever greater amounts. Therefore, although labor shortages were a constitutive feature of Guatemalan history, coffee entrepreneurs were especially limited by this obstacle and Maya labor became an integral component of the liberal government's development strategies (Carey 2006). Guatemala's high-quality coffee production required large numbers of laborers, historically provided for plantation owners through coercive labor drafts, called *repartimientos* before independence and *mandamientos* in the post-independence era. According to Woodward (1999:44), the repartimiento system represented what has become "one of the most pervasive qualities of Central American society and mentality." The system provided Indian labor for landholders, miners, and government officials and slowly evolved into long-term debt peonage. In Guatemala, where the Indians were more numerous, the repartimiento survived beyond independence, and similar systems of forced labor, such as the mandamiento, persisted into the twentieth century.

Liberal presidents like Barrios viewed the Maya as a resource to be exploited, much like the nation's fertile volcanic soil and ideal coffee-growing conditions. Decree 177, issued on April 3, 1877, instituted strict labor laws. Laborers were forced to carry a *libretto* (work pass) at all times and employers were required to inspect them to ensure no outstanding debts were owed to other employers. Individuals without this work pass or a debt contract for future labor were subjected to mandamientos similar to those structuring colonial labor relations. These labor measures, combined with the expropriation of Maya lands (described below), in many cases contributed to the deterioration of highland village autonomy and effectively impoverished peasant agriculture, driving increasing numbers of smallholders to seek wage labor on developing coffee plantations (Handy 1984:69). However, while the Maya were forced to work in agro-export production for the landed elite, many also maintained their subsistence livelihoods in their highland communities. This economic strategy persisted among Juaneros through the 1970s. Indeed, although the self-government of highland villages may have been compromised by the formation of the national coffee state, many Maya communities successfully maintained their culture, languages, and subsistence livelihood. However, the profitability of this system kept capitalist relations of production from fully developing in the agro-export sector of the Guatemalan economy (McCreery 1986, cited in Moors 1988).

Despite, or perhaps because of, their dependence on indigenous labor, the coffee elite consistently maintained that the nation's Maya population presented a barrier to economic modernization, and they persisted in stereotyping the Maya as lazy, stupid, dirty, and drunken (Handy 1984; McCreery 1995; Topik and Clarence-Smith 2003b). For the coffee elite, relegating the Maya to the status of "subhuman" Indians rationalized their exploitation as the cheap labor that made underproductive coffee plantations profitable (Watanabe 1995:31). The liberals tried to show that the mandamiento system was a painful but necessary measure for the development of agriculture, trade, and industry (Cambranes 1985:183). However, what is striking about the liberal regimes is the complete absence of any serious attempts to indoctrinate the peasantry in a vision of development and modernization. The elite of the day looked upon the Indian as unalterably inferior and lacking in "civilized needs . . . that would force him to work for wages and thus be drawn voluntarily into the cash economy" (McCreery 1994:175). This perspective is echoed without irony in the Anacafé-sanctioned *The History of Coffee in Guatemala*, in which Wagner presents a sanitized, contemporary version of this "labor problem." She writes: "The root of the problem was the opposing philosophies of indigenous and Ladino. The indigenous were dedicated to maintaining their culture, lifestyle and traditions and to this end they concentrated on subsistence farming on their communal lands . . . to say the least, this suggests *a lifestyle worlds removed from the modern and capitalistic western world*, characterized by a reverence for entrepreneurial ambition and a focus on international markets" (2001:90, emphasis added).

At the same time, Maya labor, even when harnessed by *finqueros* (plantation owners) and politicians, was held in opposition to elite notions of modern personhood. Over time a national project emerged that struggled to transform the Mayas into new subjects through the extraction of labor, the introduction of national education, the conversion to Protestantism, and incorporation into military service in the 1800s (Woodward 1999; Euraque, Gould, and Hale 2005). Whether as apathetic and stupid or committed to cultural maintenance, the coffee elite's portrayal of the Maya population informed a national doctrine of racism and ethnic exclusion that ultimately culminated in Guatemala's twentieth-century genocidal civil war. Although Juaneros reportedly complied with the forced labor drafts, they strictly policed the cultural and physical boundaries of their highland community through prohibitions against selling land to outsiders and the encouragement of inmarriage to mitigate the external climate of repression, inequality, and domination.

Guatemala's agro-export-based economy continued to grow after Guatemala's independence from Spain in 1821. However, in the 1860s more than two-thirds of the high-altitude land suitable for coffee cultivation was still owned by municipalities or Maya communities, and this shortage of suitable land posed a second significant challenge to the coffee elite's expansionary visions. The first attack on village lands occurred under the liberal regime of Mariano Galvez (1831–1839), who passed a series of laws allowing outsiders to rent and acquire *ejidal* (communally owned) landholdings for the cultivation of commercial crops (Williams 1994:56). Later, in 1862, under the Carrera presidency (1839–1865), coffee growers pushed through an order further encouraging Maya villages in the coveted piedmont region to open uncultivated lands for lease to coffee growers (Williams 1994:60). The coffee state resolved the land shortage by defining as "idle" all lands not planted in coffee, sugar, cacao, or hay and by 1873 reclaimed them as national property, including more than 200,000 acres in the predominantly Maya western highlands (Williams 1994:61).

The loss of smallholder and communal lands was not evenly distributed across the western highlands as some villages effectively organized to retain their property, or even extend their landholdings, at the expense of neighboring communities. Towns such as San Juan, which were wholly in the highlands and held no active claims to low-elevation lands, did not suffer a large loss of land during this period. In fact, in some cases liberal efforts to measure and title land ended ancient disputes. However, for many communities, even San Juan, difficulties fixing community boundaries and ownership within these boundaries continued (McCreery 1994:247). In addition to land reforms, the regime also developed the banking and credit system through the establishment of the Ministry of Development, expanded port and railroad construction, established a military academy, reorganized the education system, and limited the power of the Church. Each of these measures increased the power and legitimacy of the coffee elite, led by Barrios.

Although there were isolated uprisings, Barrios prevented wholesale rebellion by increasing rural repression, and his military budget grew to 60 percent of total expenditures (Williams 1994:63).

The years of liberal reforms and political power before Jorge Ubico's rise to power in 1933 are described by San Juan's elders as particularly painful ones filled with hunger, suffering, and near slave-like forced labor conditions. For example, one elder shared how under the presidency of Carlos Cabrera (1898–1920), Juaneros were forced to eat orange rinds and banana peels because they did not possess sufficient corn and beans. Another explained during an interview, "In the time of Cabrera the Ladinos were favored by the government and we, the *indígenas*, were exploited and humiliated. Much earlier my father told me that if you encountered a Ladino carrying suitcases, he could make you carry them wherever he was going without pay and you had to obey because if you didn't they would take you to jail."[1] During an interview, one Juanero elder recalled that his grandparents and parents told him Cabrera enslaved the Maya, forcing them to work on the coffee plantations. Although this may seem hyperbole, in reality it is not far from the truth. According to Paige, a North American visitor observed in 1908 that Guatemala had so many soldiers that it looked like a penal colony. He describes the Guatemalan coffee elite of the day as a "[b]ackward, semi-feudal landed class" that faced little opposition from its captive labor force and had no parallel in other coffee-producing countries (Paige 1997:75). This echoes Cambranes's claim that "from the nineteenth century to this day, the finqueros have arrogantly believed that Guatemala and its working class belong to them and that they have some God-given right to do with it as they see fit" (1985:189).

THE ERA OF "EL BUENO SEÑOR UBICO": LABOR MIGRATION AND MILITARY SERVICE

In 1931, Jorge Ubico began his thirteen-year-long presidency, a period largely remembered by contemporary Juaneros and other Maya as a time of law and order (Warren 1978:148). Ubico assumed the presidency during the Depression, which hit Guatemala especially hard between 1929 and 1932, when export revenues fell by 40 percent. During the same time period, in El Salvador declining export revenues fostered tense political conditions. In 1932 the military-led government responded harshly to a relatively small Communist-inspired insurgency in rural areas, murdering between 15,000 and 20,000 civilians in a brutal act now known as La Matanza ("The Massacre"). Within this regional context, local and international business

elites as well as the U.S. government supported Ubico because of his reputation for maintaining order with force and his well-integrated system of
intendentes (municipal-level administrators) in communities throughout the
highlands (Little 2008). In Guatemala, Ubico struggled to expand the Guatemalan coffee market. He implemented new taxes and signed trade agreements allowing coffee and bananas to be exported to the United States
duty-free. However, these favorable terms of trade forced him to abandon
previous trade agreements with European states and served to effectively
tighten U.S. trade and capital dominance in Guatemala (Handy 1984:94).
In 1934, Ubico abolished the previous system of debt peonage, replacing
it with the Vagrancy Law, which required landless peasants to work for an
employer 150 days a year (Handy 1984:98). However, he impressed labor
from Ladino and Maya peoples alike for his massive state projects, such as
road building, thus "equalizing" the ethnic groups (Adams 2001).[2] Ubico
maintained his popularity in rural areas by visiting isolated villages, holding
charismatic public meetings, and personally (and selectively) intervening in
response to petitions from villagers. His trips through rural towns had tremendous influence on rural attitudes toward Ubico in the early years of his
rule, contributing to the indigenous sentiments that the government had
their best interests in mind despite their harsh daily experiences (Carey 2001).
Drawing on Kaqchikel oral histories, Carey (2001) explains how Kaqchikel
feared, respected, and in some cases despised Ubico; however, because on
an individual level he was known to defend Maya and his authoritarian rule
reduced crime, Mayas' memories of him were sometimes positive.

In addition to law and order, interviewed Juaneros recalled the Ubico
years as a period of migration, military conscription, the introduction of
formal education, and road building. In their historical narratives of the
Ubico years, many interviewees stressed the fact that they could safely walk
through the streets without fearing crimes. Ubico's "law" meant, according
to one elder I interviewed, that "[t]he person who kills will also be killed.
He who robs will immediately be taken to prison and he who gets drunk
on the days of work will also be taken to prison." In addition to strict labor laws, Ubico also instituted moral codes limiting alcohol consumption
to Sundays. The ethos of hard work cloaking the labor laws also impressed
another Juanero elder who responded, "For us, the indígenas, he was good
. . . for me, the government is like a father of the family who has children
and he has to look for a way to make his children do their work and that is
what this president did with the people. He gave an order that any person
walking in the street should be immediately questioned about what he is
doing in the street, why isn't he working?"

Ubico presided over more road construction than any other president, and the development of the road system expanded the regime's reach and control. Ubico imposed a two-dollar road tax on all Guatemalan households. If the household could not pay the tax, it could be worked off with two weeks of unpaid labor on the roads (Warren 1978; Moors 1988). Because many Ladinos could afford the tax, Guatemala's roads were primarily built using the forced labor of indigenous communities, including Juaneros. Although some interviewed elders complained about the arduous work, others pointed out that the construction of the Pan-American Highway, which today links Lake Atitlan to Guatemala City and Quetzaltenango, and other roads throughout the highlands served to integrate their rural village more firmly into the national economy by easing the arduous travel of both seasonally migrating plantation workers and itinerant vegetable and craft traders.

Elderly Juaneros' narratives of the migratory plantation labor characterizing their youth demonstrate that, far from peripheral rural peasants, Juaneros were in fact central actors in Guatemala's early twentieth-century history, as Maya communities and coastal plantations formed an interdependent, and yet highly uneven, economic system. Residents say that during these years of seasonal migration en masse (ca. 1920–1970), the town was frequently silent. In the first half of the century, most Juaneros migrated to work on plantations for pay; however, as years passed, some began to rent land from large-scale finqueros on the coastal plains, where they planted corn to sell or bring home for family consumption.

Perhaps surprisingly, interviewed elders were hesitant to criticize the labor laws or the required 150 workdays each year they were required to provide to plantations (or 100 days if they could prove they cultivated at least ten *cuerdas* [0.97 acre] of *milpa* [maize]). One elder explained: "The people began to criticize Ubico's law, saying it was slavery. But when one analyzes this law, it was much better because all of the people had work. There were no robberies or murders." Today, stories about the years of migration to the plantations form part of the town's communal historical narrative and the experiences are celebrated during public events such as the Flower of San Juan Pageant, during which groups of teenagers dress in historical *traje* (community-specific dress worn by Maya) and dramatize their grandparents' and parents' years of travel and hard work through skits. However, as demonstrated in the following chapters, interviewed cooperative members were also adamant that it is better to be self-employed than work for someone else. This universal sentiment is undoubtedly informed by the community's long history of participation in this coercive plantation labor system.

Interviewed elders may not interpret the labor laws as repressive because they migrated out of perceived household economic necessity instead of coercion. As the rural indigenous population began to grow across the highlands, land and labor opportunities became increasingly scarce in communities such as San Juan, essentially transforming many Maya, including Juaneros, into a semi-proletarian workforce relying on cyclical migration to sustain households and supplement subsistence production. Furthermore, between 1871 and 1940, Guatemala suffered repeated corn shortages, which directly contributed to the growing plantation workforce (Carey 2001, 2006). By the early 1920s, more and more inhabitants of the highland villages were unable to survive without plantation wages because of a growing population and shrinking resources (McCreery 1994:304). Elderly Juaneros' stories of childhood years punctuated by bouts of severe hunger also support the argument that Juaneros migrated out of both necessity *and* coercion. For example, one interviewed elder recalled: "I had family members that died of hunger because there was no corn. We were given [as children] at most two tortillas, which we ate with a cup of cooked herbs and when they ground the maize they also ground it with banana peel and we ate the roots of different plants." Another stated, "When I was a young girl we suffered a lot of hunger and because of this, at a young age, I went to the coast to work."

Two other factors may have contributed to the growing necessity of seasonal migration within San Juan. The growing highland population and resulting corn shortages forced many Maya to shorten their fallow periods, directly contributing to ecological degradation, declining land productivity, and, as a result, seasonal migration. In addition to the necessary goods purchased by Maya with their wage-labor incomes, seasonal migrants also likely acquired new tastes and new needs as a result of their exposure to plantation life and money (McCreery 1995:218). As a result of this ratchet effect, they might continue to seek work in order to meet material consumption expectations (Wilk 1991). However, I do not have evidence to directly support these alternative explanations. Furthermore, even though coastal plantation labor provided a means of survival for Juaneros, labor conditions were far from idyllic, the pay was low, and, if one possessed sufficient, fertile lands, the returns of subsistence agricultural labor were reportedly higher than those of seasonal migration. I am wary of interpreting Juanero seasonal migration as being solely motivated by consumerist desires. Seasonal labor migration and paid employment also contradicted the Juanero agrarian ethic of subsistence milpa production. Interviewed Juaneros nearly universally agreed that working for one's *propia cuenta*, or for one's self, is much preferred to laboring under the watchful eye (and sometimes painful whip) of overseers in the fields belonging to others. Several elders recalled how they and their parents became sick as a result of the hard work (and, most likely, lowland diseases) performed during these years. This oppressive, interdependent structure of subsistence agriculture, seasonal plantation labor, structural racism, and endemic poverty limited the political power of Juaneros within the larger sphere.

As a result of the Ubico years of seasonal migration, poverty, and relative powerlessness, many Juaneros lost their land to neighboring Pedranos, a finding corroborated by earlier research in the community conducted by Sexton (1972:23). Although the wealthier Pedranos told the anthropologist Benjamin Paul that they purchased the land fair and square from their drunken and lazy neighbors (personal communication, May 2001), Juaneros recall a different history of those impoverished years, and not surprisingly, old animosities die hard. A run-down store sits on the road between the two towns with a rusty sign above its doorway marking *la frontera*, or the border separating the two communities. San Juan has long been San Pedro's smaller, less prosperous little brother, and during the twentieth century, this was truer than ever. As a result of corn shortages and widespread illnesses, Juaneros not only traveled to plantations for work but also began to sell parcels of land to Pedranos in exchange for the corn grown by their more prosperous neighbors. As one informant explained, "They sold their land very cheaply to the Pedranos; they sold it for ten pounds of corn, nothing more." Some interviewed Juaneros claim their neighbors were forced to sell their land in order to fulfill their *cargos* (appointed service positions) in the community's civil-religious hierarchy. For example, one stated, "Other people sold their land for customs or traditions and they didn't think about the future of their children or grandchildren . . . they didn't think hard about what they were doing when they lent their service to the community."

Other interviewed Juaneros claim Pedranos took advantage of San Juan's seasonal near abandonment and began to cultivate not only land they had rightfully bought but also land they illegally appropriated. Juaneros of all ages repeated stories of the notoriously corrupt mayor of the time and his assistant who accepted bribes and gifts (and many claim copious amounts of alcohol) in exchange for signing land titles granting Pedranos parcels of land owned by absentee Juaneros. One elder recalled, "Some Pedranos only bought two, three or five cuerdas but when they arranged their documents they put down ten, fifteen, or twenty cuerdas and the community suffered then and we continue to suffer because our fathers and grandfathers could do nothing to rescue these lands."[3] Ultimately, the mayor was reportedly murdered by a group of irate Juaneros who were unable to reclaim their lost land.

The work of other anthropologists suggests that such battles for land were not necessarily rare. For example, Watanabe maintains that in Chimbal, "[c]ompetition for land with neighboring Maya communities was nearly as intense as contention between Maya claims and Ladino commercial interest elsewhere in the Cuchumatan Highlands" (1992:167). Little describes a similar process of land shrinkage for another Atitlan community, Santa Catarina Palopo, which, like San Juan, is next to an economically dominant community (Panajachel). In 1911, K'iche' Maya from Santa Lucia Utatlan bought from Catarinecos roughly 1,000 acres of fairly level land nearly 600 meters above Santa Catarina, and in 1936 Catarinecos rented out eight terraced fields to Panajachelenos, who planted onions. Furthermore, the shortage of land in Santa Catarina was exacerbated as most of the real estate along the town's banks was purchased beginning in the 1950s by wealthy Guatemalans and foreigners for the construction of vacation homes, a process that is ongoing today in San Juan (Little 2004:232). The transfer of Juanero lands into the hands of Pedranos is a clear example of a local factor that directly contributed to the growing necessity of seasonal migration in addition to national political, economic, and demographic trends.

The other enduring legacy of the Ubico era is the period of required military service many young Juanero males endured. In a survey of San Juan inhabitants conducted in the early 1970s, Sexton found that forty-four out of seventy-three male informants had served in the military, "[a]n unusual record for the Indian towns around the lake" (1972:23). My research corroborates this earlier data. Although some former soldiers I interviewed spoke ruefully of their forced conscription and the hard life they endured, others recalled the years of travel outside the community with obvious excitement. Far from passive observers, Juaneros serving in the military were active participants in Guatemala's history and not all of their years of military service were characterized by brutality and harsh conditions. Several former soldiers learned how to read and write while serving in the military, valuable and rare skills within the community at the time. In addition, serving side by side with Ladinos, some Juanero soldiers reported gaining a sense of familiarity with members of the dominant ethnic group. Recalling his conscription at age seventeen, one elder (a cooperative founder) explained to me that in addition to learning to read and write, he was taught many skills in the army. However, he pointed out, "They teach you many things but it depends on the person, if he pays attention to what they teach or not, but everything they teach will help you live your life." One elder's story of conscription details the extent to which national politics influenced the daily lives of rural Juaneros. He recalled that on his eighteenth birthday he went to the commander of arms to put his name on the list. Every June 30, the new soldiers would begin their service, and so he traveled to the army base with his *compañeros* (fellow Juaneros), where he worked for three months until the October Revolution of 1944, an event he described in much detail. This revolution in turn ended forced conscription and his brief military career.

TEN YEARS OF SPRING

In 1940, the first of five International Coffee Agreements allowed for nearly 16 million bags of coffee to enter the United States: Brazil's portion was 60 percent; Colombia, 20 percent; and the remaining twelve Latin American signers shared the final 20 percent. Until this time, Europe's discriminating consumers purchased estate coffees according to quality, in contrast with U.S. consumers who were less particular. The ICA enabled a small number of U.S. coffee firms to set a single price for all of the coffee produced in a region. The years leading up to this agreement had been especially tumultuous ones for the world coffee market, and the uncertainty plagued Guatemalan producers and laborers alike. The agreement effectively stabilized Latin American coffee production, albeit with some loss of the more discriminating European market.

However, at the same time as the international coffee market was stabilizing, the growth of commercial agriculture in Guatemala stimulated the development of a new class of artisans, professionals, businesspersons, university students, and industrial workers that grew impatient with Ubico's inability to free the national economy from the vicissitudes of the world coffee market and from the operations, legitimate and illegitimate, of the United Fruit Company (Wasserstrom 1975:448). Although students initiated the opposition to Ubico (Handy 1984:105), the emergence of the labor movement among urban workers in 1944 ultimately forced him to resign and provided the new president, Juan José Arévalo (1945–1951), with the support needed to decrease his political dependence upon national political parties. Furthermore, the coffee elite, who resented the exorbitant freight rates they were forced to pay the International Railways of Central America (owned by the United Fruit Company) for transporting their crop, granted Arévalo limited approval (Wasserstrom 1975:449). Arévalo created a new constitution and voting regulations, enacted a series of health and social reforms, and increased education spending by 155 percent between 1946 and

1950 (Handy 1984:107). Daily life in San Juan was more directly influenced by the social and labor reforms than the agrarian ones. For example, one elder recalled during an interview how the "good Doctor Arévalo" eliminated the lice that previously plagued rural inhabitants by instituting the regular fumigation of rural homes across the countryside. In 1945, the new constitution abolished vagrancy laws and forced labor. As a result, although Juaneros continued to seasonally migrate to coastal plantations in search of work, they were no longer required to do so by law. One elder explained, "In this time there was liberty, everyone began to work for himself and had total control over his labor."

The agrarian reform began in 1949 with the largely ineffective Ley de Arrendamiento Forzos, which required large-scale landowners to rent uncultivated land to neighboring peasants (Wasserstrom 1975:452). In 1951, Jacobo Arbenz Guzmán was inaugurated with the heavy support of sectors of the divided labor movement and middle-class progressives; under Arbenz Guatemala moved sharply to the left and into a close relationship with the Soviet Union, although the new president did not openly profess Communism (Woodward 1999:240). Under his direction, the agrarian reform was carried to the countryside.[4] Arbenz combined agrarian reform with support for agricultural diversification and expanded access to agricultural credit (Handy 1984:114), hoping that progressive legislation would enable his government to organize peasant and labor movements on which he could depend while he reorganized Guatemala's economy along more just and efficient lines.[5]

Arbenz enjoyed only scattered support in many municipalities,[6] but during his administration more than 900,000 acres were expropriated from more than 1,000 of the largest fincas, the majority of which were lowland plantations producing export commodities other than coffee, and were redistributed to 87,000 individuals. Although only 16 percent of the country's total lands were expropriated, much less than eligible under the terms of the law, the redistribution prompted opposition from landowners, the Church, and the military (Handy 1984:128–132). The biggest loser was the United Fruit Company, which lost 372,000 acres of uncultivated land. It is generally argued[7] that this expropriation convinced Eisenhower to agree to Operation Success, a U.S. military invasion spearheaded by Allen Dulles, the head of the CIA who owned significant shares of United Fruit Company stock, and the secretary of state, John Foster (Handy 1984:139). With the help of the United States, the ex-colonel Castillo Armas took power in 1954 and 90 percent of the expropriated lands were swiftly returned to their previous owners. Operation Success was the CIA's most ambitious and covert operation and served as a model for future actions. It lasted for nearly a year and relied on the Organization of American States (OAS) to isolate Guatemala diplomatically, worked with U.S. businesses to create an economic crisis there, and funded and equipped an exile invasion force based in Honduras (Grandin 2004:77). The overthrow of Arbenz restored the coffee planters, large landholders, and foreign capitalists to power and protected them under military regimes (Woodward 1999:245).

THE MILPA MIGRATION

The failed agrarian reforms did little to alleviate the ongoing pressures facing highland communities that were a consequence of population growth, declining soil fertility, and decreased local wage labor opportunities. In the western highlands, the average farm size decreased from 1.3 hectares per person in 1950, the middle of the "Ten Years of Spring," to 0.8 hectare in 1975. At the same time, the highland population increased at a rate of 3 percent per year (Jonas 1991:79), partially as a result of increased longevity resulting from expanded access to health services in rural areas. By the mid-1960s the Guatemalan National Planning Council estimated that 90 percent of rural families possessed insufficient land for subsistence (Jonas 1991:65), and by 1976 there were more than 400,000 landless farmers in Guatemala (Jonas 1991:79). Guatemala possessed one of the most inequitable systems of land distribution in all of Latin America with indigenous farmers surviving on what Galeano poetically termed "plots of land the size of graves" (1967:5). Over time, population growth effectively eliminated subsistence production as a viable alternative to wage labor. Not surprisingly, some national commentators attributed the growing landlessness and poverty in highland areas to the innate backwardness of Maya communities and traditional farming methods. However, Maya subsistence farmers not only produced a higher yield per dollar invested and cultivated a substantially greater proportion of their holdings than owners of larger fincas but also achieved yields up to twenty times more per hectare than the largest farm size, despite inferior land and limited use of chemical fertilizers and pesticides (Handy 1984:211). Therefore, it is more probable that increasing land pressures accounted for the pressing problems of rural hunger and poverty, not ignorance or poor production methods.

Along with many other highland Maya, Juaneros continued to seek employment on coastal plantations in the postwar era and this semi-proletarian workforce continued to subsidize a system of large-scale agricultural export production rooted in the exploitation of underpaid labor. The rapid expansion of sugar, beef, and cotton production in Central America after World War II began to challenge coffee's reign, and the 1950s and 1960s proved to be boom years for the Central American agro-export economies (Paige 1997:229). Whereas in the past labor contractors were reportedly external agents, beginning in the early 1960s, Juaneros were increasingly recruited for plantation employment by local labor contractors, first from San Pedro and later from San Juan. When they signed on with a contractor they were given a small advance of five or ten quetzals for the promise of fifteen days to one month of work. These labor contractors formed part of what some have identified as a growing divide in the egalitarian ethic of highland Maya communities. Previously, economic divisions resulted from the size of landholdings; however, now a new class of wealthier individuals emerged as a result of non-subsistence activities. Grandin (2000:223) argues this phenomenon was widespread and, as some community members increased their non-subsistence economic activities, social stratification and capital accumulation slowly increased. Some communities became divided between a newly empowered bourgeoisie and an impoverished campesino class. However, as a result of extended familial relationships and customary obligations, local labor contractors were often more likely to treat laborers fairly and pay an honest wage than outsiders. Furthermore, better transportation and communication increased seasonal migrants' knowledge of the labor market and, as a result, they ceased to remain at the mercy of labor recruiters (Watanabe 1992:145).

Interviewed Juaneros recalled traveling to the coastal plantations in buses holding forty or even fifty people. Of the fifty-three surveyed cooperative members (out of 116 total members) forty-two, or 79 percent, reported that they had worked outside of San Juan (with the vast majority traveling to the southern coast). Seasonal labor migration clearly radicalized some Guatemalan Maya, such as Nobel Peace Prize winner Rigoberta Menchu, who tells of watching her brother die under a cloud of aerial pesticides while working on a plantation in her testimonial *I, Rigoberta Menchu* (1983); however, because many communities migrated in family groups and spoke a language different from Ladinos and other Maya, their exposure to new ideas and experiences remained limited. By and large, Juaneros traveled together to work on plantations; however, family groups sometimes split off in search of better offers. As one elder explained, "We weren't always together, one group would go to one finca and another group would go to the other finca when they heard that there was a good harvest and they paid well."

Echoing earlier patterns of seasonal migration under the forced labor drafts, interviewed Juaneros explained that they migrated out of necessity, not desire. During an interview, one elder recalled, "When our people went to the coast it was because there was not sufficient work here and there was no way to earn the money to sustain our families." The little wage labor to be found in San Juan or surrounding communities paid substantially less, reportedly fifty centavos per day, than the wage in the coastal region, one quetzal per 100 pounds of cotton picked, which meant stronger men could earn upwards of two quetzals a day at a time (1930s) when the quetzal was equivalent in value to the U.S. dollar (Little 2008). However, seasonal employment on coastal cotton plantations did not end the endemic hunger facing the community members. One interviewed elder told me with tears in her eyes how her twin boys died from hunger while her husband looked for work on the coast in order to buy corn to feed his family.

The large percentage of migrating Juaneros undoubtedly stressed community and family relations in addition to the maintenance of the religious *cofradías* (religious brotherhoods and organizations) and Catholic Action as many individuals were forced to miss community celebrations and events such as Holy Week and patron saints' days. Furthermore, as in years past, working conditions on plantations continued to be intolerable. For example, one elder recalled: "Because we weren't living in a house we suffered a lot. There were many flies and sometimes they found our tortillas and food. They gave us only beans to eat three times a day for thirty days and sometimes we were desperate for food because they would give us uncooked or spoiled beans." Another remembered starting work at three in the morning in order to avoid the intense midday heat on the coast. Many Juaneros suffered from disease and others acquired vices, such as alcoholism, which increasingly plagued the male members of the community and strained family relations. One cooperative founder reported suffering greatly while working as a young child on coastal plantations. He recalled: "The first time I went with my brothers I was eight or nine years old. I remember crying a lot for my mother and I was very sad. She probably cried as well." Much of the abuse that Juaneros experienced on the fincas was structural and perhaps unconscious: because the landed elite's racism led them to assume that Indians lived in filth and ignorance, they refused to provide humane working and living conditions (McCreery 2003).

Despite the hardships, many Juaneros would likely agree with the statement made by one older cooperative member: "This work was worth it. If you didn't suffer, you didn't eat corn." Work in coastal plantations was a proven survival strategy in the face of debilitating poverty, and although it did not rescue all families from the routine hunger they faced, it did enable others to improve their conditions. One interviewed elder told me that when she and her husband first traveled to the plantations, they were inadequately clothed because of their poverty, a situation they quickly alleviated upon receipt of their first paychecks. Another recalled how after her family's first trip to the coast (around 1960), they were able to buy construction materials for their future house, and after their second trip they succeeded in building it. Some Juaneros remained in the coastal region, managing to save money in order to buy land there and begin a new life. Elders found great delight in regaling disbelieving *gringas*, like me, with stories of coastal towns populated with farmers wearing San Juan traje and speaking Tz'utujil.

In the 1970s and 1980s, Central America became the third largest exporter of beef to the United States after Australia and New Zealand (Edelman 1995:27). As the world market commodity prices for Guatemala's leading export crops (cotton, coffee, and sugar) declined, many plantation owners shifted production to less labor-intensive crops such as soy, sorghum, and beef, thereby reducing the demand for a migrating workforce (Green 1999:34). Cattle grazing was particularly attractive to Guatemalan producers because it allowed for the retention of large (albeit degraded) tracts of land, demanded little direction from absentee landlords, and required little capital investment and relatively few laborers (Handy 1984:199).

In their search for a viable alternative to coastal migration, Juaneros participated in the shifting focus of Guatemala's agro-export economy. Beginning in the 1970s, many male Juaneros began migrating to the coastal region in order to work for their "propia cuenta" (to work for themselves) as tenant laborers, planting milpa in the fields owned by wealthy plantation owners transitioning to beef production. Instead of paying rent to finqueros, they planted *zacate* grass during the rainy months of June and July between the rows of maize. After harvesting, they cleaned the milpa away, leaving grass for the cattle. Some Juaneros hired day laborers to help them tend their milpa, while others worked in solitude. Working by himself, a Juanero was reportedly able to plant and harvest six cuerdas, and ten with help. This tenancy was also common in Costa Rica, where landowners found it a virtually cost-free method of expanding pastures that provided the added benefit of enabling them to test soil fertility by observing peasants' crops. However, once landlords had cleared properties of forest and brush and planted pasture, they had little reason to continue lending land or hiring workers (Edelman 1992:257).

Despite that in the long run they were contributing to their own obsolescence as workers, planting milpa on coastal plantations benefited Juaneros in a number of ways. First, they were able to mitigate the growing shortage of land locally while simultaneously engaging in culturally meaningful milpa production. In addition, on the coast they were able to plant two harvests a year. The men traveled monthly to the lowland plantations to tend their plots. They cleaned the milpa in March, planted in April, and harvested in August. Beginning in September, they replanted and enjoyed a second harvest in January. Some sold their corn on the coast while others transported it back to San Juan (often on a truck collectively hired for the purpose) to feed their families and sell in local markets. The latter proved very profitable during the lean months of January, February, and March, when highland corn supplies were beginning to run dry and local prices began to rise. In fact, the "milpa migration" of the 1970s was a harbinger of the economic changes in store for Juaneros. One cooperative member explained, "There we found the good life, I sold some for my costs and fed my family well." Others used their profits to increase their landholdings, plant coffee, or make improvements on their houses, such as adding tin roofs. The money earned during the years of milpa farming on the coast helped fund a revival of local agriculture, subsidizing the introduction of chemical fertilizers and coffee production. In essence, the coastal milpa became the capital used to diversify local production and hence it contributed to the eventual end of seasonal migration by community members.

"MANUEL ABONO"

Multiple sources in San Juan corroborate the story of chemical fertilizer's introduction to the community. In the mid-1960s an enterprising Pedrano, Don Manuel Gonzales, reportedly introduced local farmers to chemical fertilizers, thereby acquiring the nickname Manuel Abono (abono means "fertilizer"). One elder told me, "We didn't know where he brought it from, but he told the people that there was this new type of fertilizer and it was very easy to apply, and he gave a little to the people to try and it did provide good results." Some Juaneros quickly adopted the new product though others reportedly balked at its introduction. For example, a cooperative member recalled, "My father was very bothered when the fertilizer came; he didn't want to use it." This initially mixed reaction to chemical fertilizer is echoed in the findings of Carey, who claims that in a nearby Kaqchikel community many refused to use chemical fertilizer, despite the immediate benefits it produced (2001:104).

Chemical fertilizers reportedly helped indigenous farmers living in the highlands to significantly increase production levels, thereby enabling them to feed their families with less land. For example, Watanabe's ethnographic research demonstrates that in Chimalteco, milpa production jumped from

60 pounds per cuerda in 1964 to 150–200 pounds per cuerda by 1979, allowing Chimaltecos to plant only between fifteen and twenty cuerdas of milpa to feed their families, half to a third less than they needed ten years earlier (1992:134). Furthermore, chemical fertilizers also reportedly enabled some Juaneros to diversify their agricultural production; in addition to milpa some began to cultivate horticultural crops such as tomatoes and onions to sell in local and regional markets. One elder recalled, "The people began to plant onion in large quantities because the application of chemical fertilizer was fast and easy and it produced a good harvest." However, at this point, San Juan still lacked paved roads and horticulturalists were forced to transport their crops on foot or by boat. The introduction of chemical fertilizers benefited not only landowners but landless day laborers as well who profited from the increased local employment opportunities resulting from the introduction of cash crops, such as onions and coffee. The majority of Juaneros reportedly ceased to migrate in search of work in the late 1970s and early 1980s. However, Maya from other highland communities continued to migrate to pay for their chemical inputs as cash became, for the first time, a necessary component of subsistence agriculture. Financial resources were also required to purchase desired consumer goods, subsidize children's education, and cover emergency expenses, such as those resulting from illness. As cash needs increased across the highlands, for some it became increasingly difficult to maintain the economic autonomy they sought.

Eventually the miracle harvests began to decline as a result of soil depletion and increasing problems with pest and disease. One cooperative member who now produces coffee organically told me that, at the time, "[n]obody knew it would waste the land and that it killed the nutrients in the soil." Others wistfully recalled how in years past, "[e]verything we ate wasn't contaminated with these chemical products, but now everything is changing." Although some romanticize the days when they were able to farm with only compost or chicken manure, the majority of non-cooperative members I spoke with told me that because the earth is accustomed to chemical fertilizers they cannot stop using them. A few even embraced a conspiracy theory, claiming the introduction of chemical fertilizers was a tactic employed by foreign manufacturers and governments who wanted to persecute highland Mayas. This contemporary theory resonates with the initial reluctance of some Maya to embrace chemical fertilizers as they represented yet one more foreign thing forced on them.

Chemical fertilizers significantly altered agricultural production in Maya communities; however, despite their widespread use poverty remains endemic in rural Guatemala and the historic inequities in the land tenure system endure. Furthermore, the growth in organic production among smallholders, described in Chapter 5, cannot entirely be attributed to market opportunities and instead indicates that there is increasing awareness of the ecological damage and subsequent declining yields that result from intensive chemical production methods. On the other hand, coupled with the capital earned through milpa migration, chemical fertilizers did help reverse the century-long pattern of seasonal labor migration by increasing local milpa yields, diversification of production, and local wage labor opportunities.[8] The irony of chemical fertilizers is that they enabled Juanero farmers to reproduce a distinctively Maya agrarian lifestyle that was in jeopardy of slipping away, much in the same way that broccoli (Fischer and Benson 2006) and handicrafts (Little 2004) have provided an economic base enabling contemporary Maya to retain their traditional domestic values.

LA BOMBA DEL CAFÉ

Although coffee has been the "heart of Guatemala" for more than a century, until the 1970s it was, by and large, a market almost exclusively controlled by the wealthy landed elite. However, beginning in the 1970s, coffee reportedly "exploded like a bomb" in San Juan. Despite coffee's turbulent history in Guatemala, it became an increasingly attractive agricultural commodity for smallholders because it is easy to store and handle, its value has historically surpassed that of comparable agricultural products, it can be grown on steep slopes, and once neglected it can be fairly easily rejuvenated (Sick 1999). Juaneros attribute the local introduction of coffee to different individuals. Some claim that Don José Gonzalez Mendoza planted the first coffee in San Juan, bringing small plants from the coast on his mules in the 1960s. However, Paul reports that Pedranos attribute coffee's local introduction to the first Protestant convert in the community, Julian Cotuc: he converted in the 1920s and first planted coffee in the 1930s (1999).

Guatemalan coffee finqueros controlled more land and laborers than their contemporaries in neighboring Central American countries. For example, the mean coffee land area controlled by individual estate owners (342 *manzanas*) was 1.5 times the mean size of large estates found in other Central American countries (Paige 1997:66).[9] Additionally, the Guatemalan coffee elite controlled approximately three times as many resident laborers as the Salvadoran elite between 1935 and 1942 (Paige 1997:68). According to the 1979 agricultural census, when the coffee bomb began to explode in San Juan, smallholders produced less than 16 percent of the total national exports.[10] In 1975, coffee's price in the international marketplace rose dramatically as a result of a Brazilian frost. Using money earned through migration, milpa harvests on the southern coast, and local vegetable sales, Juaneros, like many small farmers across the highlands, began to plant increasing numbers of coffee trees to profit from the relatively high prices. Subsistence agriculturalists who converted to coffee production in the late 1970s and early 1980s entered a market dominated by a small number of large producers and members of the coffee elite. It would be many years before small-scale producers began to successfully carve a niche for themselves in the international marketplace.

Although coffee eventually exploded on the market, its initial introduction to the community was not so forceful. The low prices (some recall prices as low as one quetzal and fifty centavos per quintal [100 pounds]) and the long-term investment demanded by coffee (trees do not produce until two to four years after being planted and coffee is considered permanent in contrast to single-season crops) meant that Juaneros did not immediately convert all their land to coffee production, instead choosing to plant a few plots here and there in order to diversify their production. Unlike other cash crops locally cultivated at the time, such as tomatoes, onions, and chickpeas, there was no local market or demand for coffee. Therefore, Juaneros were forced to sell their coffee to street corner *coyotes*, the buyers employed by local beneficio owners who processed the coffee and then sold it in parchment form to regional dry-mill owners. Because Juaneros could not negotiate the price for their product or even shop around for better offers (because coffee spoils, it has to be processed within twenty-four hours of being picked), the returns for coffee remained lower in relation to other cash crops. However, in the mid-1970s as the price climbed to between eight and ten quetzals per quintal (at a time when the quetzal's value remained on par with the U.S. dollar's), the local coffee market began to more firmly establish itself.

As the local coffee market expanded, increasing numbers of Juaneros converted their milpa and agricultural plots previously planted with various horticultural products to coffee. As coffee prices rose, so did land prices, and Juaneros, already facing land shortages by the 1970s, began to clear the previously forested slopes of the volcanoes looming above the community. One cooperative member maintained that in the past when this land remained uncultivated, "[t]here was more freedom and there weren't so many private landholdings." The forested slopes of the volcanoes were unsuitable for milpa or horticultural production but were well-suited to coffee trees, which prefer high altitude and can grow on steep slopes. In years past, community members cut firewood, harvested wild greens, and grazed their animals on the uncultivated land. In fact, several interviewed cooperative members told me they eventually sold their horses and cattle, or failed to replace them when they died, because there was no longer any place to graze them. However, they might also have sold the animals because they no longer needed their manure for fertilizer as a result of the introduction of chemical inputs. Furthermore, in later years as transportation and local roads improved, farmers did not require large animals to transport products beyond the village. Only 32 percent of surveyed cooperative members reported owning a horse or donkey.

Although Juaneros converted fields to coffee as a result of rising prices, two other factors also contributed to this trend. First, beginning in the early 1980s the price of onions, which were grown for sale in regional markets, began to steadily decline. During this time period increasing numbers of farmers across the highlands began to acquire irrigation systems, enabling them to produce crops that demand constant water, like onions. More supply resulted in lower prices and effectively eliminated the advantage Juaneros previously enjoyed from the easy irrigation of lakeside living. Second, because coffee is a taller crop than most others, when planted next to an onion or tomato field, it reportedly blocks sunshine from neighboring plots. As a result of partible inheritance, in which agricultural plots are evenly distributed among an heir's offspring, San Juan resembles many highland Maya communities in the patchwork of small agricultural plots covering its hillsides. One cooperative member explained, "What happened is that even though I didn't want to plant coffee in my land, when my neighbors planted coffee, my land was surrounded and the other crops didn't produce because of the shade." On average, the fifty-three surveyed cooperative members reported that they had cultivated coffee for twenty years, or since approximately 1982. Furthermore, of these surveyed members, forty-three, or 81 percent, reported that they themselves planted this coffee (versus buying or inheriting it). The expansion of the local coffee export market hastened the Juaneros' nearly full integration into the cash economy. Because milpa was cleared away in favor of coffee, many cooperative members now use coffee profits to purchase supplemental maize for their families. Income earned from coffee sales supplements their household milpa production, much in the same way that seasonal migration once supplemented subsistence agriculture. The introduction of coffee effectively ended seasonal migration and brought a relative degree of prosperity to the community. Not only did the success of the new cash crop foster the formation and maintenance of the coffee cooperative, with coffee profits many Juaneros were able to construct solid cement-block houses, send their children to school, and purchase consumer products such as televisions or even pickup trucks.

ECONOMIC DEVELOPMENT THROUGH COOPERATION

Beginning in the late 1960s and concurrent with coffee's growing attraction for smallholders, the U.S. Agency for International Development (USAID) mission to Guatemala and other lenders began prioritizing rural development. In 1970, USAID approved a $23 million rural development sector loan for the development of cooperatives (Handy 1984:240), the first time substantial development resources were earmarked for indigenous highland communities. USAID's interest in cooperatives and rural development reflected the post-Cuban revolution concern expressed by the Alliance for Progress that rural poverty would potentially provide the fodder for Marxist guerilla revolutions. By fall 1975 nearly 20 percent of highland Maya participated in some form of cooperatives (Handy 1984:240), and after the 1976 earthquake and the influx of additional lenders, Guatemala boasted 510 cooperatives, 57 percent of them in the highlands with more than 132,000 members (Brockett 1998:112).

Simultaneously, the Catholic Church of Guatemala made a concerted effort, beginning in 1946 with the foundation of Catholic Action, to increase the number of priests in small villages across the highlands. In 1955 there were 242 priests and by the late 1960s there were 415 scattered across the country. Nearly 84 percent of the Guatemalan clergy were foreign-born, and therefore, these immigrant priests (mostly of European origin) were less aligned with local and national elites. To compete with Protestant missionaries, who were increasingly seeking converts in highland communities, and as a result of Vatican II, the Church also promoted the formation of local associations and cooperatives.

La Voz Que Clama en el Desierto was founded with the encouragement and aid of a micro-credit lending institution located in Santiago Atitlan and operated by Caritas International, a confederation of relief, development, and social service organizations operated by the Catholic Church. In the late 1970s this organization provided small low-interest loans to Lake Atitlan residents for projects and the purchase of agricultural inputs. Caritas was the first micro-credit program to provide loans to residents of San Juan. The director, Don Diego, reportedly urged a group of community members to form a cooperative to establish its own revolving credit fund because at the time it was difficult for disenfranchised indigenous farmers to secure personal loans from banks. More than seventy community members attended the first meeting, and in 1979 twenty-five men founded the cooperative, inscribing several younger brothers and wives in order to reach the minimum membership of thirty required by INACOP, the National Cooperative Registry.

Although the cooperative was officially founded as an agricultural organization, the group's first effort was a consumer cooperative, consisting of a small store and a diesel-powered corn grinder. However, when these initiatives did not prove financially remunerative, the group transitioned into coffee processing and collective sales. In the mid-1980s cooperative members began to individually de-pulp their coffee by hand and sell it to a coffee exporter in Santo Tomas La Union on the southern coast. As a result of their success in the coffee market and the failure of their small store and corn grinder, the cooperative began to focus exclusively on coffee production at this time. In 1990, it became a founding member of the Group of Fourteen, an alliance of small-scale coffee-producer organizations in Guatemala. The group collectively exported coffee primarily to Holland with the assistance of the Dutch fair-trade NGO, Max Havelaar. For the first time, during the 1991–1992 coffee harvest the majority of La Voz's coffee was certified organic by the Organic Crop Improvement Association (one of the first Guatemalan cooperatives to achieve this certification). The organic certification and membership in the Group of Fourteen enabled the cooperative to secure a prominent spot in the emerging fair-trade and organic-coffee export market.

As a member of the Group of Fourteen, La Voz enjoyed networking opportunities, which eventually led to a long-term relationship with San Diego–based Elan Organic Coffees. Once La Voz achieved organic certification, Elan began to import an increasingly larger percentage of the group's coffee into the United States. However, La Voz continued to export a portion of its coffee through the Group of Fourteen until 1995, when it began to sell its coffee exclusively to Elan. Shortly thereafter, the Group of Fourteen collapsed amid rumors of corrupt management and a high world market price, which encouraged members of the (then more than twenty) federated associations to sell their coffee to local coyotes and resulted in the group's failure to fulfill export contracts. La Voz's early forays into the organic and fair-trade coffee market helped the cooperative to secure a strong market position in the rapidly emerging U.S. certified-coffee market in the late 1990s. With the help of supportive importers, roasters, and development agencies, the cooperative firmly integrated itself in the international coffee economy.

THE GUATEMALAN CIVIL WAR AND SAN JUAN

Throughout Guatemala's history, the existence of an agricultural frontier muted many of the conflicts and disruptions created by the fast expansion of coffee capitalism. However, by the 1970s, the possibility for flight or migration had greatly diminished, forcing the rural poor, Ladino and Maya alike, to engage more directly the promise of state-administered justice (Grandin 2004:2). As noted above, following the failed Ten Years of Spring, many highland Maya became increasingly impoverished and dependent on seasonal labor migration. Between 1950 and the mid-1980s the Guatemalan population grew from 2.8 to 8.5 million and per capita access to land steadily declined (McCreery 2003). Even though recent studies do not portray the coffee fields as breeding grounds for revolutionaries (Topik and Clarence-Smith 2003a), the unequal distribution of land and the legacy of racism fostered by the nation's coffee economy did fuel the swelling ranks of guerilla combatants. However, a closer interpretation of events demonstrates that the thirty-year-long civil war (1976–1996) resulted from a more complex interplay of forces than this would imply. Ethnographic data indicate that levels of poverty varied significantly within and among communities. Contrary to popular opinion, many Maya, including the founding members of La Voz, enjoyed increasing economic prosperity and organizational strength during this period. Therefore, the origins of Guatemala's civil war lie not simply in growing rural impoverishment and widespread discontent but also in the alliance of the nation's coffee elite and the Guatemalan military combined with the extensive funding provided by the United States under the guise of fighting Communist insurgency.[11]

Guatemala's armed insurgency began primarily as a movement led by urban Ladino revolutionaries inspired by Cuba and other regional revolutionary movements, such as the Sandinistas in Nicaragua. In January 1972, the Guerrilla Army of the Poor (EGP) emerged in the highlands and began to build support within some indigenous communities.[12] The EGP was joined by three additional guerrilla groups: the Rebel Armed Forces (FAR), the Guatemalan Workers' Party (PGT), and the Organization of People in Arms (ORPA), the last of which organized in Chimaltenango and Sololá (the department in which San Juan is located) with a majority indigenous membership (Handy 1984:240). In 1982, these four guerrilla movements united to form the Guatemalan National Revolutionary Union (URNG).

In response to this collective mobilization, Lucas Garcia and Rios Montt initiated a scorched-earth campaign across the highlands. The 1981–1983 genocidal campaign was designed to counter what strategists perceived to be the closed, caste-like isolation of indigenous communities, which was identified as the reason for the supposed collective susceptibility of the Maya to Communism (Grandin 2004:14). In order to integrate indigenous communities into the state apparatus, all opposition had to be destroyed. This was accomplished not simply by eliminating the guerrillas and their real and potential supporters but also through the colonization of the spaces, symbols, and social relations believed to be outside state control. As Grandin describes it, "Terror was made spectacle" (2004:129). Montt destroyed the legal basis of municipal government by dismissing village leaders and replacing them with his own appointees. He also established a military zone in each of the country's twenty-two departments to replace the former nine and resettled rural residents into model villages subject to constant surveillance.

The result was a massive loss of life: in the aftermath of the civil war the extent of the human rights abuses was exposed. In 1999 the Report of the Commission for Historical Clarification published evidence of massacres in 626 villages and placed the number murdered during the war at close to 200,000. Among the victims, 83 percent were Maya and 93 percent of the human rights violations were attributed to the army (CEH 1999). Individuals who participated in successful community projects and organizations, such as agricultural cooperatives like La Voz, consistently faced accusations that they were engaging in subversive or guerrilla activities (Sanford 2003). Villages with autonomous local organizations were specifically targeted by government military forces. For example, from 1976 to 1978 in the department of El Quiché (near the department of Sololá) 168 cooperative and village leaders were murdered (Handy 1984:244).[13]

Green writes that when she asked her ethnographic informants about the civil war and the violence, they responded, "Pues, tranquila [calm, peaceful]" but that this was a fragile calm: "In fact, the unspoken but implied conclusion to the statement 'pues tranquila' is 'ahorita, pero mañana saber?' [for now, but who knows about tomorrow?]" (1999:69). more than ten years later, Juaneros responded the same way when I queried them about the war and its impact in the community. They commonly said, "Oh thank God, nothing happened here." Of course, horrible things *did* happen in San Juan, but they were speaking relatively, implicitly acknowledging that the violence in communities such as Santiago Atitlan (the site of a horrific massacre) eclipsed the local tragedies.[14]

Although La Voz successfully weathered the civil war, the organization's *tienda* (store) was robbed by soldiers, and the agricultural monitor, Santiago, was imprisoned at the military base in Santiago Atitlan for several days after he was denounced as a guerrilla. Santiago told me that he convinced the officers there that he was not a guerrilla and instead was simply interested in organic agriculture and dry latrines. In fact, they were so impressed with his knowledge of latrine construction that they had him build them one before setting him free. The fact that La Voz successfully weathered the civil war, although other cooperatives did not, is partially a testament to the group's internal cohesion and partially a result of serendipitous forces in that members were not directly targeted by civil patrols, the guerrillas, or the military. In other parts of the highlands, such as the Ixil triangle, smallholder coffee production and cooperative efforts were effectively halted. Because this was not the case in San Juan, the cooperative was strategically positioned to take advantage of the emerging organic and fair-trade coffee markets in the late 1990s with the end of the civil war.

Guatemala's civil war tore at the fabric of Maya communities and in many cases weakened the strength of cooperative practices and shared identities. As Fischer and Benson explain, the surveillance culture characterizing the war at the local level dismantled the trust upon which reciprocity relies, replacing it with a more narrowly defined self-interest. Therefore, they argue, the violence was more successful than intended in supplanting communal tendencies with neoliberal capitalist relations (2006:119). As a result of the war, San Juan and surrounding communities were plagued by ongoing fear and mistrust, which partially constrain community organizing and development efforts to this day.

A FRAGILE PEACE

Several interrelated forces contributed to the final end of the civil war in 1997. First, the URNG acknowledged its defeat at the hands of the military regime and leaders gradually adopted a strategy of gaining a share of the power through the sanctioned political process (Jonas 2000:223). Second, the United Nations intervened as a result of the increasing international pressure fostered by organizations in exile and the popular support resulting from Rigoberta Menchu's 1992 Nobel Peace Prize. Guatemala was seen as a test case for the international community. Throughout the prolonged peace process, there was a deliberate attempt to avoid competition between the United Nations and international financial institutions. Of critical importance was the shifting attitude of the nation's coffee elite who previously supported authoritarian rule. They eventually came to see the pariah status of the country as a liability for their business dealings and pressured the government to end the civil war and restore economic and political stability (Warren 1998; Jonas 2000).

Although the Peace Accords, fostered by the combination of global economic and human rights interests, failed to restructure the Guatemalan state, they officially provided political spaces for public debate where civil society theoretically can make demands for development and democratization

(Pearce 1998:596; Green 1999:49). However, one legacy of the nation's civil war is the contemporary violence plaguing the country, which combined with the residual fear of government reprisal, especially prevalent in rural areas, serves to curtail grassroots mobilization and community-generated development projects. In Central America violent crime has skyrocketed and Guatemala now has a murder rate of 26 per 100,000 (in comparison, the U.S. murder rate is 6:100,000 and Colombia's, a nation in the midst of a civil war, is 72:100,000). Guatemala currently ranks among the most dangerous nations in the world for which standardized data are available (UN 2007). The murder rate is significantly lower in the majority indigenous departments. For example, Sololá, the department in which San Juan is located, has the lowest murder rate in the country at 9 deaths per 100,000 (UN 2007).[15] Furthermore, despite the Peace Accords, the nation's military and police forces remain strong and well-funded: in 2005 the United States resumed direct military aid to Guatemala following a ten-year postwar hiatus while drastically cutting development aid (Fischer and Benson 2006:111). This enduring violence impedes economic development by destroying social and human capital, undermining the government, and discouraging investment. The United Nations Development Program (UNDP) estimates that violence costs Guatemala close to $2.4 billion every year, or 7.3 percent of the nation's GDP.

CONCLUSIONS

During the 1970s and 1980s, anthropological thinking about indigenous peoples was radically altered by world system studies and theorists who argued that even isolated communities were caught up in the very global historical processes that transformed them (Dove 2006:193). For example, Wolf argued, "The more ethnohistory we know, the more clearly 'their' history and 'our' history emerge as part of the same history" (1982:19). It is undoubtedly clear from the partial and highly situated narrative of Guatemalan history presented in this chapter that I find this argument compelling. However, its logical conclusion, that indigenous identity itself is a historical product, raises complex questions of authenticity, and it is perhaps more beneficial to focus on the articulation of indigeneity and the agency of ethnographic subjects.[16]

For centuries Juaneros have contributed to larger processes and been intimately connected to northern consumers through transnational economic and political forces. The community's history demonstrates how Juaneros have long labored to help produce the tropical commodities that are so central to northern cultures and diets, and beginning in the twentieth century the daily life within the community has been intimately shaped by the political agendas and development and military aid flowing from the United States. The members of La Voz are active agents in the fair-trade coffee market, not simply the passive recipients of external beneficence. The community's history demonstrates that their participation in the economic, cultural, and political flows that cross national borders and constitute fair-trade networks is not a drastic departure from past circumstances (which northern fair-trade consumers might imagine were ones of spatial and cultural isolation). At the same time, close attention to the community's historical transformations underscores some of the concrete ways in which fair-trade market participation *is* radically different from earlier patterns of economic and cultural exchange. Furthermore, identifying the problems that have long plagued this community, such as endemic poverty, the insecurity of land tenure, structural racism, discrimination, violence, and political powerlessness, illuminates the economic advantages that fair trade offers cooperative members.

3

"Trade Not Aid": Assessing Fair Trade's Economic Impact on Cooperative Members and Their Families

Guatemala is one of the most impoverished nations in the Western Hemisphere and, like many Latin American nations, a region of stark financial inequalities. Approximately 75 percent of Guatemalans live below the poverty line, meaning that they cannot afford to regularly purchase a basic basket of goods. Conditions are even bleaker in rural indigenous communities such as San Juan. However, statistics like these do little to illuminate the harsh reality of this poverty that exists in the shadows of the posh hotels and eateries lining the streets of Guatemala City's Zona Viva. Guatemala currently has the fourth-highest rate of chronic malnutrition in the world and the highest in Latin America and the Caribbean (WFP 2009). Unlike in the United States and other developed nations, there are no social safety nets in Guatemala, such as WIC (Special Supplemental Nutrition Program for Women, Infants, and Children) or school lunch programs, to help alleviate this hunger, which is especially acute in rural communities. Therefore, the true face of poverty in

Guatemala far eclipses what most of us have experienced in our own lives and communities. Quite simply, in virtually every rural community across Guatemala, children die regularly as a result of malnutrition and illnesses (such as diarrhea), which could be easily prevented and cured with access to basic health care.

I did not truly appreciate the potential power of fair trade until the day, several years before I moved to San Juan, when I sat on a hard, cold bench in a small chapel nestled among the coffee trees in a rural community. I struggled to hold back my tears during the funeral of a toddler who had starved to death (for it felt somehow impertinent for me, a foreign gringa, to cry in front of the child's grief-stricken parents). Afterward, the priest who had brought me to the service railed against the injustice of a coffee economy that does not provide farmers with enough money to feed their children. Experiences like this make clear that fair trade is about much more than celebrity endorsements, glossy packaging, and feel-good consumerism. In the poverty-stricken coffee-growing communities of Guatemala and elsewhere it is about staving off death. In San Juan, fair trade has enabled the cooperative members not only to make a living but to make that living meaningful as they gain satisfaction from their agricultural labor and organizational efforts. This chapter does not present a rosy and celebratory portrayal of fair trade—the guaranteed price remains far too low and the market's coverage is far from adequate—however, it is important to keep in mind the desolate poverty that, at its root, the movement is attempting to erase.

Fair-trade certification and its complements within the North American market, organic and shade-grown certification, reach far beyond the economic realm and have profound impacts on the social, political, and ecological realms of coffee farmers' daily lives. However, because the primary goal of fair trade, reflected in its hallmark slogan "trade not aid," is poverty alleviation, it makes sense to begin our evaluation of the movement by examining two commonly cited economic benefits of fair trade, higher prices and access to credit. Members of La Voz do benefit from both, although the advantages may be less significant than northern consumers believe. Moving beyond these economic benefits, this chapter investigates how fair-trade market access helps ensure the land security of cooperative members and enables them to educate more of their children for longer periods of time. It also explores the struggle over credit within the cooperative and how it shapes cooperative relations among members. The consequences within these domains move beyond simple financial considerations to shape social relations and processes of cultural identification at the level of the individual, family, and the cooperative itself.

During the primary research period (2001–2003) the cooperative had 116 members. In recent years, the membership has expanded to include 160 coffee producers, a testament to the group's strong and long-standing market connections and guaranteed minimum prices. Even though the membership may seem small in comparison to the local population, it has a high profile and strong influence within the community and its economic benefits extend beyond the members and their immediate families. This is because of three circumstances. First, the tight-knit, extended family relationships structuring community life mean that virtually every resident has a family member in the group. Second, the cooperative is one of the longest-running organizations within the community. Third, although not every community member belongs to the cooperative, the organizational activities of the group benefit nonmembers through the local multiplier effects of the extra income earned through fair-trade sales and development projects initiated by the cooperative and funded with fair-trade coffee market proceeds in the areas of environmental conservation, infrastructural improvements, and emergency relief. Although the focus of this chapter is limited to the impact of fair trade on cooperative members, the group's economic well-being reverberates through the larger community.

"FAIR" PRICES AND PRODUCER INCOME

The most direct benefit to individual producers is the guaranteed price of $1.21 per pound paid by northern buyers (as explained in Chapter 1, the base price for fair trade coffee has since risen to $1.25; however, for the sake of consistency I refer to the prices paid during the primary research period). During the research period, certified organic and fair-trade coffee earned a price premium of $0.15 per pound. In addition to the guaranteed price, producers received a social premium ($0.05) to be used for community development. When market prices rise above the guaranteed floor price, an additional premium is paid. The guaranteed price helps to sustain rural communities and households and, when invested in land and education, can support effective local development. However, it is somewhat misleading to state that cooperative members earn $1.41 per pound because they actually earn significantly less than that amount. Before cooperative members were paid in June, the cooperative first deducted its operating expenses, taxes, transport costs, and fees paid to the exporting and processing company, Excagua, and to the importing firm, Elan Organic Coffees. These expenses and intermediaries within the fair-trade chain limit the amount of money cooperative members actually earn through certified coffee sales.

While I was conducting research in San Juan, international coffee prices, established on the New York Coffee, Sugar and Cocoa Exchange and the London International Futures Exchange, declined to a 100-year low when adjusted for inflation (Lewin, Giovannucci, and Varangis 2004). At the height of this crisis, during the 2001–2002 coffee harvest, members of the cooperative were paid a price of $0.16 per pound (for unprocessed coffee; the $1.41 figure is for processed, but not roasted, coffee) after taxes and the cooperative's operating costs were deducted. This price was double that paid to non-cooperative members by *coyotes*, or the representatives of local coffee processors who in turn sell the coffee through conventional market outlets. This higher income enabled cooperative members to continue repaying their debts, maintain their standard of living, retain their landholdings, and pay for their children's education during a period in which many of their less fortunate neighbors were forced to sell their land and withdraw their children from school.

Forty percent of the fifty-three surveyed cooperative members stated that higher prices were the primary benefit of cooperative membership, indicating that they recognized the higher incomes they earned through cooperative membership. Despite this, when asked the price they ideally would like to receive for their coffee, 83 percent of the surveyed members named a price slightly higher than what they earned during the 2001–2002 harvest. During interviews and casual conversations cooperative members repeatedly stated that their earnings enabled them to maintain their families but not necessarily get ahead. For example, thirty-nine-year-old Luis, who is a tailor and has been a cooperative member for eleven years, has nine children, four enrolled in primary school and one enrolled in junior high at the time of our interview. He explained his ambivalent feelings regarding the price the cooperative paid,

> We've done the math and there [in the street] they pay Q60–70 [per quintal of coffee] and in the cooperative they pay us Q130. That difference of Q70 helps us . . . It helps pay for my children's education. The first of the year they need their clothing, their books . . . This price isn't very fair and you feel the difference from 1999 when they paid us Q188. The truth is that the family needs many things. You have your washing machine, your water heater, your television—better living conditions. These years it [the price] only covers the expenses at the level of the general population. Right now what I'm doing is paying for my children's education. I am only trying to cover the first necessities right now.

Luis argues that the price the cooperative pays is not high enough and it is forcing him to focus his spending on necessities, such as his children's education. However, two of the consumer goods that he thinks a family "needs," a washing machine and a water heater, are not common household items among cooperative members or community residents, indicating that he enjoys a higher relative standard of living despite the temporarily low coffee prices.

Although they may earn higher prices for their coffee than their neighbors who do not belong to the cooperative, it is misleading to portray cooperative members as constituents of an upwardly mobile middle class. For the most part, members remain *campesinos* who invest in land and production rather than their meager household possessions. In fact, only 60 percent of surveyed cooperative members owned televisions, the most common consumer good in their households. Fifteen percent owned phones, 4 percent owned computers (primarily for their children's use), and 2 percent owned pickups. However, like Luis, many members acknowledged that they were better off than nonmembers who were forced to sell their coffee to *coyotes*. For example, one explained: "There is no price for coffee. I hope that they help us a little now with the price. But it's worse for the poor people who aren't in the cooperative. If they have an employee they pay him twenty quetzals [per day] and only receive fifty quetzals for their coffee, leaving them with only thirty quetzals." During the height of the coffee crisis, I had many casual conversations with residents of San Juan and neighboring San Pedro about the low coffee prices. Several individuals reported that they simply were not harvesting their coffee that year because they could not afford to pay the wages of day laborers and did not have enough available family members to perform the work for free.

Interviewed cooperative members primarily understood fair trade as a market transaction paying slightly higher prices than conventional coffee markets. Many had a fatalistic attitude toward the prices they received and frequently discussed their earnings in terms of the prices that buyers "gave" them and that they "received." They provided little indication that they felt empowered by fair-trade principles to negotiate higher prices and instead portrayed themselves as subject to the whims of northern buyers. On the other hand, some cooperative members (generally those who were better educated or had either worked for the cooperative or served on its board of directors) acknowledged the complexity of the coffee commodity network and argued that it was intermediaries, such as the cooperative's former exporter Excagua, who were responsible for lower prices, not their buyers (such as Green Mountain Coffee Roasters). For example, a former cooperative manager (and current member) explained: "There's no potential for them to give the cooperative a better price. They can't manage the New

York coffee prices and we have intermediaries. It would be better without them. We have to pay taxes as well . . . and the company [the exporter] takes advantage and the higher prices stay with them, not with us." Similarly, one day the cooperative's agricultural monitor, Pedro, accompanied me on an interview with a cooperative member. When I asked the member about the price the cooperative pays for his coffee, the member responded with the familiar refrain that, yes, he was happy. However, he followed this by explaining, "Organic coffee requires a lot of work . . . what we want is that they take us into account. We need more for our family expenses, for our pruning, our cleaning, all of this work." Pedro then agreed with this sentiment and explained to me and the member that "there are still intermediaries in our chain" who reduced the members' profits. This emphasis that some cooperative members placed on the negative role of intermediaries provides insight into their understanding of fair-trade market principles. Although cooperative members experienced difficulty in defining fair trade or their own role within this alternative market, their focus on the role of intermediaries reveals that they understand through personal experience the importance of the market's most basic principle of shortening the commodity chain and returning higher profits to producers.

LAND SECURITY, SUBSISTENCE AGRICULTURE, AND DIVERSIFICATION

In Tz'utujil, the word for land, *chenooj*, is the same as the word for work, but as my Tz'utujil instructor, Francisco, pointed out, "Only for us campesinos." Many cooperative members indicated that their identity as farmers lies at the root of their community membership and, by extension, their identification as Tz'utujil Maya. The critical importance of land ownership was a recurring theme in my conversations with cooperative members. Land ownership held both cultural significance and economic consequence as access to land is a critical component of total income across rural Latin America (deJanvry and Sadoulet 2000:400). Even though this is an increasingly relevant issue in light of contemporary global economic integration and not unique to Maya communities, for many Guatemalan Maya communities, including San Juan, land ownership was also an influential historical factor. As explored in Chapter 2, during the 1930s and 1940s many highland communities and coastal plantations formed an interdependent, and yet highly uneven, economic system dictated by the seasonal migration of low-paid indigenous workers. Many Juaneros were forced to migrate seasonally because they did not own enough land to feed their families. The land pressures on highland communities increased throughout the twentieth century as the rural population expanded and agrarian reforms were reversed.

Although cooperative members were not universally content with the income they earned through the fair-trade market, they did acknowledge that they were better off than nonmembers who were forced to sell their coffee in the street for frighteningly low prices during the 2001–2002 harvest. Across the highlands and Central America as a whole many small-scale coffee producers were reportedly forced to sell off portions of their land during the coffee crisis. However, as a result of their higher incomes and the promise of a future guaranteed market, few cooperative members faced this difficult choice. Therefore, the security of their landholdings is a significant benefit of the higher fair-trade incomes. In fact, I knew of several cooperative members who were purchasing the coffee fields owned by nonmembers in surrounding communities who were forced to sell because of low prices. On average surveyed cooperative members owned twelve *cuerdas* of organic coffee and eight cuerdas of transitional coffee, meaning they are in the three-year process of earning organic certification.[1]

The high value placed on land ownership is reflected by the large percentage of surveyed cooperative members (76 percent) who agreed that, given the opportunity, they would like to own more land. The cultural and economic importance of land ownership is not unique to Maya communities and is in fact a common facet of agricultural livelihoods across Latin America and the world. However, like many rural smallholder communities producing agricultural commodities for export, it can be difficult to find affordable land for sale in San Juan.[2] Furthermore, as the permanent expatriate and upper-class *Ladino* resort communities grow, the price of lakeside properties (coveted by community members for fresh vegetable production because of the ease of irrigation) has increased dramatically in recent years. For example, in June 2006 a friend offered to sell me a cuerda of lakeside land for $20,000. On the other hand, in 1999 when coffee prices were high, a cuerda of coffee reportedly cost between $1,000 and $1,200. This price declined to approximately $300 a cuerda by 2002 because of low prices. Although I did have several conversations with individuals who privately denounced community members who sold their land to outsiders, the increasing number of vacation homes lining San Juan's shore indicates that the cultural proscription against selling one's land to non-community members is slowly being abandoned.

In addition to the critical role that land plays in the security of rural livelihoods across Latin America, in Maya communities land ownership has significant cultural importance as well, especially land devoted to *milpa* production. Milpa is the Mesoamerican version of integral swidden agriculture (Warner 1991) applied in most tropical forest areas of the world. Many familiar with Mesoamerican agriculture think of milpa as simply meaning cornfield, but it is not primarily a spatial concept—instead it is a cultural institution and process (Alcorn and Toledo 1998). In addition to the coffee they produced, all but six of the fifty-three surveyed cooperative members owned milpa and all but five owned at least one cuerda of land devoted to vegetable cultivation. The five members who did not cultivate vegetables were also non-milpa cultivators who owned fewer than ten cuerdas of organic coffee each and four of the five reported non-agricultural income sources (two of the members were female and produced weavings for sale). Although today cooperative members produce significantly more organic coffee than corn, on average they own four cuerdas of milpa and two cuerdas of vegetables (such as onions and tomatoes). Of the surveyed cooperative members, 64 percent reported that their milpa and vegetable crops were consumed solely within their households and the remainder reported selling the surplus to regional buyers who resold the products in Guatemala City.

The continued cultivation of milpa and vegetables is a livelihood strategy that better enables small producers to cope with uncertain prospects: when coffee revenues decline, members can rest assured that they can feed their families despite decreased access to cash.[3] This production strategy provides a local answer to what Wolf terms "the perennial problem of the peasantry" (1966:15), or the struggle to balance the demands of the external world against the peasants' need to provision their households. This sentiment was expressed by cooperative members who made statements such as "I plant milpa so my family doesn't suffer" and "It is better to plant milpa and beans. Even though we don't have money, we have food." As previous generations of anthropologists have argued, culture plays a significant role in milpa management and, in turn, milpa affects culture. Redfield and Villa Rojas (1934) noted for the Yucatec Maya "to abandon one's milpa is to forsake the very roots of life," and Rodas and colleagues (1940) note the K'iche' do not raise maize to live, they live to raise maize. Similarly, Nigh (1976) states that the making of milpa is the central, most sacred act, one that binds together the family, the community, and the universe—in short, milpa forms the core institution of Maya society in Mesoamerica and its religious and social importance often appears to exceed its nutritional and economic importance (in Alcorn and Toledo 1998).

Anthropologists have long argued that in Maya communities land embodies culture as a site of the production of both subsistence and cultural meaning and that agriculture remains the heart of symbolic and material existence for most rural Maya.[4] However, they have also debated the significance of milpa production and the resulting food products. For example, in his analysis of the "milpa logic" found in Maya communities, Annis argues that milpa production absorbs inputs that might otherwise be wasted, such as odd hours of time, household waste, or accumulated knowledge. He argues that milpa production differs from commodity production in one significant manner: because milpa product was traditionally consumed by the family or traded within the village, it worked against capital accumulation and entrepreneurship, thereby reinforcing the egalitarian nature of the community (1987:37). However, other anthropologists disagree with this line of reasoning. For example, Cancian (1965) argued that corn was both a food product *and* an important cash crop. The income generated through its sale was used to fuel the traditional *cargo* system, which produced stratification within closed corporate communities. Similarly, Bossen (1984) argued Annis's "milpa logic" was in fact a romanticization of the lack of economic security and market access Maya communities suffered.

The production and consumption practices of cooperative members indicate that Cancian's and Bossen's analyses are closer to the contemporary reality: cooperative members both consume and sell milpa product. As described in Chapter 2, many cooperative members once cultivated milpa on the coastal cattle ranches and used the product as their capital for planting coffee and expanding their production in San Juan. Today, their current integration into fair-trade and organic coffee markets ensures the future viability of milpa production for both household consumption and market exchange. Therefore, cooperative members do not necessarily interpret coffee and milpa as diametrically opposed spheres of production. Instead, they are viewed as being intimately linked: fair-trade coffee sales supplement subsistence agricultural production and help secure land ownership, allowing members to maintain their agrarian traditions.

To be an effective economic strategy, controlling one's means of production must be linked to secure market access, something that fair-trade certification aims to provide to small producers. The importance of market access in addition to land ownership was readily acknowledged by many cooperative members. For example, one told me: "Here the campesino is dead. The land of Guatemala produces all the agricultural products but there's no price. We produce quality products but it's not worthwhile because there is no market." Even though the cooperative provides members with a relatively secure market through their long-term relationship with Green Mountain Coffee Roasters, 90 percent of surveyed members expressed a desire to diversify their production and explore additional market opportunities, whether in artisan sales or vegetable production. The coffee crisis revealed the market's long-term fragility and some cooperative members doubted the long-term prospects of the crop. Although 67 percent of surveyed members reported that they planned to plant different crops if the price of coffee continued to drop, in practice coffee farmers are often reluctant to diversify because of the time and money they have already invested in their trees.[5]

Some cooperative members do invest a portion of their coffee profits in small businesses, such as *tiendas* (general stores located in the street-side room of the home) or transportation. In fact, 45 percent of surveyed cooperative members reportedly combined their farming with wage-earning activities or small businesses. For example, one member informed me of his plan: "[I will] maintain my coffee, invest a little money in my family [through education], pay my expenses, and invest in a business. If the price of coffee falls, I will have another way to support myself." In the late 1970s when the cooperative was founded, there were no tiendas in San Juan and, for this reason, the founders originally decided to focus the group's energies on a cooperatively owned and managed tienda before later switching to coffee production. Today there are tiendas on virtually every corner in town. These stores range from small window-sales enterprises, such as the one owned by my neighbor who sold fresh eggs and small bags of chips and candy, to larger stores, such as the one that I and the two Peace Corps volunteers living in San Juan jokingly called Super Walmart. It was owned by the family of the cooperative's former agricultural monitor, Santiago, and it sold farming implements and food next to computer disks and printer cartridges. When I returned to the community in 2006, the family had relocated the store out of their house and into a freestanding building four times the original size. In addition to the large number of tiendas, contemporary San Juan now boasts two Internet cafés, several restaurants and hotels, and various smaller businesses established since the primary research period.

EDUCATION

A significant number of cooperative members reported that the relatively higher fair-trade coffee prices they earned enabled them to educate more of their children for longer periods of time, and education was a popular topic of conversation during both interviews and everyday exchanges. The importance cooperative members (and Juaneros more generally) place on their children's education contradicts sharply with their own childhoods, which in general were devoted to productive labor in fields, homes, and *fincas*, not learning. Nineteen percent of the surveyed cooperative members never attended school and 42 percent completed only three or fewer years, meaning many possess only basic literacy and mathematical knowledge. Only 10 percent of surveyed cooperative members completed high school.

These low rates of education among cooperative members are attributable to San Juan's historic lack of post-primary education, severe poverty, and the seasonal migration many families engaged in that prevented children from regularly attending the existing grade schools. The low educational attainment of the cooperative members is on par with Guatemalans as a whole, especially indigenous Guatemalans, who in 2000 had an average of 2.5 years of schooling compared to 5.7 among non-indigenous adults. In fact, Guatemala's education indicators place it behind every country in the Western Hemisphere except Haiti (McEwan and Trowbridge 2007). In Guatemala today, studies indicate that indigenous children, like the sons and daughters of cooperative members, are less likely to be enrolled in school, more likely to be overaged and to repeat grades, and more likely to drop out of primary school without achieving literacy (Patrinos and Velez 2009). As in the past, schools in indigenous communities are provided with fewer instructional materials, lower quality infrastructures, and less qualified teachers. The financial impact of this systemic educational failure cannot be overestimated—economists have determined that more than half of the earnings gap between indigenous and non-indigenous adults can be explained by differences in years in schooling (McEwan and Trowbridge 2007). Against the backdrop of these statistics the significance of the financial commitment cooperative members make to their children's education is revealed.

San Juan had only a one-room school prior to 1940, when it was divided into first and second grades. Over the decades additional grades were added, and the primary school offered six years of education by 1967 (Sexton 1972). There are now five primary schools in San Juan (three public and two private), five junior high schools (four public and one private), and one private high school. Although education is primarily in Spanish, some efforts are made at bilingual education through the third grade. This bilingual education is a recent development dating to the implementation of the Peace Accords, which mandated that all languages were to be used in the school system to develop literacy in the students' own language or the language usually spoken in the community (Cabrera and Cifuentes 1997). Although it may seem counterintuitive that bilingual education can be used to improve overall literacy and education rates, especially because Spanish is the language of power and economic success in dominant Ladino society (Garzon

1998), students of bilingual schools have higher attendance and promotion rates and lower repetition and dropout rates. Furthermore, bilingual students receive higher scores on all subject matters, including mastery of Spanish (Patrinos and Velez 2009).

In the past public school teachers were Ladinos from distant communities; however, today the majority of teachers are from San Juan and surrounding communities. The importance cooperative members place on their children's education cannot be solely attributed to their increased earnings through higher fair-trade coffee prices. Although these do play a significant role, there have been decisive shifts in the quality of the offered education and the community's attitude toward formal schooling. One cooperative founder, Benito, expressed this well during an interview in his home. He abruptly rose from his chair mid-sentence and walked across the room to a bookcase leaning against the wall. He pointed at the well-worn dictionaries and classroom textbooks haphazardly populating the shelves and told me: "What I'm saying is that now a child is stupid if he can't learn. Look at all the books they have now, they just have to copy information out if they need it. Before there were never books there. We only had little chalkboards and we had to copy everything the teacher wrote, read it, memorize it, and erase it."

Despite their own low levels of educational attainment, 42 percent of cooperative members have at least one child who has completed secondary school and works in an office, as opposed to pursuing traditional agricultural pursuits or caring for the home.[6] Although the fees and supplies for primary school education are minimal, the financial expenses increase incrementally as a student enters junior high. In 2003 the community's only high school graduated its first class of accountants. However, the school is private and therefore inaccessible to many potential students. Students pursuing degrees in teaching or occupations other than accounting are forced to leave the community and must pay board and lodging expenses in addition to tuition and fees.

Although cooperative members are currently able to sustain their families through fair-trade and organic coffee production, it is unlikely that the coffee market will expand to the extent that each of their children will be able to successfully follow in their footsteps. In fact, the fair-trade model of alternative development is criticized as being a stopgap measure in the eventual need for agricultural diversification among the world's millions of small-scale coffee producers. For example, Sidwell (2008) argues that fair trade does not aid economic development; rather, it sustains uncompetitive farmers on their land, holding back diversification and mechanization.

In doing so fair trade denies future generations the chance of a better life. Although it is undeniable that in its current guise fair trade "only offers a very small number of farmers a higher fixed price for their goods" (Sidwell 2008), the case at hand directly contradicts the argument that fair trade harms the life chances of rural youth. On the contrary, although cooperative members may not actively be diversifying their agricultural production, they are using their fair-trade profits to ensure that at least a segment of the future generation will have a wider variety of occupational opportunities. Seventy-four percent of the surveyed members expressed the hope that their children would become professionals (as opposed to campesinos).

This household strategy is aimed at reducing the overall economic risks that families face. Although many cooperative members invest their coffee profits and loans in their children's education with the belief that this will provide the key to secure, high-paying jobs in the formal sector, parents also hope their children's higher wages will at least partially be reinvested in the family farm and help provide for their own needs in old age. Furthermore, in many families the children themselves were the motivating force behind their own educational attainment and they pressured their parents to allocate scarce resources to fulfill their own dreams of professional careers. For example, one afternoon I interviewed a cooperative member whose ten-year-old daughter had been driven inside by the rain pounding down on the corrugated roof. While we spoke in the house's front room, she perched herself in a doorway and observed as I asked her father about his hopes for his children's future—did he prefer for them to become professionals or campesinos? He waffled a bit on his answer, and while he hesitated, his daughter softly attempted to sway his opinion by interjecting, "Professional, Papa, professional." Although a lucky few students may be awarded academic scholarships, in general until children obtain their own resources, such as full access to inherited land, their ability to formulate their own economic strategies is constrained by parental control. Cooperative members ultimately decide how the fair-trade coffee income is allocated and many decide to invest it in their children's education.

The reverence cooperative members express for education and their hopes for their children's professional futures should not be interpreted as an abandonment of the community's traditional agrarian-based identity. Seventy-six percent of surveyed cooperative members agreed future generations will continue to farm and nearly a quarter of respondents said they hoped their own children would combine professional careers with their agricultural pursuits. During conversations, several cooperative members expressed their own conceptual reconciliation of these seemingly

FIGURE 3.1. *Juanero schoolchildren dressed in traje, advertising their hopes for a professional, rather than campesino, future in the annual parade.*

contradictory futures. For example, my Tz'utujil instructor, Francisco, who helped four of his children successfully complete high school, told me that he hoped his children will someday become professionals who hire day laborers to farm their land for them: "Land is an investment, and I hope my children invest their money in buying land. The best thing would be to be a professional and buy land and hire workers." In a manner suggesting that he had thought this future through many times, Francisco continued to explain how he would teach his children's day laborers the complicated aspects of organic coffee production and help oversee their coffee trees so that his children could join him as cooperative members.

In conclusion, despite higher rates of education among cooperative members' children, the importance of agriculture within the community is unlikely to significantly diminish in the near future. This sentiment is well-expressed by a cooperative member who, when asked about the future of farming in the community in light of the growing number of well-educated youth, responded, "A good percentage are going to continue with this tradition—as *indigenas* we have always dedicated ourselves to our fields; this isn't going to disappear."

CREDIT AND THE COOPERATIVE

DeJanvry and Sadoulet argue that access to credit is minimal among the rural poor in Latin America and that this lowers the "income generating capacity of the meager asset endowments that the poor possess" (2000:396). However, participation in fair-trade markets can enhance the legitimacy of producer organizations, thereby granting them access to credit institutions and international lenders (Raynolds, Murray, and Taylor 2004), a key benefit for small-scale producers who were often historically excluded from formal lending institutions. Many fair-trade producer organizations use loans from external institutions to establish micro-lending to help members improve their production quality and quantity, thereby strengthening their market potential. However, these loans must be carefully managed by both the cooperative and the members who borrow in order to be effective tools for community development. Unlike programs managed and funded by outside lenders, community-initiated and -administered micro-loan programs can pose distinct challenges to producer groups, including the potential for interpersonal conflict and declining profits. The failure of many members to repay their large outstanding loans to the cooperative was a key challenge facing the group during the research period. However, the resolution of the conflicts engendered by this insolvency demonstrates that the process of democratic decision making and collective management can strengthen an organization through the continued articulation of cooperative principles and mutual aid.

Small-scale farmer credit programs in low-income countries have a long history dating back to the early 1900s. However, after World War II, interest in micro-lending surged within the burgeoning postwar culture of development. Many programs were patterned after lending institutions found in donor countries. For example, the United States promoted supervised credit programs throughout Latin America based on the Farmers' Home Administration (Adams 1992:1463). Contemporary micro-lending programs aim to direct money into the hands of needier community members and effectively eliminate the negative impact of potentially corrupt program managers and local officials. They also are designed to generate a sense of collective responsibility and project ownership by enabling participants to invest their money in productive practices as they see fit and not forcing them to participate in income-generating initiatives conceived in the culturally and geographically distant offices of international lending agencies. The last decade has witnessed a veritable explosion of variations on micro-lending, such as www.kiva.org, an Internet site that enables individual donors to make micro-loans to "featured entrepreneurs" in developing countries based on profiles akin to those posted on Internet dating sites.

Micro-loan programs can be the key components of local agricultural development in impoverished communities. In Guatemala it is often difficult for rural indigenous farmers with little education to solicit loans directly from banks and large lending institutions because they do not have the proper guarantees, do not have an existing credit history, do not understand the extensive paperwork that is required, lack confidence in their Spanish language skills, or simply do not relate well to Spanish-speaking professionals. During an interview, one member expressed the important role local lending organizations can play within this context, stating, "[t]he cooperative helps associates . . . It's not like in the banks where they don't give us anything." Access to credit is especially important for producers of high-cost, high-reward crops, such as coffee, which requires a significant initial investment and regular maintenance throughout the year. In light of the low prices characterizing the world coffee market in recent years, successful micro-loan programs within coffee cooperatives may become even more important in the future. Increasingly in Guatemala, larger lenders are reportedly unwilling to provide loans for the improvement and maintenance of coffee plots because they believe the market has no future. One member reported, "The banks told me it is better to forget agriculture, but at least I have confidence in the cooperative, it has to help me." Coffee production has historically fostered large debt loads among both small- and large-scale farmers because of high initial expenses and maintenance costs, and the members of La Voz are no exception to this rule.[7]

Beginning in 1989, La Voz received several long-term loans through the USAID Small Coffee Farmer Improvement Program. These loans enabled the cooperative to establish an internal micro-loan program, which has proven critical to the group's ongoing success and central to its identity and operations. In fact, 54 percent of interviewed cooperative members named access to credit as the primary benefit of cooperative membership, compared to the 40 percent who named higher prices. Members apply for both short- and long-term loans that they pay back with their annual coffee profits, and in addition to the promise of future profits, the cooperative requires guarantees in the form of titles to land or houses. The goal of the cooperative's micro-loan program is to provide members with year-round access to money that they can use to improve their coffee quality. For example, members can use this money to purchase organic fertilizer from the cooperative if they choose not to make their own (the cooperative sold 100-pound bags of *bokashi* fertilizer for thirty quetzals each); pay day laborers (twenty to thirty quetzals per day) to help them with pruning, the planting of shade trees, or other physical improvements; and to purchase new land or coffee trees to expand their production. Ninety percent of surveyed cooperative members reported using their credit to purchase organic fertilizer from the cooperative and 34 percent used it to fund renovations or new plantings. In addition to these officially sanctioned uses, 26 percent used their credit to help cover family expenses during periods of illness and 11 percent invested their credit in their children's education.

Because school supplies and fees must be paid in January, before or at the start of the coffee harvest, when household cash reserves are at a yearly low, it is understandable that many members divert their credit to cover these expenses. In fact, there seemed to be an unspoken acknowledgment that members frequently use this money to pay for their children's education and family expenses, and this was common practice in some nearby fair-trade coffee cooperatives as well. For example, during an interview the accountant of another local fair-trade cooperative explained, "We know everybody here in town so it's not a big deal if they use the credit for coffee or education." The average debt load of surveyed cooperative members with children currently studying at the secondary level or those whose children have completed their high school degree was $1,035.83 in 2001–2002 while the average debt load for all cooperative members was $870.48.[8] This indicates that cooperative members may have underreported their non-sanctioned diversion of cooperative credit toward educational expenses.

In light of the importance that many cooperative members place on their children's education it is understandable that they are willing to sacrifice their future profits and perhaps even their social standing within the cooperative by taking out large loans that are difficult for them to repay. As one father told me, "You know the life of students, for this I have credit in the cooperative, for the four of them." The story of my Tz'utujil instructor Francisco and his four children illustrates the lengths to which some cooperative members will go to provide for their children and the long-term repercussions of these decisions. Throughout 2002 I took daily Tz'utujil lessons from Francisco in his home and he also helped me conduct interviews with monolingual elders in the community. In addition to my daily visits, I spent time with his family at community events and during Sunday and holiday meals when their children returned to visit; I also became close with his wife, who taught me a great deal about natural dyeing techniques and weaving. Francisco was born in 1953 and married his wife, Cristina, in 1975. He attended six years of primary school in San Juan and his wife completed one year of primary school. Despite his low level of education, in the early 1970s Francisco was awarded a position at the Proyecto Lingüístico Francisco Marroquín (PLFM). The institute recruited locally nominated Mayas, such as Francisco, between the ages of twenty and thirty-five with strong social ties with their home communities and no more than six years of education. The PLFM is an Antigua-based language institute founded in 1969 that is dedicated to the preservation of Mayan languages.[9] Rather than intervening directly in communities, as was the norm for Peace Corps volunteers and missionaries, the institute decided to train Mayas in skills not available in Guatemala and to encourage participants to make their own decisions about community projects. After intensive course work, the students produced studies and educational materials based on language practices in their communities (Warren 1998:x). The institute funded the writing and publication of Maya-language dictionaries and grammars and created the written versions of Maya languages that were eventually adopted by the Guatemalan government. For six years Francisco worked with a Pedrano to develop the Tz'utujil dictionary and grammar while living in Antigua and returning to San Juan periodically to visit family and conduct recorded interviews with community elders. This experience instilled in him a strong appreciation for the importance of education, and in 2002 he was attending night school to earn his junior high school degree and was highly motivated to provide an education for his own children.

Francisco and Cristina have four children: Maria, who at the time of the research was a twenty-four-year-old kindergarten teacher living in the capital and studying psychology at the university on the weekends; Imelda, a twenty-one-year-old accountant who also lived in the capital and studied business administration at the university on the weekends; Ana, eighteen years old and finishing her last year of high school training to become a primary school teacher; and their youngest child, Antonio, seventeen years old and beginning his first year of training to become a primary school teacher. Francisco and his wife paid for their children's education through the high school level and then helped them as they could with their university studies; however, their two oldest daughters worked full-time and primarily supported themselves.

Their children were well-educated and hardworking. However, despite the numerous scholarships they had been awarded and the part- or full-time jobs that each worked, Francisco had accrued one of the higher debt loads in the cooperative primarily because of education-related expenses. In the 1999–2000 cooperative fiscal year Francisco owed $4,673.93 (compared to the $870 average debt noted above). This amount would not be an undue burden for a member with large landholdings and productive coffee.

However, as Francisco explained, "I used to have fifteen cuerdas of organic coffee but now I only have four. I sold it to associates though so it's still part of the cooperative. They [the cooperative] didn't lose any of their organic land." His small landholdings mean that Francisco does not produce enough coffee to pay off his loan: "I've had credit with the cooperative for about ten years and I used to pay it off every year. But then one year came and I couldn't pay it off and that's when the interests started adding up and now I can't cancel the debt." During the 1999–2000 harvest Francisco did not turn in any coffee to the cooperative; during 2000–2001 he turned in 27.51 qq (quintals), and during 2001–2002 he turned in 5.29 qq. This means that even though he owed more than $4,500 to the cooperative, he only earned Q687.70 from cooperative coffee sales in 2001–2002 and thereby reduced his debt by approximately $87.00. Perhaps out of embarrassment, Francisco told me that during the 2001–2002 harvest his coffee ripened before the cooperative opened its beneficio and he was forced to sell it in the street. However, he had earlier invited me to help him and his wife pick coffee in February, indicating that at least some of his coffee did not ripen until later in the season. Although I did not press the point, most likely he sold a portion of his organic coffee in the street (for significantly lower prices) because, like other cooperative members, he needed immediate access to cash and could not afford to wait until June to be paid by the cooperative when all of his proceeds would be applied to his credit. Because he owns so little coffee, Francisco sought out additional sources of income, and before I began paying him for Tz'utujil lessons, he devoted the majority of his time to cutting firewood by hand, earning 500 or 600 quetzals each month, approximately the amount a day laborer would earn working six days a week in the fields of cooperative members.

In addition to the anxiety that this debt generates for Francisco and his family members, it influences his standing in the cooperative. In 2002 he was nominated to serve on the board of directors but he was forced to stand in front of all in attendance at the general assembly to publicly explain: "I cannot serve. According to the statues of the cooperative, members who are not solvent cannot be on the board of directors." Like other indebted members Francisco also felt a growing resentment toward the group and once told me: "I'm thinking of renouncing in the cooperative once I've paid off my debts. Coffee production is so variable." Furthermore, as one of the more heavily indebted members, Francisco formed part of the larger problem of insolvency that the group was struggling to address throughout the research period. Although the accounts were not public knowledge, cooperative members knew approximately how many cuerdas of organic coffee each other owned, how much land they had sold recently, and how many children they had in school. Therefore, even before Francisco was forced to acknowledge his insolvency in front of the general assembly, members frequently identified him as one of the offenders when privately discussing the cooperative's credit problems.

Despite the financial difficulties he faced, Francisco viewed his education-related expenses as an investment in the future rather than a drain. He explained: "I prefer working for myself. In the first place, I'm trying to improve my own life and I'm working to benefit my family. Maybe with the investment I've made in my children's education, maybe one day they'll help me with a business or something. This investment in their education, it's like a crop, we're investing and investing in them." His daughter Imelda indicated that she felt mutually responsible for her father's debt. She told me: "It is my responsibility to help pay these loans. I'm now helping to pay off the loans. We got in debt together and we have to leave these debts together." She plans to keep working until she is thirty years old to help her parents and she will put off her own personal goals, such as marriage, to help them. She explained: "If I'm going to get married in a year then my parents will be left with many debts. It's better that I work until then [her thirtieth birthday] to help them pay off those debts. I always have responsibilities to the household." This case makes clear that the cooperative debts have long-term effects on both the members and their families as multiple compromises and concessions are made by all to pay back the money.

Micro-lending programs administered by cooperatives can potentially provide the means through which members can improve the quality and quantity of their coffee production, thereby strengthening the organization's market potential. However, these loans must be carefully managed by both the cooperative and the members who borrow. In the case of La Voz, the group's profits were significantly lowered when members defaulted on their personal loans and the cooperative was unable to collect the money it needed to repay the high interest and balance of its large USAID/Anacafé loan. Debt repayment has become a common problem among coffee producers in recent years and 94 percent of surveyed cooperative members agreed that the cooperative had a problem with insolvency. However, the reasons cooperative members defaulted on loans are varied. An analysis of the cooperative's micro-lending program revealed seven principal factors contributing to high rates of insolvency among members:

- Harvest takes place from December through March; however, members must wait until June or July for full payment.

- High interest rates: 85 percent of surveyed members reported the rate was exorbitant (as high as 18 percent).
- Allegations of loan mismanagement by administration and borrowers.
- Poor harvests because of hurricanes Mitch (1998) and Stan (2005).
- Loans used for unproductive purposes (such as education or medical bills).
- Loans are larger than capacity to repay.
- Members borrow from multiple lending institutions, exceeding repayment capacity.

Varangis (2003) reports problems with loan repayments among coffee producers in all Central American countries, and the debts held by cooperatives and their members have been demonstrated to significantly reduce the income-generating potential of fair-trade markets (Utting-Chamorro 2005). There have been several allegations of mismanagement and lack of transparency made against producer groups in Central America and Mexico. The problems associated with internal micro-lending programs such as La Voz's may result from inefficient and poor management within groups. Some argue that fair-trade certification encourages a cooperative structure dependent on an expensive top-heavy entrepreneurial hierarchy with a large administrative staff and consequently a higher overhead (Mendoza and Bastiaensen 2003). However, others maintain that problems with the cooperative structure and democratic decision making should not be viewed as weaknesses specific to fair trade and point out that fair trade could potentially address this weakness through heightened transparency requirements (Murray, Raynolds, and Taylor 2003; Taylor 2004). La Voz's experience with debt management lends support to both positions: although there were allegations of loan mismanagement, cooperative members collectively addressed the problem through transparent decision-making processes.[10]

Large, unpaid loans lower a group's profits and members' income. In addition to lowering profits, large numbers of defaulted loans can weaken the group's organizational capacity and hamper its market success. This can also encumber the group's morale and sense of unity as solvent members begin to feel they are being taken advantage of and indebted members begin to feel the group's management is unresponsive to their needs. Additionally, members deeply in debt to their association may actually begin to have a vested interest in the group's failure because it would potentially erase their own debts. Over the course of the research period discussions among cooperative members regarding insolvency increased in frequency and the group's collective deliberations on the ongoing problem provided a unique lens through which to view democratic participation and decision making in action. The group debated the relative strengths and weaknesses of two strategic approaches to debt reduction: an attempt to socially pressure insolvent members to repay their debts through public calls for individual responsibility or a legal enforcement of cooperative lending procedures that would result in the repossession of insolvent members' properties.

According to the statutes of the cooperative, the manager is responsible for determining the amount of credit available to individual members. This caused a great deal of conflict between the management and unhappy members and contributed to allegations of mismanagement (which will be more fully addressed in Chapter 4). These allegations extended to members of the board of directors as well. For example, one member told me: "What I see is that those on the board themselves are taking advantage. The cooperative gives the members nothing. They take advantage. The manager gives money to them and if a member comes [to ask for credit], they don't accept him, they don't pay attention to him." Another member maintained that there needs to be better control over each consecutive board of directors to stop elected representatives from saying, "Oh, I'm a *compadre* with him, I'm his cousin; I'm going to give him money."

Some interviewed members felt the credit system was unjustly administered and others contended that members with unpaid loans might feel ashamed or feel that the management does not understand their personal circumstances. When confronted with these allegations of mismanagement during an interview, the cooperative's former manager readily defended himself and his difficult position, stating, "If the member is insolvent he asks for more. They spread many bad things in the cooperative about the management. Only the people who are heavily in debt come in and ask for more loans and when we can't give them money they say bad things to the board of directors about the management. People who bring in all of their coffee and pay off their loans, well they don't complain about anything. You didn't hear them crying out in the [general] assembly did you?"

In their discussions of their own insolvency and that of others, members provided contrasting definitions of what it means to be a good cooperative member. For example, some interviewed members viewed credit as a contractual obligation between the individual and the cooperative as an institution. They consequently did not feel that individual insolvency was an affront to the other members. However, others remained steadfast in their belief that cooperative members are mutually responsible for one another's debts and that the insolvent members were hurting not only their own prospects but those of the cooperative itself. The fact that only 19 percent of interviewed members favored heightened institutional control and rule enforcement and only 8 percent believed the cooperative should take legal action demonstrates members' reluctance, on the whole, to police and discipline one another. Interestingly, there was no significant difference between the solutions offered by all interviewed members and the twenty-three members whose loan balance exceeded US$1,265.82 (Q10,000) during the 2001–2002 harvest.

Cooperative members who believed that insolvent members should take personal responsibility for repaying their loans (43 percent of interviewed members) stressed the group's founding principles of mutual aid and collective responsibility in their discussions of the issue. For example, one member, who at the time worked two jobs in addition to his agricultural labor, stated: "The cooperative isn't the building, it's me. If I repay my debt, I am helping myself." However, other members maintained that when some people defaulted on their loans their own coffee profits were decreased, as the cooperative was forced to siphon income from all members to service the interest on the defaulted loans of a few. Members who attempted to reinforce the ethic of mutual aid were also reluctant to enforce cooperative regulations and repossess the property of insolvent members. As one explained, "It's difficult [to say] 'Look you, get out of your house, get out of here' . . . But where are they going to live?" In an attempt to set an example, several years prior to the research period the cooperative repossessed the land of a member who was deeply in debt. Although his brother, also a member, bought the land, the whole experience was demoralizing for both the punished associate (who no longer participates in the cooperative) and the assembly in general. A cooperative founder and former president told me: "It was a shame to make this decision but we had to do it. He always did the same thing and didn't turn in his coffee. He didn't cover his debts and didn't fulfill his promise to the cooperative."

Solutions for member insolvency and debt repayment were regularly discussed among cooperative members in informal venues, for example, while pruning coffee trees in a member's field. After much informal discussion and through a process of public democratic decision making during the general assembly, the group collectively decided against the legal enforcement of cooperative lending procedures and the potential repossession of insolvent members' properties. Instead, members and the board of directors repeatedly stressed the need for individual responsibility during cooperative meetings. This strategy became more viable after the board of directors and administrative staff successfully solicited a low-interest bank loan, which they used to pay back the cooperative's high-interest USAID loans and subsequently lower the interest rate they charged cooperative members. The group's secure international market undoubtedly heightened their credibility in the lender's eyes and the transparent fiscal policies the cooperative adopted to earn and maintain fair-trade certification proved their ability and willingness to responsibly manage an additional loan. Fair trade therefore directly assisted them in this process and enabled the cooperative to continue its community development efforts and maintain the social bonds uniting the membership, which past events indicated would be critically threatened by the legal enforcement of lending procedures and property repossession.

CONCLUSION

Fair trade's primary goal is poverty alleviation through trade rather than international assistance. Therefore, in critically evaluating the movement's impact on small-scale coffee producers it is vital to determine first the extent to which this objective is fulfilled. There are two primary ways that fair trade improves producers' livelihoods: higher prices and access to credit. In the case of La Voz both of these aims are being met; however, there are steps the fair-trade movement could take to heighten these economic benefits. Although the fair-trade prices paid to cooperative members are higher, especially during market downturns, than those paid to non-members, they do not necessarily enable cooperative members to dramatically increase their standard of living. On the other hand, in addition to helping maintain producer households, the guaranteed fair-trade income can be used for productive purposes, such as investments in land and children's education, which in turn help ensure the long-term viability of the community's agrarian lifestyles. The fair-trade movement has more recently taken steps to increase the earnings of certified-coffee farmers. The terms of exchange for fair-trade-certified coffee have deteriorated over the past decade. The base price for fair-trade coffee remained stagnant at $1.21 a pound from 1989 to May 2008, at which point it increased to $1.25 a pound. However, this represents only a 3 percent increase during twenty years (Smith 2010). Although the fair-trade price paid to coffee farmers has not increased significantly, fair-trade certification and quality demands continue to increase.

Access to credit is also a critical component of fair trade's success and it serves important purposes, such as increasing the quality of coffee production and supplementing family spending on education. However, microloan programs must be carefully managed by cooperatives to avoid financial catastrophes and interpersonal conflict. Although fair trade's impact on producer livelihoods cannot be overstated, the movement's influence reaches far beyond this narrow realm.

4

Obligatory Burdens: Collaboration and Discord within the Cooperative

In April 2002 the cooperative held a general assembly meeting in the empty coffee warehouse that the group had recently built with members' voluntary labor and the funds remaining from the construction of the additional drying patio provided by Green Mountain Coffee Roasters. It was a warm and dusty day as the heat of the dry season settled over San Juan and the lingering smell of last harvest's coffee permeated the room. The meeting began midmorning on Chapino (Guatemalan) time, meaning two hours late. Some male cooperative members came alone while others brought their wives, many with babies tied to their backs in colorful rebozos (shawls) and young children at their feet. The board of directors and the management sat at the front of the room, and in a mixture of Tz'utujil and Spanish they presented a seemingly endless number of large sheets of paper with the cooperative's accounting figures scrawled on them in colored markers. The heat and the monotony were broken with a mid-meeting snack of warm sodas in glass bottles and sugary cookies.

At several points during the meeting cooperative members stood to challenge the board and the management, but none so forcefully as Santiago, a cooperative founder and the group's then agricultural monitor. At the time, fair trade had become the development cause de jure around the lake, and various international organizations were actively promoting the formation of coffee associations with the intention of securing fair-trade premiums. For example, within San Juan the World Vision–funded NGO Cotz'ija was actively soliciting coffee from the parents of children enrolled in the group's child-sponsorship program. La Voz's statutes explicitly state that cooperative members are not permitted to participate in other agricultural cooperatives, and at a time when the cooperative was struggling to fill its orders, selling coffee to an outside organization would be especially unwelcome. Despite this, I had heard several rumors that cooperative members or their *mozos*, day laborers, had been spotted carrying bags of coffee to Cotz'ija's makeshift *beneficio* on the other side of town. As the agricultural monitor, Santiago was responsible for ensuring that the certified-organic coffee grown by members actually arrived at the cooperative. He emphatically stood and explained the problem in a mixture of Spanish and Tz'tujil, ending his outburst by exclaiming (in Spanish), "I know there are people on this very board of directors that are selling their coffee to Cotz'ija and this is a large error; we have to unite ourselves and stop this!" A member of the board replied, "Who are these associates with commitments to Cotz'ija?" Unlike many Juaneros, Santiago did not shirk from public confrontation. He boldly faced the board of directors and in front of the entire assembly accused the cooperative's president, Juan, of sending his mozos to sell his coffee. A sheepish grin appeared on Juan's face yet he deftly defended himself by arguing that this coffee came from plots inherited by his wife who was not a cooperative member and therefore there could be no conflict of interest. Choosing not to pursue his allegations, Santiago instead continued to plead with cooperative members to unite themselves, furiously crying out in Spanish, "We are cooperative members or we are nothing!"

Despite the community's history of mutual assistance and service, as the events of the general assembly relayed above demonstrate, cooperation is hard work for members. Positions on the elected board of directors are referred to as *cargos*. As the literal meaning of the word implies, a cargo is best understood as an obligatory burden; similarly, the everyday practice of cooperation is a weighty responsibility that entails balancing the sometimes conflicting demands of the external market and community interests. For the members of La Voz the meaning of cooperation was intertwined with the long-standing cultural traditions of service maintained through the constantly evolving cargo system. Historically the cargo system was a community-wide structure that relied on the public service of Catholic male Juaneros and the private labor of their wives. Over time, this service ethos expanded to encompass cargos in municipal committees, Catholic Action, Evangelical churches, and cooperatives. Fulfilling cargos was the primary means through which Juaneros earned community authority and power within the local spheres of influence.

This chapter analyzes both the meaning and practice of cooperation within the group and assesses the organizational capacity of the cooperative. It closely examines internal relations, the flow of information, and the sharing of decision-making power among the management, the board, and the general assembly to question the extent to which cooperation promotes democracy and transparency within local spheres. The events that unfolded at the general assembly illustrate that rather than an intrinsic and static value of indigenous communities, cooperation is instead an ongoing process of negotiation and conflict resolution. Furthermore, cooperation within the organization does not unfold in isolation from the larger relationships and norms of behavior structuring everyday life in the community at large. On the contrary, it is instead a reflection of Juanero customary behavior that emerges from local understandings of community authority, appropriate forms of respect, sanctioned paths toward progressive power, and finally clear demarcations between insider and outsider status. The consumers in the global North who purchase fair-trade coffee may assume that cooperation comes naturally to the small-scale producers who grow their beans. This stereotype is especially potent in northern constructions of indigenous coffee producers. However, for cooperative members the act of cooperation itself can be as laborious as carrying 100-pound bags of organic fertilizer on their backs up the steep trails that lead to their high altitude coffee fields.

There are emerging tensions between La Voz's membership and the increasingly powerful cooperative management. Decades of research on cooperatives reveal that virtually every organization at one time or another suffers from internal power struggles and La Voz is no exception to this rule. To successfully compete in the international fair-trade coffee market and fulfill certification and quality requirements, the cooperative steadily increased the responsibilities and power of the manager and the board of directors. In addition to contributing to emerging stratification within the group, the emergence of a managerial elite could potentially threaten the cooperative practices and participatory democracy that collectively form the groundwork for the group's success. Cooperative members actively worked to check administrative power through calls for transparent book-keeping and gossip, which in 2002 consisted of often-repeated rumors of managerial corruption.

Finally, scrutinizing the daily practice of cooperation sheds light on the failure of fair-trade coffee networks to adequately protect and promote gender equity among producer groups. This is one of the deepest cracks in the façade of FLO certification practices and promotional materials, both of which sanitize the messiness of small-scale farmer collaboration and help to prop up the market fantasy of idyllic peasant coffee growers laboring together to create a better world for their families and northern consumers. Although fair-trade standards state that "there must be no discrimination regarding membership and participation" (FLO 2007a), women do not fully participate in the cooperative's democratic decision-making process nor does the group adequately promote non-agricultural income-generating projects to meet their needs. This problem is hardly unique to La Voz. To address these issues, fair trade cannot simply rely on a "trickle-down effect of male income into the household" (Shreck 2002). Instead it should actively bolster gender equity through a more participatory certification process that circumvents the failures associated with snapshot auditing.

When I asked members what cooperation really meant, they often peppered their answers with words such as "unity," "equality," "mutual assistance," and "shared mindsets." To many these concepts defined cooperation and set the parameters for appropriate conduct among members and management. However, not all members subscribed to such romantic notions and instead some spoke of cooperating solely for financial rewards and to improve their coffee quality. One interviewed cooperative member explained how difficult it was to define, let alone practice, cooperation stating, "We're all different therefore every single person has his own thoughts about what his organization is." The FLO minimum standards for small farmer certification state:

> The organization must be an instrument for the social and economic development of its members, and in particular the benefits of Fairtrade must come to the members. The organization must therefore have a democratic structure and transparent administration, which enables effective control by the members and its board over the management, including the decisions about how the benefits are shared. Furthermore, there must be no discrimination regarding membership and participation." (FLO 2007b)

According to certification requirements, these conditions must be met through the formation of an elected board (and a staff that answers through the board to the members) and a general assembly that meets at least once a year at which time the annual reports and accounts are presented and approved. FLO standards suggest that associations make progress toward transparent planning, training and education, internal control mechanisms, policy discussions during meetings, and improved flows of information from the board to the members (FLO 2007b). These standards are carefully designed to promote democracy, participation, and transparency within FLO-certified organizations. However, the process of cooperation that is the very lynchpin of fair trade (meaning cooperation among producers *and* between producers and buyers, which will be discussed in Chapters 6 and 7) is highly variable and depends on the individual beliefs, histories, and cultural traditions of the producers who live in any one of the fifty-eight countries covered by FLO certification (FLO 2007b).

FILLING CARGOS:
COOPERATION AND SERVICE IN SAN JUAN

Anthropologists have long maintained that a central component of Maya social structure is participation in an evolving cargo system (Tax 1937). Historically the cargo system consisted of civil-religious hierarchies in which male community members alternated between ranked positions in religious brotherhoods and the civil government (with the assistance of their wives). Over time cargo systems evolved and most contemporary communities maintain only religious hierarchies, as the functions of civil hierarchies diminished with the introduction of formal electoral processes and national politics to the local sphere (Chance 1990). In many contemporary communities, including San Juan, membership in committees that monitor community projects and public works and service on the boards of cooperatives and associations is elective and unofficially substitutes for the previous civil positions now occupied by politicians (Stepputat 2001; Kovic 2005; Stephen 2005). Although marked differences exist between the historical hierarchies and their current manifestation, the ongoing significance of the behavioral ideal of communalism based on individual service permeates the cargos that community members fill, whether in a *cofradía* (religious brotherhood) or the cooperative; it is evident in the rituals of social recognition and public initiation (Annis 1987; Watanabe 1992), the performance of shared morality (Cohen 1999), and the reinforcement of community values (Cancian 1965).

The historical Mesoamerican cargo system has several essential features: it involves voluntary service without remuneration (although there may be social pressure placed on individuals to participate); tenure in offices is rotated, usually annually, to other members of the community; participation is costly in terms of time or money; and participation is an important means of acquiring prestige within the community (Dewalt 1975; Carmack 1995). Service within the fair-trade coffee cooperative in the form of positions on the board of directors shares some of these essential features: service is voluntary and not remunerated, tenure is rotated annually or semiannually to other cooperative members, participation can be costly in terms of time, and service on the board of directors is rewarded with prestige and decision-making power within the organization. Cooperative service also brings practical and tangible rewards to members, such as the formation and maintenance of networks of reciprocity, respect, and trust, which serve to unite non-kin community members. Historically, the cargo system limited outside intervention in community life through the local resolution of internal differences (Greenberg 1995; Cohen 1999). As an authority system, its legitimacy depended on how successful leaders were at resolving internal conflicts and divisions *and* winning political contests with external adversaries (Carmack 1995). Similarly, fair-trade cooperatives with a strong board of directors are better able to maintain their autonomy within the global market and resist external control at the hands of development organizations, managerial staff, and buyers.

Service in public positions, whether in groups such as the cooperative or in religious hierarchies, can be interpreted as a conservative force. Those who serve sacrifice for the community through financial investments, labor, or time. This sacrifice is essentially an investment in the continuity of the system that ensures them their local social rewards (Cancian 1992:94) or, in the case of the cooperative, their financial remuneration. This analysis of service as an investment and reward cycle is reflected in the claims made by many community elders during interviews that serving cargos requires both obedience and respect for the position, the responsibility it entails, and the elders who have filled it before you. Unlike other forms of local participation in the transnational economy (migration, service jobs in the tourist industry, and drug trafficking), which often present alternatives to community-based economic strategies, participation in the fair-trade coffee market embeds members more deeply in local economic and social spheres because it is contingent upon an individual's membership within a democratically organized cooperative. In essence, cooperative members' success in the marketplace requires an allegiance to the group itself. The adaptability and yet continued importance of service to both the community and the cooperative help ensure that those who participate remain invested in the local social structure and its continued cohesion in the future.

Three-quarters of the fifty-three interviewed members had served on the cooperative's sixteen-member board of directors at least once over the course of their cooperative membership (average length of membership is fourteen years). On average they fulfilled two terms of service, each lasting one or two years. A similar rate of participation is evident in the community and religious service records of cooperative members: 83 percent served a cargo in a religious organization or on a municipal committee. These high rates of participation demonstrate that the ethos of service and mutual aid remained a highly potent symbolic component of cooperative membership, one that helped mitigate tensions among members. In interviews, members frequently reiterated the importance of mutual aid by explaining, for example, "The cooperative helps you at the same time that you have to help it." Members also employed culturally distinct negotiation styles in general assemblies: before making decisions those in attendance took turns voicing their opinions regarding the matter at hand. Special respect was given to the opinions of elder cooperative members, although all who wished to speak did so (however, as will be demonstrated in the following, this was primarily a male sphere of participation and women were effectively silenced). After thorough discussion, decisions were made through public voting procedures. This practice theoretically helped to diffuse tensions or allegations of injustice within the group as it ensured all opinions were heard in an open forum. While the cooperative undergoes the process of self-transformation into a business association that successfully negotiates the international coffee market, members collectively ensure that the group remains a mutual-aid society through their service. This experience is supported by similar studies indicating that Latin American cooperatives that combine cultural norms of reciprocity and service with contemporary business activities are often more accountable to the needs of their communities and better grounded in local social processes (Bebbington 1996; Nigh 1997; Hernandez Castillo and Nigh 1998).

Despite the premium placed on service within the cooperative, not everyone enthusiastically jumped at the opportunity to fill cargos, a fact cogently expressed by a cooperative member who told me, "Not everyone has this love of the group." In fact, at times, it was difficult to recruit members to serve on the board of directors. Some individuals served repeatedly while others provided excuses for why they could not fulfill their elected cargo (viewing it literally as a burden). For example, many of the long-term members of the cooperative told me they fulfilled their responsibilities and should not be required to provide future service. In addition, those already serving cargos in Catholic Action (generally two-year posts) or one of San

Juan's four cofradías (one-year posts) are excused from cooperative service obligations because of time constraints. Because surveyed members have nearly equal rates of cooperative and non-cooperative service (77 percent and 83 percent, respectively), external commitments often limit the prospective pool.

The fact that nearly 60 percent of the surveyed cooperative members attended three years or less of school and may be illiterate or have poor Spanish skills also contributed to their reluctance to serve cargos in the cooperative. The cooperative faced increasing pressures to meet market demands for certification and quality, and as a result service on the board of directors now involves regular contact with foreign buyers and certifiers, a mastery of Spanish, an understanding of contractual obligations, and familiarity with financial accounting. This effectively precluded the participation of illiterate or monolingual Tz'utujil speakers and those who were uncomfortable associating with Ladinos and foreign businesspersons. When members who were illiterate or who lacked bookkeeping skills were elected to the board of directors, their service appeared perfunctory to some critics. For example, I was told a rumor by several people that a past president allegedly signed whatever checks the manager placed in front of him because he did not firmly grasp the details of the group's financial expenses.

Ironically, some of those best prepared for service, those who were educated and relatively comfortable negotiating cross-cultural social relations and business transactions, were not disposed to accept positions because they are "professionals," as opposed to *campesinos*, and cannot miss work in order to attend the frequent meetings. My neighbor Edgardo's paternal uncle and father (from whom he was estranged) and maternal grandfather were cooperative founders. His maternal uncle (and my landlord), José, was also a member of the cooperative's board of directors. Edgardo was in his early thirties, and after leaving San Juan to earn a high school degree in education, he returned to the community and began teaching at the Catholic elementary school. In addition to his work he was actively involved in the Catholic Church's choir. He and his wife, Ana, had two young sons and a third child on the way in 2002. At the general assembly a cooperative member shouted out Edgardo's name when the president solicited nominations for the board of directors; however, Edgardo quietly declined the nomination that day. The next week he told me: "They have nominated me but thankfully they understand that I don't have the time. I can't . . . One can't send his mozo [day laborer] to fulfill the cargo and because of my job I'm always going to meetings at the school." Although the educated and professional cooperative members might be better equipped to monitor the group's management and financial transactions, their lack of participation might not be an entirely bad thing.[1] Even within the traditional Mesoamerican cargo system in which participants alternate between religious and civil service, the expanding scope of bureaucratic authority vested in the civil positions contributed to the expectation that officials should be better qualified to carry out the assigned duties. For example, Carmack argued that in Momostenango, while control over the local authority system was historically a central object of the community power struggle, this intensified in tandem with heightened bureaucratization (1995:391).

On the basis of a longitudinal study in Zinacantan, Mexico, Cancian (1965, 1992) argues that changes in macro-level systems, including state politics and the global economy, have contributed to decentralized political and social relations in Maya communities and the slow erosion of the traditional bases of community identity. This finding is echoed in Zorn's research on cultural heritage tourism projects in Taquile, Peru. She finds that an increase in income correlates with a decline in communal institutions as wealthier Taquileans say they are "too busy" to attend assemblies and serve in leadership positions. She argues this breakdown in social structure may be especially critical because the ability to act collectively is a key component of the existing social gains (2004). Although the experience of La Voz's membership does not contradict these findings, it does illustrate that alternative models of engagement with the global economy, such as fair-trade markets, can actually serve to increase solidarity among participating members rather than threaten it. However, not every resident is a member of the cooperative and there is little empirical research demonstrating that fair trade reinforces political and social relations or the traditional bases of identity at the community-wide level.

EXPANDING ORGANIZATIONAL CAPACITY AND COMMUNITY IMPACT

Fair-trade consumption in the North is predicated on consumers' access to information regarding the conditions of production and, increasingly, the social circumstances and cultural traditions of producers themselves (Lyon 2006). Therefore, participation in international fair-trade markets can lend legitimacy and protection to democratic producer associations, which in turn are able to create safe opportunities for members to work together and reproduce long-term traditions of horizontal cooperation, reciprocity, and mutual aid. This organizational capacity building can translate into enhanced external civic engagement: for example, some Mexican fair-trade cooperatives are involved in national coffee, credit, and small-business associations (Taylor 2002).

Although not every Juanero belongs to La Voz, the organizational activities of the group benefited non-members through the local multiplier effects of the extra income earned through fair-trade consumer markets. The wider community also benefited from development projects initiated by the cooperative and funded with fair-trade coffee market proceeds in the areas of environmental conservation, infrastructural improvements, and emergency relief. For example, the cooperative played a leading role in the municipal government's 2002 successful effort to organize a weekly trash collection effort in the community. The cooperative was also engaged in an ongoing reforestation project in which seedlings were donated to cooperative members and their extended family members to plant in the agricultural plots surrounding the community. In addition to these environmental conservation programs, the cooperative worked with the National Coffee Association to initiate a coffee tourism project, which will potentially attract additional visitors to the community and increase the income of both members (through tour sales) and non-members, who will have an expanded market for their artisan crafts and service sector, including newly built (and locally owned) hotels, restaurants, and Internet cafés.

The cooperative also played a leading role in securing emergency relief funds and assistance in the wake of Hurricane Stan's October 2005 devastation. The municipal government estimates that more than 30 million quetzals (or $4 million) in agricultural crops were lost during landslides and more than 2,000 residents were displaced after 259 homes were destroyed.[2] After the devastation, the cooperative immediately contacted Green Mountain Coffee Roasters, who sent financial assistance and a group of employees who worked with members to rebuild several homes for displaced families. These efforts were funded by GMCR profits earned largely through fair-trade coffee sales.

In addition to their support of community-development projects, the cooperative capitalized upon the organizational capacity and administrative skills it built through participation in the international fair-trade market to increase its political presence within the national coffee sector. The group regularly sent board members and staff to attend the National Coffee Association's annual conference in Guatemala City and in past years sent administrative staff to the Specialty Coffee Association of America's annual meetings in the United States. The cooperative also regularly hosted and advised groups of smallholders with an interest in developing a fair-trade coffee cooperative. After many years of participation in the certified cof-

FIGURE 4.1. *Municipal employee respon-*
sible for collecting trash and sweeping
the streets of San Juan in 2006.

fee market, the cooperative also successfully applied for its coffee export license, enabling it to directly export to roasters. The elimination of export-er and importer intermediaries increased the group's profits and fostered a stronger relationship between the cooperative and its roaster.

MANAGING THE MANAGER

In order to successfully compete in the international fair-trade coffee mar-ket and fulfill certification and quality requirements, the cooperative steadi-ly increased the responsibilities and power of the manager and the board of directors.[3] The exporter, importer, and roasters who purchased La Voz's coffee preferred to negotiate exclusively with one person year after year in-stead of a constantly revolving board of directors who lacked experience and market savvy. For example, in 2002 the owner of La Voz's exporting firm told me, "The manager has grown a lot as a person and his business skills are partially responsible for the cooperative's success." Speaking about fair-trade coffee cooperatives in general, another exporter said, "It is going to take a long time for these people to learn how to be professional in the marketplace, and it helps if they have a manager who is in charge year after year and understands how to answer bids, for example." On the other hand, because the outside buyers communicated solely with the management, it was at times difficult for the board of directors and the assembly to effectively monitor and manage their employees.

Out of necessity, the cooperative hired its first paid manager in the late 1980s during its initial attempts to secure a long-term coffee market. The first two cooperative managers were coffee farmers and cooperative members. However, the third manager, Guillermo, came to La Voz in 1993 and, even though he grew up in San Juan, was neither a farmer nor a cooperative member. At thirty-four years of age in 2002, Guillermo had a high school degree in accounting and belonged to the first generation of educated Juaneros who benefited from the region's coffee boom and the resulting cash influx (described in Chapter 2). As one of a small number of educated professional Juaneros living and working within the community, Guillermo represented the occupational ideal to which many local youth aspired. At the same time, even though he was Tz'utujil, the membership's unease with him and his authority reflected the fact that in many ways he was still culturally an outsider because of his education, frequent associations with foreigners, occupational status, and bureaucratic role. Therefore, the conflicts within the cooperative parallel those that historically structured relations in indigenous communities dominated by Ladino bureaucratic authorities. For example, in 2002 several cooperative members expressed their unease about the fact that they were currently represented by a non-farmer who they believed was not as trustworthy as a hardworking campesino. Questioning the manager's loyalty to the cooperative, one member told me, "Well, I've never seen *him* heading to his fields with a hoe." Many cooperative members who primarily performed agricultural work believed professionals live a life of leisure, protected from the elements and growing fat as they take daily lunch breaks in *comedors* (small restaurants) and drink numerous sodas throughout the day. For example, one day in the cooperative's beneficio, as I helped the former agricultural monitor weigh members' coffee, an associate joked with us about how soft and easy it is to be an employee instead of a farmer. He said: "It's not like it is for us farmers. In the countryside we feel everything, the air, the weather, the sun, but here it's soft." Although the differences between campesino and professional life may be a source of humor, they can also fuel tension. As discussed earlier, many members financially struggled and sacrificed in order to provide their children with an education they hoped would spare them the hardships and poverty associated with the farming life. Therefore, it is unlikely that cooperative members would condemn the manager solely on the basis of his professional occupation.

However, the members used his non-farmer status as a proxy to express their anxiety over Guillermo's performance and growing power, feelings that some were perhaps uneasy expressing more explicitly (although others held no such reservations).

La Voz's internal structure is typical of most agricultural cooperatives: the general assembly is the base of the organization and is represented by a sixteen-member board of directors elected to fill two-year positions. Although the board meets weekly throughout the year, the cooperative's daily operations are administered by the manager, accountant, and the agricultural monitor. The board members exert varying degrees of power within the cooperative, but the form of this power is distinct from that of the management. First, board members serve two-year positions, thereby eliminating the potential for oligarchy. Second, for the most part, individual progression through cooperative cargos resembles the graded progression through the ranked statuses of the community's religious hierarchy, statuses that are associated with different degrees of respect, prestige, decision-making power, administrative obligation, and ritual association (Carmack 1995). With age and experience, members are typically elected to increasingly more powerful and important positions. In contrast, the thirty-four-year-old manager effectively sidestepped the traditional age hierarchy in assuming a position of authority and respect at a young age. Guillermo also was the cooperative's public figurehead in the international coffee market. Although he was not a coffee farmer, Guillermo represented the members and the cooperative in banks, development agencies, contract negotiations, public relations, and in the meetings of associations, such as those held by Anacafé and the Specialty Coffee Association of America (SCAA), whose annual gathering in the United States he attended three times. At the 2002 SCAA meeting in Anaheim, California, Guillermo gave a talk titled "The Complete Circle of the Origin of Sustainability." This was understandably a proud moment for him, one that he asked me to memorialize by snapping a photo that he could show his friends and family.

In the nascent years of the cooperative, the general assembly convened monthly; however, with the introduction of management, the number of meetings declined significantly to one or two a year at most. Although nearly three-quarters of interviewed members said they would like to convene more often, in practice some members seemed content to fully relinquish administrative authority to the manager and elected officials. For example, during an interview, one member stated, "The manager and the board of directors are the only ones who know the true situation of the cooperative." Rhetorical maneuvers such as these enabled members to disavow responsibility for the problems facing the institution. The manager was responsible for enforcing the rules and decisions made by the board of directors. Through this enforcement he assisted members who might prefer to avoid confronting and regulating one another. In fact, for the manager this task was potentially made easier precisely because he was *not* a cooperative member. As discussed earlier, many cooperative members exhibited a reluctance to move into positions of authority—for example, by serving on the board of directors or supervising the production practices of their fellow associates (which will be described in Chapter 5)—because this felt like betrayal. In their reluctance to individually discipline one another, the members of La Voz resembled the inhabitants of Tzintzuntzan, the southern Mexican indigenous community researched by Foster. He maintains that community members avoided confrontation and opposed decision-making practices: "A direct confrontation in which two candidates are in direct opposition—and hence one must lose—or in which in public discussion one tries to have his ideas take precedence over others, is disturbing to all, since an equilibrium is destroyed . . . Hence, decisions must be based on consensus, gradually achieved" (Foster 1967:172).

However, consensus-style decision making, such as that practiced in the general assembly, is not a viable strategy for the management of daily operations. For example, the manager was responsible for approving credit applications from members. Decisions such as these could not be made by a group vote (or, truly, even by committee). One individual must hold the authoritative power because members would be extremely uncomfortable publicly discussing the financial business of their fellow associates.

In contrast to members who contentedly surrendered administrative control to the manager, some associates were decidedly unhappy about his growing power. On one particularly gray afternoon at the tail end of the 2002 rainy season the agricultural monitor, Pedro, and I dodged puddles in the cobblestone streets and back alleys as he accompanied me on my visits to cooperative members' homes. He had recently accepted the position and was slowly learning his responsibilities while just beginning to understand the complexity of his new situation: a long-term cooperative member he suddenly found himself occupying a supervisory role. As a result he possessed significant insight into the frustrations of members and the administration and how these shaped the practice of cooperation on a daily basis. After sitting in on an interview I conducted with a cooperative member who loudly complained about the manager, Pedro relayed a recent conversation he had with Guillermo in which Pedro suggested a slight change in the cooperative's policies regarding organic certification. The manager responded, "Okay, well I have to check with *my* board of directors." To Pedro, this choice of words was indicative of Guillermo's professional attitude. Pedro explained, "He should have said *the* board of directors because he is an employee, not the *owner*." Pedro's concerns were echoed by many members during both interviews and more informal conversations. For example, one told me, "It would be better if the [elected] president had a little more power to make contacts in the capital because *he* really has a love of the cooperative and the associates." Another explained: "Since the beginning, the manager has had the upper hand. Maybe this is because of his academic studies and the fact that those on the board are afraid to speak Spanish." Similarly, a former board member complained: "We are here only to keep up appearances. What we do is give him a legal voice in everything . . . I am beginning to think he is the true owner of the cooperative." However, when I confronted Guillermo with these accusations one afternoon he vehemently disagreed, arguing, "I don't have a voice, or a vote, nothing more than an opinion . . . I inform them and they are the owners of the cooperative."

FEARING CORRUPTION

I began my research in San Juan in December 2001. For the first few months I primarily spent my time at the cooperative's beneficio in the afternoons, observing the harvest activities, while in the mornings I studied Tz'utujil with Francisco for several hours. In addition, I spent a lot of time hanging out with my neighbors and acclimating to my new living circumstances (e.g., cold showers in the outdoor bathroom) and a seemingly endless number of chores such as washing my clothes by hand in the *pila* (outdoor sink), chasing my neighbor's chickens out of my kitchen, and mopping my floors daily to combat the film of dust that seemed to invade every crevice during the dry season (see also Hendrickson 1995). I was slowly getting to know the cooperative members and the individuals who would eventually become my friends and informants, and it was not until March 2001, four months after my arrival, that I heard the first whispers of managerial corruption. Over time, these whispers grew into a roar as more and more people hinted that the manager was stealing money from the cooperative, making illicit trades with European coffee buyers, and colluding with corrupt members of the board of directors.

In hindsight it is perhaps not surprising that these rumors initially sent me spiraling into a funk. I recall writing a rather desperate e-mail to my dissertation advisor that I was afraid to continue with the research because of what I might find. At that time the fair-trade coffee market in the United

States was growing exponentially, spurred by the high-profile entrance of Starbucks and the promotional efforts of TransFair USA, Global Exchange, and other organizations. I naively feared that my research in San Juan would crack open what I increasingly believed to be a fair-trade façade. However, she wisely advised me to continue and the cooperative eventually faced this corruption head on, in the process teaching me a valuable lesson in solidarity and shaping my understanding of the fraught nature of cooperation. Despite this, the rumors continued throughout my research. Over time, I have come to understand not only the fears of corruption but the act of corruption itself differently. I know now that when they whisper into my ear, people are telling me more than just the latest gossip—they are expressing anxiety and attempting to control a situation that seems beyond their reach. I also realize that even though the current fair-trade coffee market has many flaws, single acts of corruption do not negate the model's future potential.

In regions with a history of targeted rural violence, such as Guatemala, the international nature of fair-trade networks can buttress the strength of cooperatives and the secure civic spaces they foster. Although many Guatemalans see democratic organizations as essential to confronting poverty and precarious economic circumstances, because any social organization not under army control during the war was criminalized, fear remains a significant obstacle to rural organization (REMHI 1999). As discussed in Chapter 2, Guatemala's civil war created a climate of distrust and insecurity in many indigenous communities. The contemporary rumors and discourses of corruption that permeated the cooperative membership in 2002 should be understood as an outgrowth of this insidious and long-standing fear. Part of the burden of cooperation is working together to surpass the mutual misgivings and suspicions that accompany so many rural development efforts in Guatemala today. Furthermore, just as the Guatemalan civil war unfolded against the global backdrop of cold-war politics, local rumors and fears of corruption must be understood within a larger geopolitical context in which developing nations such as Guatemala are publicly chastised for their high levels of corruption by the leaders of northern countries (despite the fact that their own administrations are rarely free of scandals and recrimination) and international organizations such as Transparency International exist to challenge "the inevitability of corruption."[4]

Fair-trade and organic coffee certifiers and cooperative members themselves place a high degree of importance on transparency. This is codified in the FLO certification requirement that "[t]he organization must have a democratic structure and transparent administration, which enables an effective control by the members and its Board over the management" (FLO

2007a). However, despite this emphasis on transparency, both allegations and acts of corruption are not uncommon in fair-trade coffee networks. As Scott argues, "Corruption, like violence, must be understood as a regular, repetitive, integral part of the operation of most political systems" (1972: viii). Although certified coffee commodity networks are not political systems per se, they are democratic institutions and within both the local and international economy serve many of the same purposes, such as regulation and enforcement.

Fears of corruption (and actual corruption) are more prevalent in nations such as Guatemala, where secrecy, uncertainty, and fear represent the enduring legacy of the three-decades-long civil war. Guatemalan political and legal systems are widely acknowledged in public venues as suffering high degrees of corruption. Before the Peace Accords, Guatemala had no national police force, and in many indigenous communities today inhabitants give officers a wide berth. Far from providing an aura of safety, I found many of my friends and neighbors (including myself) actually feared the local police (all non-local Ladino males), who swaggered around town in crisp blue uniforms carrying shiny rifles. In fact, I heard several rumors of policemen raping indigenous girls and harassing villagers in various lakeside communities. My own fears of the police were undoubtedly heightened by the nights I was awoken by my neighbor, who, after working four day-long shifts as a policeman in a distant community, would return to San Juan and drink excessively, beat his wife, yell loudly, and even fire his gun and throw rocks. This type of behavior and corruption reportedly pervades all ranks of the national police force and, as a result, Guatemala's international reputation has suffered.[5]

Corruption is a difficult topic to explore ethnographically. As Werner points out, defining corruption poses a conceptual problem as the boundaries between "corrupt" behavior and "cultural" behavior are not always clear. She defines corruption as the "[a]buse of public power for private gain," with the caveat that corrupt acts are not limited to the public sector and often benefit individuals other than the perpetrators (2000:16). Over the course of my fieldwork I was told numerous stories about the current and past corrupt actions of various individuals, including cooperative officials and board members (of both La Voz and other Juanero associations), politicians, local business owners, development agency employees, money lenders, and ordinary Juaneros. These stories were all relayed in the form of gossip and I rarely bothered to corroborate them: under the anthropological mandate to do no harm to our subjects, discussing and publicizing cases of actual proven corruption at the local level would be ethically and professionally questionable scholarship. However, I would like to stress that virtually every single community development project and political administration was tainted by rumors of corruption at some level.

In this case it is not the *act* of corruption that is of anthropological interest but instead the *discourse* of corruption, in which community members pass moral judgment on one another. Corruption must be understood as a multidimensional entity: it is a functional behavior (the purposes it serves for individual participants); it is a discourse that shapes political, social, and economic systems; and it is a practice capable of shaping personal attitudes and moral sensibilities. In the case that follows, I argue that the often repeated rumors of managerial corruption represent an attempt by members to mitigate their anxieties and exert power over organizational spaces, such as financial bookkeeping and coffee contracts, which were slowly slipping out of their realm of understanding and control as the cooperative became increasingly enmeshed in external markets. Several factors contributed to the insistent fears of corruption expressed by members, including the strength of interpersonal relationships and kinship ties, unfamiliarity with administrative functions, a lack of legal accountability, and the cultural expectation of corruption. The extended family networks linking virtually every inhabitant to many other households fostered fears of corruption as individuals questioned the illicit favors family members allegedly performed for one another. There is a cultural expectation in San Juan that the members of extended families help one another when need arises. Therefore, it is difficult for many Juaneros to believe that officials of any organization would refuse requests made by their relatives.

The second, and perhaps more important, factor contributing to rumors of corruption within the cooperative was members' general lack of business acumen and familiarity with administrative duties and power. Juanero bureaucrats, such as the cooperative manager, possessed significantly more academic training and greater fluency in Spanish, and thus were culturally more at ease with foreigners, Ladinos, and visiting officials. The knowledge discrepancy between the manager and many members resulted in two divergent trends. Those cooperative members who were turned down for loans or were unable to follow the complex accounting procedures described to them in the general assembly were more likely to complain during interviews that the manager was corrupt. However, a handful of members closely monitored the management and showed up at the general assembly with calculators in hand to check the manager's and accountant's math while carefully listening to their explanations of expenditures and income. They exerted their authority by publicly pointing out discrepancies during the meeting. Not all cooperative members were subordinate to the manager, either in terms of education or status. Therefore, some were able to effectively police his behavior and bookkeeping for the benefit of all. These public enactments of fiscal accountability are examples of effective participatory democracy. However, members of the general assembly were unable to continuously monitor the cooperative's daily operations or managerial authority, limiting the effectiveness of this method of supervision.

Furthermore, some cooperative members seemed to expect corruption from individuals occupying positions of power because they had served past cargos in organizations and thus well understand the temptations that accompany such jobs. As so often happened during my Tz'utujil lessons with Francisco, one morning we pushed aside the vocabulary lists and began chatting (in Spanish, perhaps an explanation for why I never developed a working fluency in Tz'utujil). He recalled a trip he took to Guatemala City in the late 1970s when he was assigned the task of collecting cash loaned to the cooperative and transporting it, by bus, back to San Juan. The bus wound its way along the Pan-American Highway. As Francisco reached Los Encuentros, a point where he could choose to travel North to Chichicastenango, continue west to Quetzaltenango, or descend to Panajachel and the boat that would take him home to San Juan, he began to shake uncontrollably from the fear that he might be robbed or succumb to temptation and take this large quantity of money and never return to his wife and young children. The many associations in San Juan, including the cooperative, received regular and large flows of development money from the agencies that operated projects in the area. As a result, many Juaneros were skilled financial and cultural brokers who redirected resource flows through a complex negotiation of customary and contractual obligations within the community. For many community members the idea that a committee leader or association president might redirect at least a portion of these funds to his own benefit was categorically accepted behavior. This expectation of corruption is echoed in the works of previous anthropologists conducting research in Guatemala and Mexico, such as Sol Tax, who wrote, "Honesty is not so firmly established in the culture that it can be taken for granted" (1953:19), and Foster, who suggests, "Small advantages accruing from a favorable position are assumed to be one's right; it is only excessive abuse that arouses anger" (1967:111).

Although the rumors and fears of corruption were at times pervasive within the cooperative, members were reluctant to share them with outsiders lest they should circulate beyond San Juan's borders. Cooperatives need to maintain a delicate balance among a professional and well-informed managerial staff, an active board of directors, and an engaged general assembly. However, this can be a difficult goal to achieve, and sometimes as a manager's control and influence grows, the general assembly becomes increasingly less informed and involved. When one individual represents a cooperative and its interests to the world at large, it also becomes easier for outsiders to question his or her honesty. Rumors of corruption may begin to tarnish reputations in the marketplace and negatively impact the cooperative's daily operations. One coffee importer who had worked closely with cooperatives across Latin America for more than a decade told me she had never maintained a long-term relationship with a cooperative without questions of corruption and mismanagement arising at some point. Other roasters and importers expressed reservations about dealing with coffee cooperatives because of similar problems. For example, a Green Mountain employee familiar with the Latin American coffee market told me he did not understand why I was researching La Voz. In his opinion, because the cooperative had enjoyed market success and not suffered from public rumors of corruption, it was an atypical case. These beliefs in the pervasive nature of corruption within Latin American coffee cooperatives were shared by some of the Ladino professionals I spoke to in Guatemala. One Anacafé extension agent who worked in lakeside communities told me, "For years we could say the Ladinos robbed the indigenous people but now they don't need Ladinos, they are robbing themselves." Similarly, a regional director of National Institute of Cooperatives (INACOP), the government organization responsible for monitoring and certifying cooperatives, claimed: "The people hire a manager with the idea that he knows a lot, he has experience, and he's going to care for the cooperative. But it's the opposite because he knows and he takes advantage of the people. There's no system of fast justice and cooperative members might not report corrupt managers to the authorities because they are afraid." These comments indicate that certain forms of behavior are commonly associated with the uneasy structural position occupied by the managers of indigenous organizations, such as Guillermo, who awkwardly straddle insider/outsider divides.

FACING CORRUPTION

The skylines of both the smallest towns and Guatemala City's opulent Zone 10 are framed by lengths of rebar reaching up to the sky from the roofs of buildings. Over the course of my fieldwork, this rebar was an ever-present visual metaphor of the hopefulness and sense of future possibility held by many Guatemalans. When building their homes, many dreamed of the eventual second story, and therefore, dismissing aesthetic considerations, they left the metal support bars in place to rust and weather with age. Without doubt, although Guatemala has experienced many recent changes and rapid growth, it has a long road to travel. For many this road appears ripe with possibility because of the democratic openings and the flourishing of civil society that accompanied the years of postwar reconstruction. However, within San Juan, although the unfinished two-story house may represent a family's hopes for future prosperity, cement-block homes, especially those with second stories, are also, for some, symbolic representations of negative trends within the community.

Elders around the world commonly lament the loss of traditional mores and morals, and San Juan is no different. During our interviews Juanero elders frequently complained of the lack of respect children showed their elders, recalling how in their own youth their parents instructed them to step aside and allow elderly Juaneros to pass on the road after kissing their hand and wishing them well. Similarly, both elders and cooperative members frequently denounced the disintegration of the community's previous system of mutual aid, which centered on communal house building; even before a house becomes a family's home, its construction holds an important social role (Colloredo-Mansfeld 1994). In years past in San Juan, when a couple built their first house or constructed a new one, they enlisted the aid of their friends and family members. At dawn, the men would head to the woods in search of building materials and enjoy, upon their return, the breakfast communally prepared by the women. Over the course of the day, Juaneros worked together to construct the new home while the owners provided food, beverages, and the promise of future reciprocal construction labor. However, among the many changes accompanying San Juan's coffee "bomb" in the 1970s was the introduction of cement-block construction materials, introduced and encouraged across Guatemala after the devastating 1976 earthquake brought fears of being crushed in falling rubble and new government regulations. Building a cement-block house requires the expertise of a trained *albañil* (mason), who is compensated with coffee earnings in the form of cash, not communal labor. In the eyes of some, the block houses, which many interpreted as signs of wealth, prosperity, and permanence, came to represent the negative influences of agro-commodity success, the growing pervasiveness of the local cash economy, and the disintegration of the labor practices that formerly bound neighbors and families together through ties of reciprocity.[6] When elders romanticize past relationships of cooperation and mutualism, "[t]hey are not simply telling us that cooperation is part of a bygone era and no longer important. Rather they are using cooperation to evaluate and organize a world that is rapidly changing" (Cohen 1999:6).

Similarly, for others the addition of the second story to a house represents not success or hard work but, instead, possible corruption. In a community of private, single-storied houses generally surrounded by concrete walls or cane fences, the houses with second stories are conspicuous public markers of wealth. Except for the largest landowners, such wealth can rarely be earned through agricultural sales of products such as maize or onions or with coffee earnings when market prices are low. Therefore, not surprisingly, when community members wanted to place the morality of another Juanero in doubt, they frequently cited the existence of a second story as tangible proof of crimes and corrupt actions. For example, in the center of town an enterprising, young evangelical couple built a three-story home with a store on the first level. They also owned a cargo truck that brought tomatoes and onions to Guatemala City and returned filled with consumer goods. In casual discussions, several Juaneros hypothesized that despite their evangelical morals, the couple must be transporting drugs cleverly tucked in around their bundles of onions, for how else would they be able to afford such an expansive new home? The uniformity of housing within a community expresses an ideology of equality, and "[c]onformity to community housing standards is a visible expression of willingness to conform to other norms and ethics" (Wilk 1997:166). Therefore, adding a second or even a third story effectively distances a Juanero from other community members in a move that is both symbolically and practically divisive (Wilk 1997).

According to several members, the rumors of managerial corruption intensified when Guillermo added a second story to his home in 2001. As one explained, "We began to wonder how he could afford to build that second story on his house. He said it was his parents' money but we knew that wasn't true, and we knew how little he earned." In an attempt to quell the rumors by presenting the membership with factual evidence, the newly elected cooperative president, Juan, commissioned an external audit of the cooperative in 2001. This audit reportedly revealed erroneous bookkeeping and missing funds. One afternoon as we rode in the back of a pickup truck down the winding road from the Pan-American Highway into San Juan, Juan shared his thoughts on the manager and his alleged corruption. Juan told me that he believed the manager intentionally mismanaged funds to his own advantage, explaining, "As the Bible tells us, we have to make clear in the morning the things we did during the night. It was obvious that eventually people would find out." Juan called a meeting of the general assembly to present the evidence and ask the members to vote on Guillermo's continued employment.

In the days leading up to the meeting, cooperative members gossiped with one another, sharing bits and pieces of information and opinions, lobbying for one position or another. Few individuals possessed the whole truth and, indeed, some of the rumors were outlandish. For example, I was told that Guillermo had been buying conventional coffee in town through *coyotes* and then selling this coffee to European importers as certified organic coffee grown by La Voz members. At the annual meeting I attended in April 2002, my two years of calculus classes did not help me understand the seemingly indecipherable series of accounting figures the manager and his assistant rushed through. In fact, after the meeting I took pictures of each sheet of paper with the hope of attaining a deeper comprehension at a later date. It is not hard to imagine that, like me, the majority of cooperative members, who had little formal schooling, were unable to fully understand the bookkeeping and contract details that the management shared with them at the annual meeting. As the cooperative's business negotiations became increasingly more complex, the daily operations slowly moved outside the realm of daily experience for the majority of members. Rumors thrive in situations like this precisely because the facts are uncertain and not easily discovered.

As explained earlier, cargo service, whether in the religious hierarchy or in organizations such as the cooperative, is a conservative force in that individuals sacrifice for the community but also invest their time, energy, and resources in the continuity of a system that ensures local social (and, in the cooperative's case, financial) rewards. Anxiety over managerial corruption was partially fueled by the fact that the young, educated manager's rise to power within the cooperative contradicted local models of authority gained through seniority and experience. One of the founding members explicitly expressed his dissatisfaction with the manager, arguing, "He doesn't understand the suffering we experienced, he doesn't understand everything we've been through for this cooperative." In the cooperative's early history, the founding members signed an act proclaiming only children of associates could be employees of the cooperative with the idea that, in the words of one founder, "[w]e had struggled to form the cooperative and if the managers and accountants were the actual children of associates, their parents would make sure their children weren't cheating the cooperative or illegally taking out loans without anybody's knowledge." Several of the older cooperative members, such as Francisco, suggested that the cooperative should enforce this act.

Despite the widespread dissatisfaction with the manager, at the meeting convened by the president the members decided not to fire Guillermo. Although I was not invited to this meeting, several members who voted in favor of the manager's continued employment shared their reasons with me in private. Some feared the cooperative would suffer financially and potentially lose its long-term market because only the manager had the outside contacts and business knowledge necessary to run the organization. Other interviewed members sympathized with the manager because "[h]e doesn't earn that much for his salary" and believed that after a public discussion he would undoubtedly correct his behavior in the future if it truly was problematic. Others acknowledged they simply did not have enough information to pass judgment. For example, one stated: "People make allegations of corruption for lack of education. We don't understand how management works. We think badly of him but it's also true that he doesn't explain himself well."

Just as corruption must be understood as a multidimensional entity, rumors of corruption also serve multiple purposes: not only do they constitute a discourse that impacts political, social, and economic systems but they also can serve functional purposes within a community or organization. Although I have argued that the rumors of managerial corruption were an attempt by cooperative members to mitigate their anxieties and exert control over organizational spaces, they also served to unite the group and solidify its boundaries as the cooperative developed increasing numbers of relationships with external agents in the marketplace.

Among cooperative members, the rumors and gossip leading up to the meeting perhaps ironically served to reinforce the unity of the group by enabling members to achieve a degree of social consensus without resorting to blatant conflict.[7] For example, while he weathered these allegations, the manager was never threatened or publicly ostracized nor did he face legal repercussions. The punishment for his alleged embezzling was the loss of his job, not jail time, and members did not stand to gain anything personal through their gossip about the manager (e.g., none of them would be given his job if he was fired). Furthermore, the gossip served to enforce the boundaries of the group precisely because cooperative members talked only with one another (or other Juaneros) and *not* with outsiders. I spent four months researching the cooperative before anyone in the community even hinted at managerial corruption, and in fact, many of the conversations that I had with individuals regarding the manager took place several months after the cooperative meeting in which his future was determined.

In June 2002, Santiago resigned from his position as agricultural monitor and the cooperative hired to take his place a new monitor, Pedro, also a member of the cooperative. One day as I was walking to Francisco's house for my Tz'utujil lesson, I bumped into Santiago in the street in front of his house. He told me that he had resigned and explained that his decision was influenced by the fact that the president, Juan, who he respected greatly (despite accusing him earlier that year of selling his coffee to another association), had earlier resigned in disgust over the cooperative's refusal to sanction the manager. (I privately, however, suspected that Santiago's decision was also the result of his desire to devote more of his time to his family's expanding tienda.) Santiago quite freely shared with me his belief that the board of directors and the management were corrupt. During the town's fiesta in June, Santiago spoke with Elan Organic Coffees representative, Carlos, in private and neither of them chose to reveal the details of this conversation. The unknown content of this conversation proved worrisome to the board of directors and the manager. In August, September, and October Pedro assisted me in my interviews with cooperative members: he sympathetically listened to their complaints and frequently expressed his agreement with their complaints in private as we walked to our next interview. Furthermore, he was unwavering in his opinion that Santiago had done a great disservice to the cooperative by sharing its internal problems with Carlos, an outsider. Pedro explained: "I don't believe in God and religious people because look at him [Santiago]. When he's singing in church, he appears so religious as he raises his arms up to God. But then he goes and does such a bad thing, telling Don Carlos about all of these problems."

Anthropologists studying Mesoamerican communities have long noted the pervasiveness of gossip, scandal, and fears. For example, Foster describes life in peasant communities as "[m]arked by suspicion and distrust . . . sensitivity to the fear of shame, [and] proneness to criticize and gossip" (1967:89). Similarly, in his study of highland Maya communities, Tax writes that the "[m]ost persistent obstacles to peace of mind are the continued vexations of social life: fear, envy, fear of envy, rumors, slander, gossip, [and] fear of gossip" (1953:13). Annis finds highland Maya relationships to be so "[d]elicate and so potentially open to conflict" that community members preface conversational references to personal desires and needs with the phrase, *man owal ok'*, literally, "There is no dispute between us," essentially stating that they are not seeking conflict and that noncompliance would not result in dispute nor the dissolution of social accords (Annis 1970:123). In short, earlier generations of anthropologists maintained that Mesoamerican communities exhibited an aversion to overt disagreement and employed informal codes to regulate the balance of individual opinions and the needs of the larger group.

Although theoretically within the cooperative all members are equal, power differences do exist, attributable to factors such as length of membership, age, sex, the status of the extended family within the community, the number of family members within the cooperative, the size of landholdings, the size of individual debts to the cooperative, repayment practices, past service on the board of directors, fluency in Spanish, and the possession of business knowledge and accounting skills.[8] Foster argued that certain Latin American communities are driven by the image of the limited good, or the idea that life is played as a zero-sum game in which one player's advantage comes at the expense of another (1972:168). More recently, Warren supports Foster's formulation, arguing that the image of the limited good resonates with Maya sense of the competitiveness and danger of interpersonal relations (1998:175). She maintains that Maya religion historically reversed the external Ladino values: poverty became purifying and good and material riches were interpreted as a result of evil (1978). As a result of Guatemala's inequitable power relations, Maya were structurally incapable of translating wealth into economic and political power in the national and Ladino spheres. Therefore, the accumulation of wealth was morally rejected in favor of reinvestment in a kind of social currency, negotiable only at the village level (Annis 1987:61).

Within communities that have experienced sharply rising standards of living as a result of the introduction of cash crops like coffee, such as San Juan, inhabitants possess an increasing number of material consumer goods. Among the interviewed cooperative members, only one owned a pickup truck and only two owned computers. However, 62 percent owned televisions, 33 percent owned horses or mules, and 15 percent owned telephones. The possession of these consumer goods is a direct result of the financial well-being generated through coffee sales and fair-trade market participation. Grandin maintains that the survival of community identity and institutions does not necessarily signal resistance to capitalism but rather forms "[t]he cultural and social matrices through which communal relations articulate(d) with market forces" (2000:128). Cooperative members (and Juaneros, more generally) are capitalist and they most definitely hope to acquire consumer goods and achieve higher standards of living. Some Juaneros with higher income levels and greater purchasing power act similarly to the Otavaleño cultural improvisers described by Colloredo-Mansfeld, sampling styles, tastes, and objects from other cultures while simultaneously investing more resources in the reproduction of native practices, such as the purchasing of the expensive Juanero *traje* for their sons and daughters. However, in a process of "fragmentation" similar to that experienced by the Otavaleños, as individuals acquire more possessions, academic training, and worldly experiences, intra-community and intra-family gaps in knowledge and experience are emerging and these may, in turn, prove the greatest challenge in the future reproduction of Juanero culture within the globalizing economy (Colloredo-Mansfeld 1999:27).

As a result, although the image of the limited good increasingly applies less and less in communities such as San Juan, the emerging stratification and blatant displays of wealth still invoke anxiety among Juaneros. For some, fears of envy and allegations of corruption foster the self-imposed regulation of conspicuous wealth displays. For example, many Juaneros kept their televisions in back rooms, out of the sight of prying eyes. Rabinow writes: "It is shame, that concern for the good opinion of one's neighbors and friends, which circumscribes behavior within the moral boundaries created by shared values. A man without shame is, by definition, capable of anything" (1977:158). In building a second story on his house, thereby flaunting his accumulated wealth, the manager acted publicly and without shame.

If a good name is the most vital social possession and is only "[d]efined by others according to shared and commonly sanctioned criteria of interest," then it follows that gossip can serve to defend or attack "good names" accordingly (Wilson 1974:100–101). Scott argues that stories circulated about powerful individuals by less powerful ones are, in essence, "[c]ornerstones of an ideological edifice under construction": through these stories, less powerful individuals attempt to create and maintain a certain view of what decent, acceptable human behavior ought to be (Scott 1985:23). Therefore, cooperative members gossiping about the manager's alleged corruption were not simply shaming his good name, they were also attempting to enforce primary community values, such as equality, mutualism, and accountability. Although fair-trade market participation brings many rewards, like modernity itself, it is experienced by cooperative members as a fragmented, contradictory, and disquieting process that produces untenable situations and power that lies beyond their grasp (West and Sanders 2003:16). The rumors of managerial corruption served to challenge the emergent stratification within the cooperative resulting from the manager's increasing power. They also challenged the growing primacy of external fair-trade market forces over local forms of social organization and community norms.

A MARKET OF OUR OWN: WOMEN IN THE COOPERATIVE

In August 2002 two aides working for the U.S. House of Representatives Foreign Affairs Committee, accompanied by several employees of Anacafé, visited La Voz as part of their research on the coffee crisis. The Anacafé staff members told me they chose this particular cooperative to visit because it was "well known" and because "people come on the pretext of working but they really want to be tourists and see the lake." The visit lasted approximately thirty minutes, and even though the cooperative's manager and board of directors had prepared a lengthy presentation covering the cooperative's history, its coffee production methods, and current market conditions, the Americans interrupted them after five minutes to say they would rather ask their own questions. Using an Anacafé employee as a translator, one of the visitors asked the male manager and all-male board of directors, "What have you done to incorporate women into the cooperative?" The cooperative's president quickly demurred, stating he did not want to monopolize the discussion and deftly passed the question to a board member, Alejandro. Alejandro did not have a ready answer and stalled a bit before hesitantly explaining, "In the beginning we had very little participation on behalf of the women but we are trying to incorporate the women into the cooperative more. We've received workshops from Anacafé which have helped us too. The women help out the most during the harvest. But now, if a man can't attend a meeting he will send his wife in his place." The aide followed up by pointedly asking, "Is there a woman on the board of directors right now?" Alejandro replied, "Right now, no, because the board changes every two years . . . but in the past, oh yes, in the past, of course." During the meeting several female cooperative members and wives waited patiently outside on the patios of the cooperative's beneficio, baking in the high-altitude sun. They were holding brightly colored weavings, which they hoped to sell to the visitors. However, their hopes were dashed when the Americans and their handlers sped away in their jeep, on to their next whirlwind visit.

Several months earlier I had interviewed Juana, one of the cooperative's ten female members and a cooperative founder. She told me: "The men have work, but us, we don't have work. The men manage all the funds. I think the female members are discriminated against—only the men participate and we don't know anything. Only men are on the board of directors. I can't be on the board of directors. We're discriminated against in the cooperative, us ten women. I want the board to pressure the manager to look for another [artisan] market. Right now I'm demanding this of the board of directors but nobody is helping in the cooperative."

Juana's claims were well-illustrated during the cooperative's annual meeting that year. Although there were approximately thirty women present, they broke their silence only to shush their children until Juana stood

FIGURE 4.2. *The weavings of female cooperative members, strung up in the cooperative's wet mill, waiting for a potential sale to a visiting coffee roaster.*

to comment on a matter under dispute. She began to speak forcefully in Tz'utujil and was almost immediately quieted by a booming male voice. Juana immediately exclaimed in Spanish (for she, unlike many other women in the community, was bilingual) that the men were discriminating against her by not allowing her to speak. After silencing the heckler with this proclamation, she continued to speak in Tz'utujil for approximately three minutes until she promptly sat down after being told to be quiet by her own elderly father, the most senior cooperative member, who, dressed in the traje he wore daily, sat in a position of honor at the front and center of the assembly.[9] Juana was the only woman who spoke publicly that day. In fact, the only participatory role given to women was to serve plates of chicken, black beans, and steaming tortillas to members and their families at the end of the five-hour-long meeting.[10]

The Fairtrade Labelling Organization International has attempted to foster gender equity through its existing certification standards. FLO identifies the "empowerment of women" as one of fair trade's ten impact areas on its website, stating, "Important investments can be made in women's income-generating activities that are not related to the farm, thereby strengthening their income, business experience and position in the family."[11] However, in practice the effectiveness of FLO's standards and efforts are debatable, especially in regard to democratic participation and the promotion of non-agricultural income-generating opportunities for women. In fact, although fostering gender equity has theoretically been a priority for fair trade, women's current limited participation in producer associations may perpetuate rather than overcome the traditional gender bias in Latin America's agricultural sector (Murray, Raynolds, and Taylor 2006). This weakness calls into question the adequacy of fair-trade certification standards and challenges the effectiveness of the certification process itself. As the above examples illustrate, despite the fact that certification systems are cloaked in a mantle of transparency and democracy, producer groups may selectively manage the information provided to outsiders. This forces us to consider whether, in light of the cultural and socioeconomic diversity characterizing producer groups, the fair-trade network should attempt to dictate and enforce generic standards of gender equity through certification requirements. Despite its drawbacks, the fair-trade movement represents one of the few large-scale, viable alternatives to contemporary neoliberal globalization. However, in order to be a truly effective alternative, fair trade must fully address the needs of all participants, not simply the men. This is especially true in Latin America where overall women's participation in the agricultural sector has been structurally limited and where women constitute the majority of the indigent, poor, unemployed, and illiterate while occupying the lowest paid and least secure jobs and suffering from higher levels of personal violence and risk than their male counterparts (Molyneux 2002:173; for a notable exception see Hamilton 2000). In general, women farmers and workers throughout the South still confront lower pay, less stable employment, widespread sexual harassment in the workplace, and a double burden of wage labor and household responsibilities (Oxfam 2004).

Similar to many agricultural commodities, gender oppression has been central to the historical development of the coffee industry (Fridell 2007), where women face lower pay and overt gender discrimination in the plantation settings.[12] Among small-scale producers, in many Latin American communities it is common for husbands to "send" their wives and children to pick coffee during the harvest; however, the men typically oversee the labor and the transferring of sacks of coffee from the fields to the beneficio or buyer (Luetchford 2008). There are several ways in which patriarchal social relations shape aspects of smallholder coffee production in Latin America, potentially limiting the possibilities for enhanced gender equity in this productive realm. For example, frequently men have privileged access to land and income while women are required to work in both the field and the home (Mayoux 2001; Redfern and Snedker 2002; Fridell 2007). Furthermore, there is evidence that the role of women in household decision making is often disproportionate to the work they devote to the actual coffee production (Fridell 2007:132). Finally, participation in the coffee industry, especially in the potentially more lucrative certified coffee markets, is accompanied by transitions in economic relations at the local level. Research in Maya communities demonstrates that economic transitions can either heighten gender disparities (Ehlers 1990; Nash 1993b) or increase gender equity (Little 2004), depending on circumstance.

Fair-trade certification standards are divided into minimum requirements, which all producer organizations must meet, and progress requirements, on which producer organizations must show regular improvement (FLO 2007a:2).[13] Existing fair-trade certification standards for smallholder organizations pertain to the generic small producers who are understood to be those who "are not structurally dependent on permanent hired labor, managing their farm mainly with their own and their family's labor force" (FLO 2007a:4). The standards state that "where workers are casually hired by farmers themselves, the organization should take steps to improve working conditions and to ensure that such workers share the benefits of Fairtrade" (FLO 2007a:21). However, the standards avoid opening the black box of household relations, including the work conditions of the "family labor force" and the distribution of economic benefits, other than to state that "children may only work if their education is not jeopardized" and that "spouses have the right to off-farm employment" (FLO 2007a:24). The generic standards for small-scale producers do require certified groups to follow ILO Convention 111, which prohibits discrimination on the basis of gender (among other factors). The existing progress requirements for this standard state that programs relating to disadvantaged and minority groups should be in place within organizations, particularly with respect to recruitment, staff, and committee membership. In implicit acknowledgement of the vagueness of this requirement, a 2007 consultation document includes a proposed change to these progress requirements: "The organization is expected to show how they directly support members from minority groups to participate actively in organizational matters, e.g., by assuming organizational responsibilities. Special attention should be given to the participation of female members" (FLO 2007b:10).

There are three central explanations for the lack of female participation in the cooperative's democratically elected board of directors and the group's associated activities, such as attending cooperative reunions, meeting with foreign visitors, and working voluntary rotating shifts in the cooperative's beneficio during the coffee harvest (December–March). First, the patriarchal relations characterizing the cooperative's organizational space subtly (and, in the case of Juana's speaking out at the cooperative reunion, not so subtly) discriminate against female participation. Second, women do not actively seek leadership roles within the cooperative because of their responsibilities within the household, which make attending frequent and lengthy meetings burdensome. Third, agricultural production, particularly coffee production, is primarily a male realm of activity in Maya communities. Female cooperative members and wives would be much more likely to actively participate in La Voz's daily operations if the organization promoted their own income-generating activities, such as weaving.

As stated above, approximately three-quarters of interviewed cooperative members served on the cooperative's sixteen-member board of directors at least once over the course of their cooperative membership. Only 7 of the 116 cooperative members at the time of the research were female. To date, none of these women have served on the board of directors: to clarify, in the history of the group a woman has never served on the board of directors or been employed in a managerial position. However, in 2004 the cooperative initiated two new income-generating programs: a coffee tour and a women's weaving project. Juana, who is quoted above bemoaning the fact that the cooperative is not responsive to women's needs, serves on the sixteen-member board of directors that administers the coffee tour. Although the weaving project remains unprofitable because of the small number of visitors and the larger cooperative's inability or unwillingness to identify foreign markets, it is run entirely by female members and the wives of male cooperative members. In this regard, the cooperative is making some effort to increase the participation rates of women and promote gender equity.

Like most weekdays, on the afternoon I interviewed Carmela her courtyard was filled with the sounds of children playing. In order to supplement her family's meager agricultural income she operated a daycare facility in her home, earning a small return while also tending to her seven (of ten) children who were in primary school or younger. Carmela told me: "I would be interested in serving a cargo in the cooperative but the truth is they don't take us into account, us women. We can't go to the reunions all the time but we do have interest." Carmela expressed a sentiment shared by many of the female cooperative members and wives with whom I spoke. They repeatedly told me that they would like to be more active but they did not feel welcome in the cooperative.

This lack of female participation is by no means universal among fair-trade coffee cooperatives. For example, a 2009 study found that 25 percent of the members belonging to Nicaragua's fair-trade cooperatives were women (IMC 2009), and Nicaragua's three largest fair-trade cooperatives are guided by female general managers (Bacon 2010). Examining cooperatives in Oaxaca and Chiapas, Lyon, Bezaury, and Mutersbaugh (2010) find that fair-trade organizational norms combine with organic procedural norms to benefit women in certified coffee networks, enhancing their control over farm practices and increasing their access to cash. However, the burden of complying with certification standards combined with stagnant real prices excluded some women who might otherwise benefit from expanded participation. Therefore, it is clear that the ability and willingness to improve the opportunities for women in certified coffee producer associations are conditioned by local cultural and political traditions. In the case of La Voz, the initial inclusion of women in the researched cooperative was not necessarily by design but instead appears to be the result of procedural necessity. As one female cooperative founder explained, "When the cooperative began, the men entered first and they began to organize and petition the government for legalization. Then we women entered, maybe because they didn't have enough people to meet the legal requirements." The ongoing lack of female participation in the group indicates that female members and the wives of male cooperative members today remain largely an afterthought, second to the business at hand, coffee commercialization.

Historically in Maya communities work was the defining quality of human beings, and men and women had almost mutually exclusive forms of work (Devereaux 1987). Gender ideology held that male and female roles should be complementary and based on the "natural propensities of each sex" (Waterbury 1989:261): men planted maize and women wove and tended the home (Prechtel and Carlsen 1988; Berlo 1991). As a result, in this peasant economy where the family productive system functioned as a cooperative unit, women's productive and reproductive labor was as valued as men's work: women were confident in their roles and had little reason to be submissive. However, with the insertion into a market economy based on commercial agriculture and productive labor outside the home (considered unsuitable for women), the sexual division of labor began to exclude women from valuable income-producing activities (Ehlers 1991). Today in Maya communities messages about gender relations—the duties, obligations, and rights of women, for example—emanate from multiple sources: the family, schools, government, churches, nongovernmental organizations operating in the area, the media, and foreigners living in the towns (Fischer and Hendrickson 2003). Furthermore, there is great variability in the acceptable boundaries of female economic behavior across different communities.

Although in many communities, including San Juan, some women may be hesitant to speak w th outsiders or travel widely, in others these are accepted practices. For example, in his research on Maya artisans and vendors working in Antigua's tourist economy, Little finds that women are the primary income earners and that their husbands play supportive, behind-the-scenes roles in family businesses (2004).

As discussed above, many Maya communities have a history of public male service roles in the civil-religious hierarchy that are propped up by female labor. In San Juan while male community members accept positions leading one of the community's cofradías, their wives prepare food for the cofradía members during their meetings; weave and sew their husbands' required clothing; and care for the saint, which includes regularly replacing the fresh flowers on the saint's altar and tidying up the room in which it is displayed. However, despite this labor, "in formal politics and the cargo system women are almost totally marginal; modern voting procedures and political parties have done little to increase the participation of . . . women" (Bossen 1984:130). The pattern of cooperative service to date mimics that of cofradía participation. The wives of male cooperative members work steadily at home as their husbands fulfill their cooperative responsibilities, whether through service on the board of directors or through voluntary labor in the beneficio during the harvest.

A second explanation for the lack of female participation in the cooperative's democratic processes is the onerous household duties that preclude their attendance at frequent time-consuming meetings. In San Juan the women appear to never stop working. Every morning they line up in the cold fog of dawn to use one of the several diesel-powered corn grinders scattered throughout the community. They return to their homes to make the morning tortillas by hand, which they do three times a day. Women perform all of the household cooking and cleaning, laboriously washing clothes and dishes by hand at outdoor *pilas* or on the lakeshore. Several women told me that even though they wanted to participate more in the cooperative, they simply did not have the time. This is undeniably true. However, I do not recall meeting one woman over the course of my fourteen months of research who did not belong to at least one of the many weaving associations in the community or who did not participate in the Madres de Familia, a female Catholic service group, or similar committees in Evangelical churches. These groups are generally all-female and therefore are most likely more welcoming environments. Income generated by weaving generally remains entirely in female control as opposed to coffee income, which is reinvested in production, spent on general household expenses, or controlled entirely

FIGURE 4.3. *Women waiting in line to grind the corn for the early morning tortillas, one of many daily chores that occupy their time.*

by men. Therefore, the willingness of women to participate in groups that directly serve their personal economic interests indicates that, although it may be difficult, women are able to rearrange household responsibilities when necessary for desirable forms of group participation.

Comparative research needs to be conducted to determine the extent to which cultural traditions shape female participation in fair-trade cooperatives' democratic processes. There are examples of coffee cooperatives that actively promote female participation through gender-issues training (Milford 2004); the formation of female-only associations; and the encouragement of female participation in cooperatives that many male members have left to search for work (Lyon, Bezaury, and Mutersbaugh 2010) or where communities have chosen to actively require female participation. For example, La Asociación Maya de Pequeños Agricultores in Santa Anita la Unión, a Guatemalan coffee cooperative formed by ex-combatants, reserves 50 percent of its elected board positions for female members.[14] However, there are also several existing studies that support the conclusion that there is a lack of female participation in the democratic processes of fair-trade cooperatives.[15]

The reliance, in fair-trade certification standards, on the generic family farmer is in some cases proving to be a disservice to the female members of producer households and a limitation on fair trade's promotion of gender equity. As Jha points out, agricultural decision making occurs within agricultural households but also within the context of collective action within communities, and "not distinguishing these two domains may lead to a misplaced sense of confidence in the role that women play in public decision making about agriculture" (Jha 2004:553). Not only do fair-trade certification requirements fail to account for gendered power inequalities within households but the existing one-vote-per-family-farm system appears to curtail women's decision-making power within the public domain as well. The ability to make decisions is the foundation of both participatory democracy and gender equity as it endows the decision maker "with a sense of independence and command of his or her own destiny" (Crewe and Harrison 1998:52–54). Therefore, the exclusion of women from the fair-trade democratic process is a fundamental flaw that should be addressed.

FLO's website highlights the market's "empowerment of women" through investments made in "women's income-generating activities that are not related to the farm." Furthermore, an appendix to the existing certification standards for small farmers states that fair-trade premiums may be used by producers for any number of projects, including "[p]rograms addressing gender inequality or promoting the participation of women [and similar programs for marginalized groups]" (FLO 2006:10). However, a review of FLO-certified producer profiles reveals that women's projects are largely focused on non-income-generating activities such as health care or subsistence farming.[16] Although La Voz has struggled to solidify a female income-generating project, other groups have been more successful. For example, across Lake Atitlan a more recently formed fair-trade coffee cooperative developed a women's program (run by three women and four men) that runs a catering service that provides meals for local groups that are having meetings and events (this cooperative also has a female accountant on its staff). Similarly, the Mexican cooperative UCIRI has developed a variety of projects "designed to ease the burden of women's work and improve the well-being of the family" (Fridell 2007:208). However, these micro-projects, such as small animal husbandry and fruit processing, do not appear to actively ameliorate gender inequality, which would ultimately "necessitate challenging local or 'traditional' notions of the peasant family being run by property-owning male 'heads of household'" (Fridell 2007:133).

Forty-five of the fifty-three interviewed cooperative members agreed that the cooperative should seek markets for non-coffee-related products.

FIGURE 4.4. *A female cooperative member organizes her thread before beginning a new weaving project.*

Of those forty-five individuals twenty thought that the cooperative should actively seek a market for the weavings made by female cooperative members and wives (as opposed to five who named onions, four who named tomatoes, and three who named avocadoes). Despite this widespread support for women's weaving, female members and wives struggled for decades to form the now existing weaving project. However, as stated earlier, to date the cooperative has not supported their efforts to find a foreign buyer and local tourist sales are minimal. The women's own efforts at finding a foreign market have been thwarted for several reasons, such as a lack of Spanish fluency, discomfort surrounding contact with foreigners, and insufficient experience. Female social vulnerability is clearest when women interact with outsiders, and as a result they often defer to men in these situations. In part, this is because they do not speak Spanish, but it also results from cultural prescriptions that deny respectability to those who openly converse with strangers (Ehlers 1991). One cooperative member's wife explained that they were not actively looking for a market because "[w]e don't know the path to take to look for a market." Finally, there is a long history of corruption and dissatisfaction within the many weaving groups that have formed and dissolved within the community during the past two decades.

Although many women officially belong to multiple groups, they do not actively participate in them because of their distrust resulting from this local history. Furthermore, as a result of past animosities there is a significant amount of competition among the contemporary weaving groups in the community for tourist dollars and foreign markets. As the seven most active members of the cooperative's weaving project told me during a focus group interview, "We don't have a market and we don't have orders. For example, ——, they have help. They have orders and sales too. The tourists go there because the two organizations are there, the tourist guides [a local tourism project organized by a former Peace Corps volunteer] and ——. And the foreigners have sent them money. They have help but we don't have help."

This issue of crosscutting memberships, competition, and distrust is important and could not possibly be adequately assessed by a foreign certifier visiting for only one or two days each year. Complexities such as these cannot be sufficiently comprehended through a certification process that largely involves questioning the manager and a handpicked group of male cooperative members. The former manager told me after a FLO certifier visited (in 2002) that she repeatedly questioned him regarding what the cooperative did to support women. He said: "I told her the majority of the cooperative members have their wives in the Artisan Association [a long-standing local group with an established foreign market]. The cooperative helped the association with a little bit of money to form a revolving credit fund in 1991." At one time or another it seems the majority of adult women in the community did belong to the association; however, as the group's market has dwindled over the years and allegations of corruption have run rampant, few members actively participate.[17] For example, each of the seven women in the focus group was officially a member of the association, despite the fact that none had attended meetings or earned income through the group in many years. Therefore, the manager was not necessarily lying to the inspector, but he also was not entirely forthright. Furthermore, the fact that the manager could only identify a small donation to a weaving cooperative over the course of ten years when pressed on the group's commitment to gender equity is indicative of the organization's weakness in this area.

The female cooperative members and wives are eager to find a foreign market for their weavings in order to increase their own earnings. In general, the women primarily use these earnings to support their children's educational goals or as a type of non-liquid savings. I once asked a woman to quantify how much she earned from selling her weavings in a month. She told me that this was difficult, because "[s]ometimes I don't sell anything. What I do earn I invest [in more thread] and hope that I am going to sell something. I save my money in my thread. If I buy thread then I can't spend my money easily on the children or on food. It's better." She, like many women I spoke with, was eager to keep her earnings from weaving separate from the household budget and entirely under her own control. A female cooperative member who belongs to the group's weaving and tourism project explained: "We have to separate the money because this money is ours—it's from our products. It's better that we manage it ourselves so that we can do something with the money. We want to be equal to them." Managing their own money also ensures that they can support their children's education, thereby diversifying the next generation's livelihood prospects.[18] A cooperative member's wife stated: "For the moment we are only selling a little bit of our weavings and it doesn't cover our needs. It's not enough to send the children to school and take care of them in the house."

Fair trade's failure to adequately promote gender equity raises several important questions regarding the goals and effectiveness of fair-trade coffee networks. For example, does gender equity necessarily have to be a central goal of the fair-trade movement? Can the fair-trade certification process help to address gender inequity or is certification not the appropriate venue for promoting this goal? Is it possible to promote gender equity though generic certification requirements given the vast cultural diversity found among producer groups in just one region (Latin America), a diversity that most certainly increases exponentially when the cultural traditions of coffee-producing households and communities in Asia and Africa are also included in the analysis? Finally, to what extent does the certification process itself (e.g., interviewing management and handpicked cooperative members) undermine the effectiveness of certification requirements by creating the potential for inaccurate reports?

The answers to these difficult questions partially lie in our understanding of fair trade's long-term goals. If we envision fair trade as a development strategy aimed at increasing the market access of a select group of small-scale coffee producers, then the movement does not need (and perhaps should not bother) to actively promote gender equity. In fact, in this instance the fair-trade movement would be better off leaving the complicated issues of gender and development to groups that are better equipped to promote equity and women's interests. However, if we believe that fair trade can become a truly viable model for an alternative globalization that challenges existing neoliberal economic relations, then the promotion of gender equity must be absolutely central to its mission.

As discussed further in Chapter 6, a participatory form of social auditing would help fair-trade coffee networks achieve this goal and would substantially improve the effectiveness of the existing certification standards. A simple first step would be to require certifiers to speak to a broad range of cooperative members and their wives (because fair trade certifies family farms, not individuals). By speaking to women, certifiers could easily ascertain that women have, in fact, never served on the board of directors or filled a managerial position at the cooperative. The discussions could be used to identify women's needs, such as "a market of our own" and more equality, and help pinpoint ways to attain these goals.

CONCLUSIONS

Many analyses of fair-trade coffee cooperatives do not adequately address the fact that the practice of cooperation and often times organizations themselves have long histories that predate the introduction of fair-trade certification requirements. For the members of La Voz the meaning of cooperation was intertwined with the long-standing cultural traditions of service maintained through the community's cargo system and cultural norms of appropriate expressions of authority, power, and participation. In prioritizing the formation of independent democratic associations, the fair-trade movement follows in the footsteps of earlier international development efforts. Beginning in the 1970s, agricultural cooperatives were increasingly viewed as the ideal organizational structure for the dissemination of technological innovations and services to rural people (Gill 1985).[19] In addition to their perceived potential for heightening efficiency in smallholder commercialization, cooperatives were also encouraged by international lenders who were attracted to the overtone of social solidarity and democracy surrounding the concept.

Despite these perceptions, some research indicates that rather than alleviating poverty, cooperative programs introduced by international lenders often serve to strengthen and entrench a small group of better-off peasants without significantly benefiting large sectors of the population.[20] This issue is one that FLO addresses by acknowledging that "[t]he Fairtrade system has been criticized for singling out producer groups that enjoy fair trading conditions while their neighbors or colleagues need to continue working under poor conditions." FLO argues that "[r]esearch has shown that benefits of the Fairtrade system often spill over and solidarity with other disadvantaged but non-Fairtrade producers can increase."[21] The debate over fair trade's impact on local inequalities is a critical one that warrants future research. Although this chapter only touches on the issue, it does examine the emerging tensions between the membership and the increasingly powerful cooperative management.

To successfully compete in the international fair-trade coffee market and fulfill certification and quality requirements, the cooperative steadily increased the responsibilities and power of the manager and the board of directors. In addition to contributing to emerging stratification within the group, the emergence of a managerial elite potentially threatens the cooperative practices and participatory democracy that collectively form the groundwork for the group's success. The rumors of managerial corruption frequently repeated by cooperative members represent an attempt to mollify their anxieties and exert control over organizational spaces, such as financial bookkeeping and coffee contracts, which were slowly slipping out of their realm of understanding and control as the cooperative became increasingly enmeshed in external markets. These rumors also ironically served to unite the group and solidify its boundaries as the cooperative developed increasing numbers of relationships with external agents in the marketplace.

It is tempting for northern consumers to romanticize the cooperative efforts of the small-scale coffee producers in Latin America who grow our coffee—to contrast our harried lives fueled by the regular consumption of coffee with what we imagine to be their simpler, slower existence, an existence we imagine is marked by cultural traditions and the kind of mutual assistance and solidarity that our own society slowly abandoned as we became increasingly disconnected from our friends, neighbors, and democratic structures—as we began to "bowl alone" (Putnam 2000). However, cooperation is hard work. Serving cargos in the cooperative and making collective decisions is an obligatory burden that cooperative members must carry. However, they do so out of an acknowledgment that this cooperation will help ensure future financial rewards and the maintenance of their community-based identity and social relations.

The Political Economy of Organic and Shade-Grown Coffee Certification, Local Livelihoods, and Identities

In the United States, a casual perusal of the fair-trade coffee offerings at the local supermarket or coffee shop will quickly reveal the extent to which fair trade and organic coffee certifications are linked in the marketplace. The majority of fair-trade coffees for sale are also certified organic and often shade-grown as well. This dual and even triple certification reflects first and foremost the desires of coffee roasters to simultaneously place products in as many market niches as possible, thereby attracting consumers motivated by a variety of personal causes and interests. However, it is also an outgrowth of the past underpinnings of the fair-trade coffee market in the United States, which was originally dominated by Latin American coffees, especially those produced in Mexico, Central America, and Peru, regions that historically have high rates of organic and shade-grown coffee production. For producers who sell primarily to the U.S. market, such as the members of La Voz, this means that organic (and in some cases shade-grown) certification is a de facto requirement for fair-trade market participation.

This chapter demonstrates that this market structure has multiple implications for the daily lives of producers who struggle to adapt universal certification standards to the particularities of their own livelihoods, ecosystems, and community histories. Although roasters, certifiers, and even consumers often think about coffee certifications as distinct processes and standards generated by separate regulatory bodies, producers experience them as an overlapping system of rules that must be abided. As described in the following, this has a marked impact on the cooperative members and the ways in which they understand the coffee market, the people who buy their coffee, and concepts such as coffee quality, defined and dictated by foreigners.

Coinciding with the widespread introduction of coffee to San Juan in the 1970s, production methods across Latin America have become increasingly more technified through the use of sun-grown varieties that require an increased use of agricultural inputs. Initially prompted by the invasion of leaf rust into the region, which arrived in Brazil in 1970 and Central America in 1976, researchers urged coffee producers to technify their coffee plots by switching from traditional *Arabica* varieties, such as *bourbon*, which require shade, to more hybrid *Arabica* varieties, such as *caturra*, *catuai*, and *catimor*, which can be grown in full sun, require more fertilizer, and produce substantially more coffee (Pendergrast 1999:399). The historical efforts of Anacafé and Guatemalan extension agents to promote the technification of coffee production are reflected in the contemporary mix of *bourbon* and *caturra Arabica* coffee trees found in the plots of cooperative members today.

Coffee is the third-most heavily sprayed crop in the world after cotton and tobacco (Pendergrast 1999:398). In addition to the heavy use of chemical inputs, numerous environmental problems are associated with coffee production, including the clearing of forest areas, soil degradation from chemical use, and degraded freshwater ecosystems as a result of dumping waste pulp (rather than using the pulp as a soil amendment, which is encouraged in organic and shade-grown coffee production). The last environmental problem is of special concern in the Lake Atitlan basin as there are multiple coffee mills in virtually every lakeside community and many residents' livelihoods depend on the lake and the resources it provides (e.g., for the fishing and tourism industries).

Recently, agriculture has been identified as the main global threat to biodiversity (World Conservation Union and Future Harvest 2001, in Giovannucci and Koekoek 2003). At present, organic and environmentally sensitive agricultural certification systems represent the most logical way to address this problem. Shade-grown and organic coffee production is one of the few forms of agriculture that potentially helps to preserve the environment, and biodiversity and could prove critical in efforts to curb deforestation in Central America, which currently has one of the world's highest deforestation rates (Infopress 2006). However, as La Voz's experience demonstrates, to fully realize conservation goals, market-based solutions must respond to local economic and cultural needs in addition to international calls for environmental protection.

The merging of the mechanisms of consumer sovereignty and tropical conservation within the institutional frameworks of organic and shade-grown coffee certification constitutes a form of structural power that entrusts the protection of nature and the well-being of producers to certifying institutions, consumers, and capitalist enterprises. Coffee producers are frequently, if not always, excluded from the certified coffee market's center of power. Although the impact of fair-trade coffee certification has been explored by a variety of researchers, the meanings, structures, and processes of identification surrounding organic and shade-grown certification are less studied. This chapter explores a number of tensions within the certified coffee market. First, there is a tension between a regional history of organic production that emerged from the cooperative efforts of *campesinos* to increase their yields while limiting their dependence on expensive inputs and the contemporary reality of organic coffee certification processes and production for export markets. This tension, which is replicated within certified organic networks in the North, has led some to argue that organic agriculture is becoming a form of eco-colonialism rooted in global class differentiations (Guthman 2003). Second, there is a tension between the pride generated by the cooperative members' perceptions of quality and the high market standards required for participation in the specialty-coffee market. The imposition of strict quality and certification standards requires internal surveillance mechanisms that reshape social relations and practices among members. Third, the certification standards designed to promote tropical conservation project a specific image of small-scale coffee producers that conflicts with the actual ways that the members of La Voz utilize the land to make a living. In other words, shade-grown and organic coffee certification straddles the divide between contradicting definitions of nature and its use-value—productive versus protective.

SHADE-GROWN AND ORGANIC COFFEE CERTIFICATION

Like many smallholders participating in the certified coffee market, the members of La Voz produce coffee that is certified as both organic and fair trade to fill multiple market niches. During the primary research period (2001–2003) the cooperative also applied for shade-grown certification at the urging of its long-term U.S. importer, who hoped to place La Voz's coffee in this emerging market niche. For small-scale producer groups hoping to access the United States specialty coffee market, dual and triple certifications are now a requirement for participation as approximately two-thirds of the certified fair-trade coffee imported into the United States is now also certified organic (TransFair 2009).

Organic coffee certification is a growing segment of the diverse, international organic agriculture movement, and there are numerous organic certifying agencies in the United States and Europe. The basic international guidelines for organic certification are determined by the International Federation of Organic Agricultural Movements (IFOAM) and its standards related to global agricultural production, which are divided into categories such as crop production, animal husbandry, organic conversion, storage and transportation of products, processing, social justice, and labelling information.[1] The standards for organic coffee production are lengthy, numerous, and exacting. To acquire organic certification, producers must undergo a thirty-six-month documented conversion period. Certification may also require significant investments in the producer's fields (if requirements are not already in place). For example, live barriers and buffer zones must be created to promote soil conservation, deter erosion, and safeguard the "organic integrity" of the certified fields. Requirements also outline soil-building and conservation procedures; the use of seeds, seedlings, grafting, and root stock; harvest and post-harvest conditions; water use and wet milling; crop protection; and biodiversity, including shade-management plans for the support of migratory bird populations. These requirements demonstrate that there is much more to organic farming than simply "forgetting" how to use chemical inputs. The memory loss needs to be accompanied by the acquisition of new knowledge, which is not a simple matter because virtually the entire system of innovation in the agri-food business is geared to generating, testing, and diffusing knowledge for the industrial food chain (Morgan and Murdoch 2000:167).

Written records, and the audit trail they form, are an integral part of organic certification. Producers are required to maintain complete information describing three (preferably five) years of production practices, which will theoretically permit the tracing of sources and amounts of all off-farm inputs, the date and place of harvest, and the coffee's physical movement through the commodity chain. Additionally, organic certification is expensive: OCIA charges cooperatives an annual fee of $450 in addition to a $200 fee per day for the inspection itself and 0.05 percent volume fee for use of the trademark.

Shade-grown coffee certification emerged in the late 1990s under the direction of ornithologists at the Smithsonian Migratory Bird Center and the members of the more than 500 local Audubon organizations in the United States, such as Seattle Audubon.[2] Populations of North American migratory birds, the majority of whom winter in the tropical forests of northern Latin America, have declined steadily in the past half century. The Green Revolution and technological improvements promoted heavily by the U.S. Agency for International Development (USAID) and other development agencies throughout the region in the 1970s introduced new varieties of coffee that yield exponentially higher harvests and are cultivated in full sun with heavy chemical inputs. Several scientific studies document a sharp decline in the diversity of migratory birds in sun-coffee systems in comparison to shade coffee (Perfecto et al. 1996; Greenberg, Bichier, and Sterling 1997), and others demonstrate that naturally shaded coffee plantations can serve as sanctuaries to protect forest species, especially in regions where natural forests are degraded or no longer exist (Pimentel et al. 1992; Rice and Ward 1996; Moguel and Toledo 1999, in Giovannucci and Koekoek 2003).

Shade-grown coffee certification was created to provide an economic incentive to small-scale coffee producers to preserve migratory bird habitat through coffee cultivation in forestlike agro-ecosystems in which coffee trees form an understory shaded by a mixed cover of fruit trees and hardwood species. Research demonstrates that agroforestry systems, such as shade-grown coffee plantations, are among the most promising land uses for both achieving conservation goals and supporting human livelihoods (Méndez, Gliessman, and Gilbert 2007). However, unlike fair-trade and organic-certified coffees, both of which offer producers fixed-price premiums, shade certification offers no fixed-price premium, only a chance to sell to a premium market. When linked to coffee quality, the premiums paid to shade-grown coffee producers commonly range between ten cents and sixty cents per pound (Giovannucci and Koekoek 2003). To compete in the North American specialty-coffee market, shade-grown coffees must also meet high quality standards. Therefore, the majority of small-scale producers cultivating shade-grown coffee belong to established coffee cooperatives that have received training and financial assistance from development agencies and coffee roasters.

The Smithsonian Migratory Bird Center (SMBC) created the initial certification standards for shade-grown coffee.[3] In order to promote a diversity of bird and animal populations, the SMBC requires 40 percent minimum shade coverage to be measured with an optical densitometer at noon time. No more than 60 percent of the shade trees can belong to the *Inga* genus, which is commonly used and fast-growing. The remaining 40 percent must comprise ten or more species, with at least ten of these trees representing 1 percent or more of all shade trees present. The backbone of the shade-tree canopy should be allowed to attain a minimum height of twelve to fifteen meters with lower and higher trees growing around the backbone totalling 20 percent of total shade. Additionally, producers must nurture epiphytic plants (such as bromeliads and mistletoes) and maintain tree borders and shrubs along roadways and field boundaries to preserve the integrity of the soil.

THE SHADE-GROWN COFFEE MOVEMENT

In the summer of 2001 I moved to Seattle to learn more about the Northwest Sustainable Coffee Campaign, which at the time was spearheaded by shade-grown coffee activists in the Pacific Northwest region. The advocates I interviewed in Seattle and surrounding communities tended to be well-educated white members of the middle and upper classes. Many of them worked in information technology and related fields, although I also spoke with artists, NGO employees, and academics who were committed shade-grown coffee advocates. The majority of them were middle-aged, reflecting the demographics of the birding community at large; however, I did encounter a handful of younger (mid-twenties and mid-thirties) avid birders and shade-grown enthusiasts. In attending campaign events and interviewing advocates and participating regional coffee roasters, I hoped to illuminate the complex portrayals and understandings of coffee producers that circulate in northern coffee-consuming communities—how did these committed individuals conceptualize and talk about the people who grew their coffee and protected the migratory birds they held so dear? Although I found a great diversity of individual opinions on this topic, there were three common framings of coffee producers that I repeatedly encountered during interviews and observations at events designed to encourage consumer participation in the movement. Shade-grown coffee producers were understood as either natural conservationists or simple mechanisms for biodiversity conservation. A third framing focused on the role of consumers and involved an almost complete disavowal of the producers' labor and their role in the circuits of coffee production and exchange.

To understand the meanings they attributed to producers it is helpful to first examine birders themselves. Birding enthusiasts, who are engaged in intense and ongoing observation of birds, often travel widely and look for as many species as possible. Many have life lists of birds they have observed and may spend significant amounts of time and money chasing rare birds to add to these lists. The U.S. Fish and Wildlife Service reports that there are 46 million birders in the United States who spent $32 billion in 2001 (Mehan 2005),[4] and birding is the second-most popular hobby in the United States (O'Connor 2005). In fact, according to the U.S. Fish and Wildlife Service, because birds are both ubiquitous and conspicuous, they have come to symbolize America's wildlife experience.[5] The number of birders in the United States has doubled since the early 1980s (Querna 2004), perhaps because of the popularity of feature films such as *Winged Migration* (2003) and *March of the Penguins* (2005); the growing number of birding-related books and field guides, which are the backbone of the nature publishing category (Danford 2003); and events such as the National Audubon Society's Christmas Bird Count, a century-long tradition that draws more than 55,000 participants into fields, wetlands, and forests around the country during December and early January to survey North America's bird population (Querna 2004).

The shade-grown coffee advocates I interviewed varied greatly in their birding practices and the length of time they have identified as birders. Some came to the hobby relatively late in life, such as Susan, who was on a whale watching trip in Baja, California, in 1984 when she became intrigued by the birds diving in the Sea of Cortes. She explained: "It was so spectacular and I thought, 'Now I understand why people go all over the place with their binoculars looking at birds and I'm going to do that too.' It was a very conscious decision in that moment, like, 'I'm going to do that.'" Others began birding at a young age, such as Doug, a middle-aged Seattle-based artist I interviewed. He became a birder when he was about twelve years old after a green heron got caught in his family's backyard chicken coop. Doug told me: "If you've ever seen a green heron up close they look embroidered . . . I became a bird watcher then and I made lists like the birders do and I kept bird watching throughout the rest of my life." However, he went on to explain: "I'm not a very good birder; if you're a birder you see the nuances of differences and I'm just an average birder. Really good birders get pretty acoustically organized and have really good language skills for birds." Doug's words provide a glimpse into the range of commitments in terms of time, money, and study among U.S. birders. Although several of the interviewed shade-grown coffee advocates traveled extensively in their search of birds to add to their life lists, others were simply backyard hobbyists.

The shade-grown coffee movement emerged from grassroots activities organized through an e-mail discussion group, which, according to one interviewed shade-grown coffee advocate in Seattle, "made the whole thing possible." Although listservs have become seemingly ubiquitous in the postindustrial urban milieu, in practice they preclude the input of small-scale coffee producers in places such as Guatemala, who rarely have Internet access and even less frequently speak English. This lack of direct input from (or contact with) coffee producers allowed some advocates to nurture a fantasy of producers as natural conservationists employing "a human-land use equilibrium [which] has evolved in coffee production over time" (Rice and Ward 1996:17). In the North we rarely think of "locals" as nature lovers in the same cosmopolitan sense that we think of ourselves as nature lovers—instead, we imagine that, unlike ourselves, they have an innate appreciation of nature (Tsing 2005:30). This image of small-scale producers is a key facet of shade-grown coffee's symbolic meaning for advocates and consumers and it is fueled with the facile representations of "local" knowledge and identity permeating the superficial observations and travel accounts of advocates, biologists, and coffee roasters who spend only weeks or months in coffee-producing regions. In turn, shade-grown coffee advocates and roasters employ this information to lend the shade-grown coffee market an aura of authority and authenticity.

On the other hand, although some advocates have framed shade-grown coffee producers as natural conservationists, others prioritized the protection of migratory bird habitat and ecological diversity. They largely understood that support of small-scale coffee producers was a simple means to this end. For example, during an interview one avid birder and shade-coffee advocate in Seattle scoffed at my plans to move to Guatemala and study coffee producers. He advised me, "What we need are more lists of birds, what birds live there in the coffee fields and in what trees." This vision of producers as a mechanism for biodiversity conservation and the corresponding focus on habitat protection rather than producer livelihoods are understandable outgrowths of birders' passions for spotting and cataloging new and intriguing birds. Susan, the shade-grown coffee advocate introduced earlier, described the "tremendous sense of sadness and futility" she felt in 1985 when she first learned about rainforest destruction and the decline in migratory bird populations. She explained: "I had just identified my first warbler and I was really into it . . . It was like before you can even get in to it, guess what! They're not going to even be here anymore. And I remember saying something to a friend at that point, 'Someday, and I don't know how, someday I'm going to get involved, I'm going to try and do something about this destruction of the rainforest that's hurting migratory birds.'" Another interviewed advocate felt that this focus on spotting rare birds and compiling lists made it difficult to interest some birders in habitat protection. She explained how she was "on the big birders list here and it literally gets like one hundred postings a day." She continued: "It's all about, 'Oh I saw a dogwood, I saw a this and I saw a that, blah, blah, blah.' I looked through all my messages—there was like five hundred messages there—[only] one person said anything about the coffee." These two contradictory portrayals of coffee producers within the shade-grown coffee movement, either as natural conservationists or as mechanisms for biodiversity protection, echo the tension underlying many conservation-based natural resource management projects that juxtapose celebrations of indigenous environmental knowledge with a focus on changing the actions and practices of local people to meet the end goal of conservation (Dove 2006; West 2006).

In contrast to these two understandings of shade-grown coffee producers, a third framing focused on the role of consumers and involved an almost complete disavowal of the producers' labor and their role in the circuits of coffee production and exchange. Interviewed advocates described how they consciously explained shade-grown coffee as a simple, guilt-free consumer action, thereby simplifying the complex webs of global capital, inequality, and exchange that bind producers and consumers. Increasingly, a commodity's value hinges on what different actors connected in spatially dispersed networks of production, exchange, and consumption know about their place in the network and their connections to other participants. The management of this knowledge and the associated sign values are constitutive features of certified coffee commodity networks. It is not so much the readily perceptible features of shade-grown, organic, and fair-trade coffees (e.g., flavor or appearance) that help distinguish them from the growing crowd of specialty coffees but, instead, the trust consumers place in their corresponding symbolic values of environmental protection and social justice. The differentiation of ethically and environmentally certified products, such as dual- and triple-certified coffees, is central to consumers' pursuit of self-expression and the formation of group identity because these products speak not only to characteristics such as taste and sophistication but also to insider knowledge and demonstrable moral values.

Many consumers associate the conditions of globalization and postindustrial restructuring with a deep sense of political fatalism and chronic insecurity in that the sheer scale of contemporary social, economic, and environmental change appears to outstrip the capacity of national governments or citizens to control, contest, or resist that change (Beck 1992; Held et al. 1999). Mass media plays a crucial role in the construction and communication of environmental problems and solutions. It also works in tandem with certified coffee advocates to discursively frame the consumption of certain coffees as a simple yet effective alternative to more exploitative forms of global trade. In recent years, hundreds of articles have appeared in mainstream newspapers and alternative publications. Almost without fail, the articles reference the small steps consumers can take in order to effect real change in distant locales. For example, one urged readers to "[t]ake a look at the label on the packet. It could tell you whether you are a responsible global citizen or party to the exploitation of Third World producers" (Dearlove 1999). Similarly, another stated: "People may think, 'What's a few more cents a cup going to do?' Well, it does a lot. It's pretty powerful what we as individuals can do, even if we don't see it firsthand" (Lobdell 2004).

In 2001, the Northwest Sustainable Coffee Campaign, initiated through a partnership between TransFair USA, Seattle Audubon, and the Songbird Foundation, enlisted stars such as Bonnie Raitt, Jackson Browne, Tom Robbins, and Keb' Mo' to play benefit concerts and publicize certified coffees during their local on-air and print interviews. For example, during one interview on June 1, 2001, with the host of the morning show on Seattle's radio station 103.7 "The Mountain," Raitt plugged shade-grown coffee:

> Actually Songbird Foundation was started and the reason it was called that is because the songbirds, which are an indicator species, which of course migrate from North to South in this hemisphere, their system of migration is being threatened because the new development of "new and improved," I mean that in quotes, sun-grown coffee, means they're cutting down a lot of the shade canopy areas of Costa Rica and parts of the path of the migrating birds and now they have no place to land and stop on their journey. So there's a terrific threat to not only the bird population, but also to the small farmers and to the ecosystem and environment of the areas where we get our, as we know in Seattle, a java motherload . . . where we get our coffee from and this is the spirit of a six-week campaign here in Seattle where we're going to be trying to put a little pressure on the coffee industry and the consumers to switch over. If we can ask for French roast and non-fat, we can certainly include fair-trade and shade-grown in it and end up doing a lot less harm to the local economies and the environment.

The publicity efforts reflected the campaign leaders' desire to present shade-grown (and fair-trade) coffee consumption as a guilt-free, feel-good issue, one that would be attractive to Seattle's middle- and upper-class consumers. In this same vein, several of the interviewed shade-grown coffee advocates described themselves as "cheerleaders to consumers." As one advocate stated, "We're promoting a feel-good commodity to on-the-go consumers who want to do something simple to help the migratory songbirds in their own backyards and stop deforestation in far-off lands." Similarly, the founder of the Songbird Foundation, the Seattle-based shade-grown coffee advocacy group, explained that his primary message to consumers is "Don't feel guilty, you don't have to; buy a quality cup of coffee and support all kinds of life systems."

After the political upheaval of the 1999 World Trade Organization (WTO) meetings and 9/11, shade-grown coffee advocates felt that Seattle consumers were searching for non-confrontational activist causes. Describing her experiences at the shade-grown coffee tables she set up at street fairs, one advocate explained, "Everybody likes shade coffee, you give them a taste and they immediately like it; there's nothing for anybody to be upset about, there's nothing controversial, it's a completely uncontroversial, feel-good environmental issue . . . nobody's mad at you and nobody's losing a job because of shade coffee and the little songbirds are so cute and appealing." These advocates intentionally framed shade-grown coffee consumption as effective action at a distance and refrained from addressing the structural inequalities of global trade, consumption practices, or habitat destruction in the Pacific Northwest. Their goal is for shade-grown coffee to become ubiquitous for consumers. Or, in the words of one advocate, the goal is "for it to be like dolphin-safe tuna."

Although this feel-good consumerism was the official campaign message, not all of the interviewed advocates agreed with this strategy. For example, Doug, the artist and lifelong birder mentioned above, stated: "I really think that the shade coffee movement needs to get aggressive. I think all left-wing politics has stalled into niceness and we're not aggressive enough." Although he continued to work with members of the Northwest Sustainable Coffee Campaign, Doug also began buying advertising space in the *Seattle Times* to publicize his own views, which, among others, included questioning the intentions of companies like Starbucks.

In his analysis of the "yuppie market segment" and its penchant for proletarian hunger killers, such as specialty coffees, Roseberry argues that consumers do not identify with the laborers who actually grow, cut, or pick their coffee but instead with the commodities' preindustrial nostalgia, and their history as exotic and expensive products within Europe's early markets, a time before mass society and mass consumption (1996:764). Similarly, shade-grown coffee advocates and roasters urge consumers to systematically associate the protection of migratory birds and their Latin American habitats with environmental health, transnational communities, and prosperity, not agricultural labor. Little thought seems to be given to the impact of certification requirements and market demands on producers themselves.

One shade-grown coffee advocate explained how her involvement in neighborhood politics surrounding the Seattle Housing Authority and the Sound Transit provided her with "a whole new perspective on environmentalism." She explained: "You can espouse a policy and say this is what we should do to try and help the earth, to try and help the environment. Whatever you advocate, if you don't have to live with the consequences of the policy . . . and other people do, then that's the problem . . . I understand the farmers in a way that I never did before." However, shade-grown coffee consumers are not asked to contemplate the destruction of nature corridors and U.S. bird habitat that inevitably accompanies urban expansion. Instead, the shade-grown coffee market reinforces consumers' attachment to far-off places and traditions and the belief that through their purchasing habits they can protect wide swaths of natural life in the developing world. Within this postindustrial imagination of nature, the small producers and their productive labor are transformed into commodities along with the shade-grown coffee they tend. This construction obscures the often contradictory reality of smallholder agricultural production and the rigid, scientifically based certification requirements certified coffee producers must meet.

ORGANIC PRODUCTION AS A SOCIAL MOVEMENT

Like shade-grown coffee, organic agriculture is primarily framed as a consumer-driven movement in the United States and organic meanings and practices historically have been defined largely in the global North (Raynolds 2004:729). However, across Latin America, organic agriculture is understood differently as a social movement aimed at improving the lives of marginalized small-scale producers. For example, in an organic agriculture manual that Santiago, the cooperative's former agricultural monitor, used for training purposes the author writes, "Before it is an instrument of technological transformation, organic agriculture is an instrument of social transformation, where the true agrarian justice that the *campesinos* look for . . . results from their own independence and liberty" (Restrepo 1996:9). Indeed, organic agriculture was not developed by the scientific establishment; "on the contrary, it was developed by ecologically committed practitioners, and later examined by the scientific establishment, with the result that the formal knowledge system lagged way behind organic practice" (Morgan and Murdoch 2000:167). Despite this potential, researchers have identified several adverse effects of organic certification among small-scale coffee producers in Latin America, including the imposition of bureaucratic and industrial conventions that may counter the norms and practices of small-scale producers, the northern bias of certification standards, burdensome record-keeping requirements, the expenses associated with certification, and insufficient compensation (Plaza Sanchez 1998; Browne et al. 2000; Bray, Plaza Sanchez, and Murphy 2002; Mutersbaugh 2002, 2004; Calo and Wise 2005; Raynolds 2004).

Latin America is the hub of certified organic production in the global South, boasting 21 percent of the world's certified land (4.9 million hectares) and 19 percent of the world's organic enterprises (110,000 producers). This reflects a worldwide trend: 75 percent of the 750 institutional and individual members of the International Federation of Organic Agricultural Movements are located in the global South (Raynolds 2004:729). In Guatemala there are 14,746 certified organic hectares farmed by 2,830 growers producing coffee, bananas, cashews, fruits, and vegetables (Raynolds 2004:735–736). However, as Raynolds argues, these impressive figures are counteracted by arguably negative commodity production trends. For example, more than 80 percent of Latin America's organic output is exported, reproducing the region's historical dependence on agro-export markets and vulnerability to their fluctuations. Furthermore, most Latin American organic products are exported in unprocessed bulk form "so that the substantial profits derived from processing and packaging accrue to enterprises in northern consuming countries" (Raynolds 2004:735–736).

Despite these issues, organic agriculture is presented by many Latin American advocates as a creative, homegrown solution to some key problems facing small-scale producers, including diminished production over time from overuse of chemical fertilizers, lack of market access, health problems, and environmental degradation. The growing popularity of organic production methods parallels the Campesino a Campesino movement initiated in Guatemala in the 1980s. The movement, which spread across Central America, promotes simple methods of small-scale experimentation and horizontal (farmer to farmer) workshops in basic ecology, agronomy, soil and water conservation, soil building, seed selection, crop diversification, integrated pest management, and biological weed control (Holt-Gimenez 1996; Desmarais 2002). Similarly, the conversion to organic coffee by small-scale producers in Mexico arose from over a decade of populist agrarian organizing and innovations. Conversion to organic production "depended upon the substantial amount of pre-existing 'social capital accumulation' in the Mexican countryside (Fox 1996), a process of self-organization and institutional learning (Folke, Berkes, and Colding 1998) and the existence of significant subsidies" (Bray, Plaza Sanchez, and Murphy 2002:431). Agrarian movements such as these place the burden of innovation and change on the farmers themselves instead of urban agricultural extension agents employed by the national government or development agencies. This can empower marginalized, undereducated small-scale farmers while fostering more appropriate production methods. According to Holt-Gimenez, rather than asking how to get farmers to participate, these movements pose the question, "How do those interested in the development of sustainable agriculture participate in farmer-led development?" (1996:2). Rather than blind trust in the technical advice of extension agents and agro-chemical suppliers, organic producers are forced to create "studied trust relations" with fellow farmers—to have confidence in the information, they must have confidence in the source (Morgan and Murdoch 2000:168). This regional-level agricultural innovation can challenge the ways in which international development efforts create "states of backwardness" (Pigg 1993:47) that need to be rescued from their "undesirable, undignified condition" (Esteva and Prakash 1998:10). Instead, auto-initiated agricultural-based development spread through peer networks may ultimately be more responsive to local needs.

In Guatemala, organic agricultural methods coupled with secure market access could potentially help reverse the negative effects of decades of increasingly intensive agricultural production and its root causes, such as population growth, the inequitable distribution of land, the introduction of agricultural commodity production for export, and the heavy use of chemical fertilizers. In Latin America the institutionalized social relations within and between populations virtually guarantee inequitable access to resources and contribute to environmental damage by both the extremely wealthy in search of capital accumulation and the impoverished in search of survival (Stonich 1994; Durham 1995). Therefore, the fact that cooperative members engage in environmentally sound organic practices to gain access to lucrative foreign commodity markets is an abrupt departure from historical patterns of exclusion, oppression, and impoverishment.

The local roots of organic coffee production run deep in San Juan. Early in the cooperative's history, members of La Voz worked with an NGO on various projects, including the construction of dry latrines and enclosed stoves, the purchase of chickens, the production of organic fertilizer, and the implementation of soil-conservation techniques. The NGO first introduced cooperative members to organic production in the early 1980s. Santiago, the former agricultural monitor and a cooperative founder, explained that agency representatives informed participating members that eventually chemical fertilizers would decrease the productivity of their agricultural plots and become increasingly expensive. With the help they received from the NGO, several members of the cooperative began to experiment with organic production and soil conservation in scattered agricultural plots. At the urging of the agency director five members began applying two pounds of the fertilizer produced by the dry latrines to each of their coffee plants. According to one of the men who made this initial foray into organic production, the health of his coffee trees improved rapidly and dramatically. In 1988 the NGO reportedly introduced the cooperative to a Mexican exporter who told the group that if they could produce certified organic coffee they would be able to find a secure market for their product. In 1990 the cooperative implemented a formal program of organic production, obtaining their first organic certification (from OCIA) for their 1991–1992 harvest. The cooperative's initial experience with organic production echoes the farmer-led agricultural movement discussed above. A cooperative founder explained that from 1992 to 1994, cooperative members received several training sessions on organic production from visiting agronomists: "We received theory, but really more practice than theory. We began in the classroom learning the theory behind organic production but then we really spent all of our time out in the fields practicing organic production. [We learned] that organic production proceeds stage through stage throughout the year and we have to follow the steps. Like, if a member looks at his coffee and says, 'Oh it's doing pretty well this year, I don't need to put on any fertilizer'—but no, he needs to. It's more practice than theory."

Although contemporary cooperative members are proud of the quality of the organic coffee they produce and laud its many benefits, most likely without this initial market opportunity they would not have taken the steps necessary to transition to full and certifiable organic production. In their analysis of the Indigenous Cooperative of the Sierra Madre de Motozintla's (ISMAM) organic coffee production in Mexico, Hernandez Castillo and Nigh stress the importance of ISMAM and its advisors choosing organic production before becoming aware of its market potential. They write, "This fact is important in establishing that ISMAM's agro-ecological techniques are not mere stratagem, mere opportunism motivated by higher prices, but rather arose as a set of solutions to perceived technical, environmental, and economic problems" (1998:142). Through this argument they imply that producers who at the outset transitioned to organic production to capture a share of an increasingly lucrative market are somehow less authentic than their counterparts who made the same decision unfettered by economic necessities.

Although the extent to which contemporary organic production represents a wholesale rejection of industrial agriculture is a worthwhile topic of discussion, within the social sciences these questions are much more likely to be posed about small-scale producers in less-developed countries rather than their better off northern counterparts. For example, in Kentucky (where I now reside) the farmers who are transitioning their fields away from the formerly lucrative tobacco crops in favor of organic fruits, vegetables, and meats are celebrated for their innovation and openness to new ideas and markets. We rarely question whether they are making this transition out of financial necessity or ideological commitment. Similarly, it follows that indigenous agrarian development in Latin America should also support the viability of rural lifeways. Coupling certified production with secure access to northern markets has proven to be a successful avenue for the ongoing maintenance of agrarian livelihoods and the associated cultural traditions of La Voz. However, the key role that market access plays in the transition to certified production methods is illustrated by the fact that four out of five of the cooperative members I interviewed routinely apply chemical fertilizer to their corn and vegetable fields, indicating that although members may recognize the benefits of organic production, they are unwilling to incur the added monetary and labor costs without market remuneration.

This strategy of producing certified products for northern markets may enable indigenous (or other marginalized) producers to circumvent the regional commodity and capital circuits that historically disadvantaged them because of structural power inequalities. As the first cooperative to successfully transition to organic coffee production in Guatemala and one of the first to secure long-term access to northern certified coffee markets, La Voz is an inspiration (or an advertisement) to cooperatives in the early stages of organizing and organic conversion. As a result, the cooperative receives frequent visits from groups of small-scale producers seeking to learn from their experiences. During one such visit, a cooperative founder, Emiliano, eloquently addressed the structural inequalities facing small-scale producers within Guatemala. One of the visitors said that it was hard for them to convince people in their community that chemical fertilizers were not necessary. Emiliano responded:

> It is foreign capital that produces these inputs. You know that Anacafé is directed by *finqueros* and business people and these big business people put it in the heads of small growers that they needed to use chemicals to produce their coffee. In the 1990s not a lot of people wanted to enter the organic market for exactly this reason . . . However, it's different now because there are foreigners who want organic coffee, not chemicals. There are also people now who have health problems as a result of twenty, thirty or forty years of chemical inputs. Now we want an organic natural product without chemical contamination.

Emiliano's analysis of the importance of organic agriculture is an example of how for him and other members of La Voz, organic production was about more than improving soil condition; it was about resisting the legacy of economic domination under which small-scale producers have suffered for years in Guatemala. In light of Guatemala's history, the true potential of organic agriculture may lie in this coupling of sustainable production methods with northern market access. On the other hand, this does not help to transform the critical flaw limiting the development potential of contemporary organic production—that the majority of certified products are exported, thus continuing the region's historical dependence on agro-export markets.

The goals and methods of organic agriculture mirror the Maya agrarian ethic of sustainable subsistence production. This twining of organic production and indigenous cultural traditions was articulated by many co-operative members, who made statements such as "We are rescuing the culture and rescuing the older system of production from before." Although they acknowledged their advanced technical knowledge, many described in depth the similarities between modern organic agricultural methods and those employed by their grandparents before the introduction of chemical fertilizers. For example, one day Francisco, my Tz'utujil instructor who was a cooperative founder, related the history of agriculture in San Juan. He reminisced about how his father and grandfather produced their crops and he acknowledged the similarities between these older methods and his own contemporary organic production. He explained:

> My grandfather and father used to grow coffee trees next to half moons in the dirt. They filled these holes with dried leaves which nourished the plant. They used this same method with tomato plants. My father had a big hole behind the house and all of the kitchen trash went into this hole and after one year when it came time to plant the tomatoes in October or November they would put this black earth from the bottom of the hole on their land. It was semi-organic you could say. Also, there weren't a lot of insects in this time because they didn't fumigate. After they harvested, they would cut all the plants and put the cuttings in the fields where he would plant his *milpa* in May when it began to rain. The land would rest for a few months.

The fact that Francisco identified these corollaries between his grandfather's production methods and his own organic techniques supports Hernandez Castillo and Nigh's argument that agro-ecological discourse can provide indigenous farmers with "an internationally recognized arena for the reaffirmation of . . . their traditional cultural values of independence and respect for nature" (1998:144). However, despite this overlap with cultural traditions and the potential of organic certification, certification requirements have a transformative impact on the "[o]uter and inner life of society" (Lukacs 1971:84, in Holmes 1989:11) as members of La Voz are forced to relinquish a portion of the independence traditionally characterizing smallholder agricultural production to succeed in the certified coffee market.

PRODUCER PRIDE AND CERTIFICATION COMPLIANCE THROUGH SURVEILLANCE

It is in the realm of coffee quality that the demands placed on the members of La Voz by the certification frameworks and competitive market conditions under which they operate become most clear. All but two of the fifty-three cooperative members I interviewed agreed that organic methods generate a higher quality coffee. This perceived high quality is a source of considerable pride. During informal conversations, members detailed the specific characteristics of organic coffee that they believed contribute to its high quality. For example, one member explained: "We have seen the difference in the quality of our organic product. The cherries are bigger, they weigh more. They are also juicier and have more water inside them. Organic production is difficult but worthwhile." Others maintained that organic production results in taller and greener coffee trees that yield consistently more than trees grown with chemical fertilizers.

Many cooperative members explained how organic methods enhance the flavor characteristics and overall quality of the final consumer product. Like the majority of small-scale coffee producers in Guatemala, Juaneros do not drink their own coffee, which they produce solely for export. However, the North American coffee importers, roasters, and certifiers with whom La Voz has regular contact routinely assert that coffee quality is dependent on production practices and, more specifically, on the attention to detail that organic certification demands. These contacts with U.S. buyers provide a valuable source of market information on quality standards and desirable flavor characteristics. Responding to an open-ended question about the benefits of cooperative membership, one member described the organization as a venue for contact with foreigners who "[b]ring us information about coffee, new techniques, and consumer demands for quality."

As discussed in Chapter 3, cooperative members believe that the hard work and attention to detail required for coffee certification should be rewarded with higher prices. When asked the price they ideally would like to receive for their certified coffee, 83 percent of the surveyed members named a price greater than what they received for the 2001–2002 crop, which was approximately US$0.16 per pound for unprocessed coffee after taxes and the cooperative's operating costs were deducted.[6] The average ideal price named was US$0.19, a relatively small increase. In follow-up conversations, many maintained that their coffee should earn a higher price because of its high quality. Similarly, research on small-scale coffee producers in Nicaragua indicates that quality demands coupled with producer education can instil pride in craftsmanship and motivation for improvement (Bacon 2005). However, this desire for higher prices may also reflect the fact, documented by several studies, that the income earned through organic coffee sales does not always cover the added costs of production (Plaza Sanchez 1998; Bray, Plaza Sanchez, and Murphy 2002; Calo and Wise 2005).[7]

In addition to market access and information, the cooperative has received significant technical and financial assistance from coffee buyers and the Small Coffee Farmer Improvement Program, implemented by USAID and Anacafé. Members understand the basic production and processing practices that influence the quality of the final consumer product. For example, they know that their certified coffee must be carefully picked to avoid contamination from over- or underripe coffee cherries and leaves. After turning in a day's harvest to the cooperative's beneficio, many sell their low-quality coffee to the *coyotes*, the street-corner buyers for local mills, who pay significantly lower prices than the cooperative. Others dry the worst of the cherries, called *k'ox*, on their patios or sidewalks for later hand roasting and household consumption. One morning, as I assisted cooperative members stripping the overripe coffee cherries off the tree branches they were pruning, I noticed them laughing as I meticulously picked each individual cherry and placed it in my basket. The owner of the field told me, "You don't need to be so careful, this bad coffee doesn't go to the cooperative, it goes to the coyote and he'll eat anything." Organic certification does not guarantee the cooperative market access. However, organic production methods do contribute to a higher quality coffee. The cooperative's former manager routinely reinforced the association between market access and quality. He frequently explained to members that the cooperative is "succeeding in the market because of the quality of our coffee." He also attempted to instil a sense of responsibility in the members by stressing the mutuality of their business contracts with the importer and explaining that the firm's international reputation is dependent on the quality of the cooperative's coffee.

Fulfilling certification requirements and meeting quality standards requires extensive paperwork and monitoring. Like other forms of auditing, organic certification involves a process of "making the inner workings of organizations more visible" (Pels 2000:142). This can be interpreted by producers as a form of surveillance that, when combined with group requirements of mutual accountability, can prove highly disruptive of local social relationships. Cooperative members share a community-based identity and are linked to one another through complex interweaving relationships of family ties, business negotiations, service in the community's religious hierarchy and secular committees, and long-term friendships. This contributes to the group's longevity and market success but it can also make it difficult to enforce production requirements and to punish one another for failing to meet quality standards.

As producers reorient themselves to the demands of transnational markets they may sacrifice some of the traditional independence enjoyed by smallholders. Because La Voz itself, and not individual members, applies for certification, each member's certification status and access to price premiums is dependent on fellow cooperative members' willingness to abide by the rules (Mutersbaugh 2002). This tension between individual effort and group compliance was demonstrated when Carlos, the agronomist employed by the importer to help the cooperative meet the shade-grown certification requirements, attempted to organize cooperative members into work groups of approximately ten members each to work collectively to improve each other's fields, apply organic fertilizer, and prune trees. The members in each group would become accountable for the quality of each other's coffee plots. Therefore, the system would effectively force them to monitor the work habits of their fellow cooperative members. The members I spoke with were universally not in favor of this intrusion into the sphere of individual labor. As one told me, "It's a waste of time. I've already done the work I need to do. The idea came from there [the buyers in the United States] and it's another requirement we have to fulfill in order to export organic coffee."

The strong relationships and shared community identity that bind the members of the cooperative to one another contribute to its financial success; however, they also make it difficult for members to punish one another for breaking the rules. To produce high-quality, certifiable coffee, the cooperative needs to maintain a clean, well-run, and well-managed beneficio and accept only ripe coffee (meaning no green or overripe cherries) free of sticks and leaves from members. Cooperative policy states that members who fail to meet these standards are theoretically fined minimum amounts. However, during hours of participant observation at the beneficio I noted many instances in which small infractions were overlooked because of lack of time and personal commitments to family and friends. The reasons for cooperative members' reluctance to supervise and penalize their associates may not be easily conveyed to outside inspectors or buyers. After watching the cooperative's former agricultural monitor, Santiago, accept a bag of unripe coffee cherries from another member, the visiting agronomist, Carlos, expressed his frustration. He relayed his conversation with Santiago: "I said, 'Santiago, why are you accepting this?' And Santiago told me, 'Well it's organic coffee and it's from an associate.' And then it happened again and I said, 'Look Santiago you can't accept this green [unripe] coffee. This is the importer's coffee and I am the importer's representative and we don't want green coffee.'" Carlos then instructed Santiago and the mill employees to pick the green cherries out by hand. Although he may have feigned ignorance, as a founding member of the cooperative and an early proponent of organic agriculture Santiago clearly understood that green cherries compromise the quality of the coffee. However, the costs of castigating a cooperative member in front of his fellow associates outweighed the benefits of meeting high quality standards that particular day.

Under the strict certification standards, cooperative members must negotiate a middle ground between the demands of transnational commodity markets and the local patterns of social life. In other less public instances, Santiago strove to enforce the production rules that he thought were most essential, such as the prohibition against chemical fertilizer use. For example, he told me that one day he was walking along the narrow paths winding through the coffee fields surrounding the community and was shocked to see the supposedly organic coffee trees owned by a cooperative member with chemical fertilizer applied at their bases. Rather than directly confronting this member, Santiago borrowed his teenage daughter's camera to take a photograph of the fertilizer, which he then gave to the former manager, Guillermo. Santiago said he told Guillermo to "[m]ake sure this member doesn't try to sell this chemical coffee as organic coffee." Guillermo reported back to him several days later that the member in question took affront at the physical evidence of his non-compliance: he tore up the photo and stormed out of the office. In presenting Guillermo with a photograph of the offense, Santiago was able to fulfill his duties without directly involving himself in the interpersonal conflict that would ensue. Of course, instances such as these may have fueled the animosity some members felt toward the former manager (discussed in Chapter 4), who was routinely forced to bear this burden of supervisory authority.

The rules of certification and the demands of quality control may also require a restructuring of the daily lives, landscapes, and work habits of producers. For example, members were encouraged to surround their coffee fields with living borders to mark boundaries and protect the coffee from passersby. However, to some this seemed like an unnecessary expense or busy work as they could easily decipher the boundaries, the owners (present and historical), and the relative quality of virtually every coffee plot in the patchwork of agricultural fields surrounding San Juan. Similarly, to monitor the work habits of producers and create written documentation of farming methods, inspectors urged cooperative members to maintain a daily written record of their agricultural activities. However, because of illiteracy or low-level literacy, for some cooperative members this would be at best a laborious and time-consuming task, while for many others it would prove impossible. Perhaps understanding the difficulty this proposed individual audit trail posed to some cooperative members, Carlos once suggested to a group that they ask their school-age children to help them with this task. Although the majority of cooperative members stressed the importance of their children's education, they were not necessarily eager to abandon their filial authority and pride in their agricultural knowledge and hard work (which funded their children's education) by placing themselves at their mercy.

Although a coffee producer who is not a cooperative member may criticize the methods employed by neighbors, his own economic well-being is not endangered by their perceived failings. However, the interdependence of the cooperative members' earnings and their group-level certification requires them to monitor and discipline each other. In a small community, this behavior can be interpreted as meddling or, worse, as a malicious pursuit of tangential feuds. It can also be employed to reinforce existing hierarchies within the larger community or as a justification for the growing power of leadership factions within the cooperative. Therefore, not only does this forced monitoring and disciplining alter the economic logic of farming (Mutersbaugh 2002), but it might also endanger the participatory democracies that fair trade intends to foster. In conclusion, it is important to note that although members are reluctant to supervise one another, they are firmly rooted in the principles of mutual aid upon which their cooperative rests. One cooperative founder expressed the significance of this ethic to the members of a cooperative visiting La Voz when he stated: "We have to work together to produce this coffee. If members don't feel like working together then they can leave. They have to want to work in a group and have a vision of the future. They have to think of the children as well and their future. If you want to go and sell in the streets instead, then go ahead and sell in the streets."

THE LOCAL CONTRADICTIONS OF
CONSERVATION AND HOUSEHOLD NEEDS

Historically, Maya identity was intimately linked to natal communities and land ownership. Although cooperative members do not ascribe an intrinsic purity to nature, wilderness, and forests, they do share an ethic of environmental stewardship and care for the land that provides their livelihood. They have also enjoyed substantial economic and technical assistance from foreign development agencies and coffee importers who place a high value on conservation. During interviews and informal conversations, cooperative members often made statements such as "Trees are an important part of being human and our equilibrium. We have to conserve the lake and the volcanoes." When walking visitors through their coffee plots they frequently pointed out the high quality of their organic soil and the large number of edible herbs growing beneath their trees. Members also spoke of the importance of forest diversity and maintained that their shade trees augment rainfall levels and help cleanse the local air. These sentiments are similar to the ones voiced by the northern environmentalists who purchase the cooperative's coffee with the goal of conservation in mind. However, a closer examination of cooperative members' understandings of the production requirements demanded for shade-grown (and, to a lesser extent, organic) coffee certification reveals that conservation and, more simply, trees have very different meanings within this local context far removed from the well-lit, climate-controlled shelves of our local supermarket.

In less-developed countries, strict environmentalism is a luxury that is difficult to meet in practice. The bulk of La Voz's members do not resemble the U.S. archetypal portrait of an environmentalist nor, for that matter, do they resemble consumer fantasies of the "green Native." Although they recognize the benefits of organic coffee production, this has not translated into a wholesale adoption of an ecologically sensitive lifestyle. During the primary research period Juaneros had no access to a landfill, no opportunity to recycle consumer waste, and limited financial resources. Across town, coffee fields were littered with household waste, including discarded plastic bags and glass bottles. Santiago unintentionally demonstrated the local nonchalance toward littering one afternoon as I helped him make organic fertilizer. As he lectured me on the benefits of organic coffee production he simultaneously balled up the paper wrappers from the blocks of yeast used in bokashi organic fertilizer production and tossed them over the fence into a cooperative member's neighboring coffee field. This is a prime example of the paradox that although cooperative members are committed to organic production methods in their coffee fields, environmentalism has not become an all-encompassing way of life for them.

Many Central American and Mexican small-scale farmers produce coffee in the traditional forestlike agro-ecosystems lauded by proponents of shade-grown coffee. In fact, for these farmers, shade-grown coffee certification is a laudable effort to reward them for the absolutely critical role they play in biodiversity conservation. However, because of the history of coffee cultivation in San Juan, shade-grown certification is not a natural fit for cooperative members. In this circumstance, rather than compensation for existing conservation methods, the importer's push toward shade-grown certification was experienced as yet another regulatory imposition from the North. The standards and the rationale supporting them were poorly understood by the members of La Voz, heightening their resistance to the diversification they were asked to implement.

When the stricter certification requirements for shade-grown coffee were published in 2001, the cooperative failed to pass its initial inspection. Like many small-scale producers in Latin America, cooperative members planted coffee en masse in the 1970s and were influenced by USAID's emphasis on technology transfer. They initially converted their milpa into plots of coffee grown with chemical fertilizers and limited shade coverage. Because they planted in existing cornfields, cooperative members' coffee plots do not have natural shade canopies nor the diversity of biological life found in forest ecosystems. To achieve organic certification in 1991, the majority of cooperative members planted two fast-growing shade-tree species, *Grevillea* and *Inga*. This lack of shade-tree diversity directly contributed to their failure to meet the certification standards. However, the cooperative's importer saw that shade-grown certification would increase the marketability of the cooperative's coffee, and to ensure future compliance with certification requirements and improve coffee quality, she employed an agronomist to visit the cooperative periodically to monitor coffee production. The agronomist, Carlos (mentioned above), was frequently described as *fuerte*, or strong, by cooperative members because of his rapid Spanish and brisk interpersonal style, which contrasted sharply with their own more reserved approach to conversation and collaboration. Eighty-four percent of the interviewed cooperative members completed six or fewer years of schooling. This lack of formal education meant that many members lacked confidence in their Spanish-language skills. As a result, I frequently observed them nod their heads in agreement as Carlos dictated the trees they needed to plant in their coffee fields, only to have them confess later in casual conversation their incomprehension. As one member told me after spending a morning with Carlos, "In terms of shade, I am on the moon."

Unlike U.S. conservationists, who celebrate the forestlike aspects of the agro-ecosystem that shade trees create, cooperative members spoke of the trees' practical role in agricultural production, emphasizing the ways in which shade trees contribute to the health of their coffee, in the form of shade, soil conservation, and natural fertilizer. For example, when asked the primary purpose of shade trees, 66 percent of members responded that the shade trees are necessary for proper coffee production, whereas only 25 percent responded that the shade trees contribute to ecological diversity. The majority of members who identified environmental benefits as the most important function of shade trees explained that the trees counteract pollution by producing oxygen and reducing contamination. For example, during an interview, one stated simply, "If there's only contamination, there is no happiness in life." However, this same individual later told me that "[t]he United States says Guatemala needs to plant more trees but they have to pay us a better price." Another who cited the oxygen produced by shade trees as a benefit argued that "[t]he buyers want us to plant shade trees because *they* pollute a lot in the United States, but then they should pay *us* more money." Comments such as these indicate that some members resent being asked to preserve biodiversity and meet environmental standards while consumers in wealthier industrialized nations continue to pollute.

Like other Central American coffee farmers, many members of La Voz believed that shade trees are beneficial to the health of the coffee agroecosystem (Méndez, Gliessman, and Gilbert 2007). However, cooperative members defined themselves primarily as campesinos, not conservationists, and they did not necessarily agree that diversifying the shade coverage in their fields would improve the quality of their coffee. They had produced certified organic coffee for more than a decade and were hesitant to accept the additional burden of habitat conservation without demonstrable financial reward. To avoid requests for higher payments, Carlos routinely described shade diversification to cooperative members as a part of the organic certification process (which does not detail ecological diversity requirements) and attempted to instil the idea that shade diversity and habitat protection would increase the quality and yield of their coffee trees. In my presence he never mentioned declining migratory bird populations, the prevailing scientific justification for the required diversity of shade coverage. This contributed to the opinion shared by many cooperative members that shade diversity was an irrational demand made by U.S. buyers who had no farming experience. For example, after a long morning of touring *cafetales* with

Carlos, one exclaimed, "We're thinking, 'How are we going to produce coffee with ten species of trees in our coffee fields?' Already, my field has eight *Chalum* trees; what good will two more trees do? But they say we need to have all ten."

Although cooperative members depend heavily on their coffee fields to supply firewood for cooking, the rigidity of the certification system designed by the Smithsonian Migratory Bird Center does not necessarily serve the needs of the members' household economies. The majority of members' wives utilize woodstoves or open hearths for cooking. Therefore, fast-growing tree species, such as *Grevillea*, fill an important niche by providing firewood. However, as a nonnative species, *Grevillea* is unacceptable under the certification requirements designed to mimic indigenous forest systems. This frustrates some cooperative members, like one who complained: "We have to eliminate *Grevillea* completely because it's Australian. The buyers want us to only have native plants, but the *Grevillea* is good for firewood. We want to leave it, but they say no." Other standards were interpreted as unreasonably demanding. For example, the requirement that coffee farmers maintain ten species of shade trees in every coffee plot is a realistic demand for those with large holdings. However, the coffee plots of many cooperative members measure a third of an acre or less. This lack of adaptability to local contexts reflects a more general emerging paradox within certification systems that are theoretically designed to serve the interests of participating farmers (Mutersbaugh 2003). This paradox emerges from the fundamental tension within certified product markets between the demands of an agro-food system that relies on impersonal capitalist relations, certifications, and rules and the ideals of social justice and environmental conservation characterizing alternative trade (Shreck 2002).

U.S. proponents of shade-grown coffee claim diversity of shade cover provides insurance against economic uncertainty (e.g., see Rice and Ward 1996). However, members of the cooperative balked at diversifying their shade cover and remained unconvinced that the benefits, such as alternative sources of food and income, outweighed the costs. Avocados are the only permitted tropical tree product with any local market potential, but low prices and saturated markets make them an unattractive investment for members. Similarly, it does little good to invest in orange and banana trees if one has no secure outlet for their fruits. Because of the guaranteed price premium of US$1.41 per pound that cooperative members received for their fair-trade and organic-certified coffee, few families were poor enough to benefit from the additional nutritional benefits that the products of permitted tropical fruit trees could provide. Additionally, hardwood planted for the lumber market requires a decade or more to reach maturity. In the meantime, trees that grow tall and straight are frequently poached from coffee fields late at night and resurface days later as television antennas or construction materials at a neighbor's house. In short, cooperative members might have more eagerly participated in the shade-grown certification requirements if this conservation strategy better reflected their livelihood needs and priorities.

In shifting their focus to the transnational marketplace in search of higher incomes, cooperative members were confronted with northern fantasies of their innate naturalism. Because their coffee is certified organic, cooperative members believed at the time that they were already protecting the environment and did not embrace the opportunity to further protect ecological diversity. Their subtle rejection of appeals to their intrinsic appreciation for nature frustrated Carlos, who repeatedly expressed his opinion that members should comply with the certification systems because environmental conservation would be good for them and their community. On one occasion, I overheard Juan, a cooperative member, respond to Carlos's ongoing explanation of the shade requirements by saying, "I understand now. This is organic coffee and so we have to respect what you, the inspector, say and we have to put in more shade trees." Later Carlos voiced his frustration, "It's like when Juan said to me, 'Now we have to change and put in more shade trees because you said so.' Well no, that isn't the point. The point is they should put in the shade trees because it is better for them, for their ecosystem and their children."

CONCLUSIONS

A common criticism of international agricultural certification systems is that the rules and regulations are largely established by northern participants and not the southern producers who must abide by them. Certification systems that people see as unduly demanding or irrational may hinder the long-term success of market-based conservation efforts. In addition to financial rewards, certification systems should provide demonstrable subsidiary benefits for local producers and their impoverished communities, such as improved product quality, the reduction of pesticide use and associated health risks, and enhanced agricultural productivity. Through their participation in the international coffee market, cooperative members are contributing to the maintenance of cultural identity and the health of their local ecosystem. However, market-based conservation efforts must be coupled with market access and secure, high prices for small-scale producers if they are to reverse historical trends of impoverishment and environmental degradation. The financial incentives ensure the ongoing maintenance of the community's material base for survival, their land and agrarian tradition.

The tension and disparities between conservation agendas and the livelihood demands of Juanero coffee producers force us to examine our own understandings of environmentalism—what does sustainable living truly mean and how is this meaning variable depending on culture and context? The members of La Voz are wholly committed to organic coffee production and can clearly articulate its economic and environmental benefits. However, it may appear paradoxical that although they espouse the virtues of organic production in their coffee fields, environmentalism has not become an all-encompassing way of life for them. Much like the idea of conservation in conservation-based natural-resource management projects (Haenn 2005; West 2006), organic production is omnipresent within the cooperative in the ways that members relate to one another and to outsiders. However, outside the living barriers of the certified coffee fields environmentalism is absent in any form that might be recognizable to U.S. consumers, such as recycling, driving a hybrid car, or using fluorescent light bulbs. On the other hand, many proponents of organic and shade-grown coffee clearly identify as environmentalists committed to the conservation of biodiversity and tropical forests. In addition to the time and energy they devote to these causes, many of them spend a significant amount of money purchasing organic products and pursuing an environmentally friendly lifestyle. Are the consumers who purchase glossy magazines such as *Organic Style*, which labels itself a "new 'eco-lifestyle' destination for people seeking high-quality products,"[8] more committed to organic principles than the organic coffee producers who throw the wrappers of their processed cookies and crackers on the ground during cooperative meetings while discussing improved production methods and reforestation? The United States has an ecological footprint of 9.7 (meaning the average citizen requires 9.7 hectares of land to produce the resources she consumes and to absorb the waste she produces) whereas Guatemala's is only 1.2.[9] This disparity speaks to the larger contradictions inherent in a system that celebrates commodification as the best solution to the environmental problems and inequalities produced by capitalism.

6

Managing the Maya:
Power in the Fair-Trade Market

The cooperative's *beneficio* is at the center of the flurry of activity accompanying the annual coffee harvest in San Juan; it is where members work rotating shifts and gather each afternoon to weigh their coffee, discuss the year's harvest, and joke with one another. Children frequently rush down the hill to the beneficio after school to chase each other around the patios and wait for their mothers and fathers to finish their work. The town's *chuchos*, or street dogs, aimlessly circulate, occasionally stopping to sniff at the coffee drying in the high-altitude sun on the cement patios. The atmosphere is relaxed and celebratory: I once heard a member describe it as "very happy." With so many individuals coming and going and only a small group of paid employees overseeing daily operations, the beneficio was also a bit chaotic, disorganized, and even messy. Backpacks were haphazardly slung on window bars and plastic lawn chairs were scattered about. Uncoiled hoses snaked around walkways and empty soda bottles and trash accumulated in corners while the bathrooms were uninviting, to say the least.

I always interpreted this inattention to detail as the necessary corollary of the casual current of team spirit and anticipation of coffee profits that pervaded the beneficio during the months of December, January, and February. However, as a representative of Elan charged with improving La Voz's coffee quality, Carlos was frustrated by the group's lack of efficiency and carelessness. He rightly pointed out that the disorder made it difficult to closely monitor the coffee's washing and drying progress. For example, just one stray rock or small piece of debris could cause several coffee cherries to linger in a washing channel, thereby contributing to the overfermentation that was creating the characteristic winey flavor of La Voz's coffee. On one of his visits to San Juan the normally cheery Carlos stomped around the beneficio, loudly dictating in Spanish a list of demands to the employees and cooperative members who awkwardly trailed after him: "Pick up that trash"; "Coil up that hose"; "Keep that dog off the coffee"; "Paint this tank"; and "Fix this bathroom." This moment starkly revealed that fair trade is about more than simply empowering farmers economically. Fair-trade coffee certification and the assistance offered to small-scale producers involves the introduction of new work ethics and an attempt to "fix" farmers' problems, political and otherwise, as they are perceived by outsiders (Nigh 2002).

Taking to heart Carlos's critiques of the beneficio and its disorganization, the board of directors spent several days tidying, repairing, and painting. In an attempt to make the beneficio more visitor friendly, they also posted handmade signs around the mill identifying the stages in coffee harvesting. The signs were constructed out of roughly cut scrap lumber and painted bright turquoise. The labels for stages like weighing and washing were shakily drawn in red paint. When I returned to La Voz's beneficio in 2006 these rustic but charming handcrafted signs had been replaced with slick new ones professionally made of stained wood with precise lettering and emblazoned with the Anacafé logo. With the hope of attracting visitors to the new coffee tour, the beneficio had been sanitized: its cement-block walls were painted white and the two bathrooms now had running water, soap, and toilet paper. In short, the beneficio's previously disordered and lighthearted atmosphere was replaced by a sterile and glossy perfection, akin to the shining lobby of the Guatemala City Marriott. The "fixing" of the farmers involved their repositioning as the small-scale coffee producers that northern consumers are encouraged to envision as they sip their fair-trade lattes.[1] This is an integral part of the mirroring process, discussed further in the next chapter, in which fair-trade products function as a one-way looking glass, reflecting back to consumers their own fantasies of smiling farmers, solidarity, and just economic relationships.

FIGURE 6.1. *The newly remodeled bathrooms in the cooperative's wet mill in 2006.*

This chapter analyzes fair-trade coffee as a commodity network, specifically focusing on the relations of governance-shaping certification practices and the quality-control methods employed by northern roasters and certifiers in their attempts to "fix" these Maya coffee producers. By "governance" I mean the rules, institutions, and norms that channel and constrain economic activity, specifically focusing on the power that coffee roasters, importers, and certifiers hold in fair-trade networks at the points of production, certification, and distribution and how this affects the network's functioning.[2] In evaluating fair-trade coffee as a commodity network, I focus on the interlinking of products and services, the organizational and spatial configuration of the production and marketing networks, and the ways in which resources are allocated among the networks' participants. Fair-trade marketing materials (discussed in Chapter 7) are designed to convince consumers that fair-trade coffee networks are shaped by what academics term "relational governance," or economic relationships between suppliers and buyers that are marked by mutual dependence, cooperation, and trust

(Petkova 2006). Although this is certainly truer of fair-trade coffee networks than conventional ones, the members of La Voz are subjected to high levels of external surveillance and control as a result of their hierarchical relationships with northern buyers and certifying agencies. In other words, there are definite power inequities underlying fair trade and these are most evident in the fair-trade certification process, which is marked by a low degree of producer understanding and low levels of producer participation in the collective establishment of standards and movement goals. The power inequities are also readily observed in the processes of quality control, which entail both external and internal forms of surveillance over coffee production and processing.

In light of these power relations, many may wonder why cooperative members willingly participate in the inequitable relationships structuring fair trade, a form of exchange that consumers are repeatedly told is more just and fair than the alternative. La Voz's long record of fair-trade participation demonstrates that the benefits, such as market information, product improvement, and economic security in the face of market uncertainties, outweigh the costs of heightened external surveillance and the stresses of certification. Moreover, the deepening relationships between La Voz and its long-term buyer Green Mountain Coffee Roasters may someday transform into something resembling the academic model of relational governance—or relationships based on mutual trust, cooperation, and dependence. The extent to which fair trade can successfully promote this shift toward greater equality within coffee networks directly impacts the movement's long-term ability to craft a viable alternative to the contemporary neoliberal economic paradigm.

GOVERNANCE WITHIN THE FAIR-TRADE COFFEE NETWORK

Commodity chain analysis (now more commonly referred to as value chain analysis) is especially useful for economic anthropology because of the centrality it gives to the key concept of value. As an analytical tool, commodity chains first emerged in Wallerstein's (1974) world systems theory; however, the framework was elaborated by Gereffi primarily for industrial products and focused attention on sets of interorganizational networks clustered around one commodity or product, linking households, enterprises, and states to one another within the world economy (Gereffi 1994). Gereffi (1994) used the term "buyer-driven global commodity chain" to denote how global buyers used explicit coordination to help create a highly competent supply base upon which global-scale production and distribution systems could be built without direct ownership. Ponte (2002) in turn argued that the coffee market is constituted by buyer-driven commodity chains greatly influenced by the product specifications and supply networks of roasters, distributors, and their brands. This is particularly the case within the specialty coffee market. Although buyer-driven commodity chains tend to be more flexible, they also contribute to an industry's vulnerability as brands and corporate image become integral components of perceived value within the marketplace.

The initial distinction between buyer-driven and supplier-driven commodity chains was eventually abandoned in favor of a theory of governance based on three factors: the complexity of information and knowledge transfer required to sustain a particular transaction; the extent to which this information and knowledge can be codified and transmitted efficiently without transaction-specific investment between the parties to the transaction; and the capabilities of actual and potential suppliers in relation to the requirements of the transaction (Gereffi, Humphrey, and Sturgeon 2005:85). Gereffi and his colleagues' model identifies five forms of governance: hierarchy, captive, relational, modular, and market, which range from high to low levels of explicit coordination and power asymmetry. Fair trade's goal is to foment relational governance through the creation of relationships between spatially dispersed producers and consumers (or roasters as consumer proxies) of mutuality and trust bolstered by the certification framework.

In many ways, contemporary fair-trade networks support rather than challenge the dictates of economic neoliberalism, and although neoliberalism may mean less government, it involves forms of governance that encourage both institutions and individuals to conform to the norms of the market (Larner 2000). The analysis of governance within fair-trade networks foregrounds the nature of power relations shaping interactions among suppliers and buyers. Within the fair-trade coffee network, the power that northern certifiers and roasters wield over coffee production and processing is best understood as a form of governmentality. A quintessentially modern phenomenon, "governmentality involves the appropriation, processing and transformation of the domains of daily life by expert knowledge and the administrative apparatuses of the state" (Escobar 1999:6).[3] Populations can be governed by institutions and agencies, including the state, and by discourses, norms, and identities (Ferguson and Gupta 2002). Within the context of neoliberal economic policies, deregulation in the agro-food sectors was particularly dramatic in recent decades. As government control decreased, new forms of governmentality (e.g., certifying agencies, NGOs, and quality-control experts) began to dominate agro-food networks, drawing the attention of social scientists.[4] Within the fair-trade coffee network, governmentality is enacted through the certification process and the surveillance of production and processing practices in the name of quality control.

Although studying governance relations within commodity networks can provide powerful insights into the ways in which power is exercised in an increasingly global economy, this framework leaves little room for the creative ways that farmers, such as the members of La Voz, interpret and attempt to bend the system to their own advantage. Cooperative members are disciplined into new forms of behavior that subtly change their subjectivity through discourses of certification and quality control. They submit to this "fixing" because the promise of a decent profit in comparison to what they might earn in the conventional coffee market reinforces their compliance to the disciplinary processes of certification. The analytic framework tends to underemphasize the agency, misunderstandings, and miscommunications that underlie the fair-trade coffee commodity network (and most likely all commodity networks). Employing a network analogy (rather than referring to fair trade as a commodity or value chain) highlights the web of social and economic actors that define and uphold these governance and commodity relations. The network approach, clearly articulated by Raynolds (2008), recognizes that market activities are embedded in social as well as economic institutions while leaving analytic room for the agency and creativity of participants.

FAIR-TRADE CERTIFICATION

The members of La Voz have sold fair-trade certified coffee directly to northern markets for more than a decade. However, even though several interviewed cooperative members could articulately analyze the inequities they faced in global agricultural commodity markets, only three out of fifty-three surveyed members were familiar with the term "fair trade." On the other hand, thirty-five identified Elan Organic Coffees as the cooperative's long-term importer. This lack of awareness of the important role they themselves play in the fair-trade movement is symptomatic of the international fair-trade structure, in which producers have limited decision-making power and administrative control.[5] This lack of producer participation in the formation of fair-trade strategies and market operations constrains the movement's ability to fully identify and represent the values and priorities of its intended beneficiaries. The certification standards, described in the book's introduction, represent the backbone of the fair-trade coffee network, lending legitimacy to the product in retail markets and assuring that adequate resources are delivered to small producers. However, the majority of fair-trade participants, the small farmers themselves, have effectively no input into the creation of these standards. This flaw in the fair-trade organizational structure contributes to noncompliance and misunderstandings.

Members of La Voz were familiar with the minutia of organic certification requirements because they were forced to incorporate the regulations into their daily production practices. However, the fair-trade certification requirements, and even the concept itself, were poorly understood, if at all, within the cooperative. Although members often employed rhetoric similar to that found in fair-trade promotional materials in discussing the rights of small-scale producers and the importance of shortening the commodity chain, not one explicitly referred to fair trade. For example, one member explained: "Anacafé is an association dominated by larger plantation owners. Yes we are a part of Anacafé as small producers but we never become members of the board of directors. They receive privileges. The small producers always receive the least." Tellingly, this member failed to acknowledge that he was an active participant in an alternative market that worked to counteract these structural inequities.

Because they do not fully comprehend fair-trade markets and their reputed benefits, many members displayed a fatalistic attitude toward the coffee market. When asked the farm-gate price he would like to receive, one member replied, "Well, whatever the people in the United States give to us, we are at their mercy." This sentiment was echoed by many interviewed cooperative members.[6] This unfamiliarity with fair trade is problematic at both an ideological and a practical level. For example, fair-trade producers who do not fully understand the market in which they operate may be more likely to leave the cooperative when coffee prices recover, choosing to sell their coffee to *coyotes* for cash in-hand (rather than selling to the cooperative and waiting several months for remuneration) and thereby avoiding administration expenses and participation requirements. Among older, well-established cooperatives such as La Voz this is less likely to occur; although members might hold little ideological allegiance to fair trade, they do respect the commitments they have made to fellow cooperative members.

The lack of producer knowledge is partially attributable to the fact that cooperative members have little direct contact with FLO because the bulk of the activities supporting fair-trade certification and marketing by necessity are managed by cooperative leadership and administration. This represents a fundamental difference from organic production, which requires producer training and individual, daily attention to regulations to achieve and maintain certification. Furthermore, unlike La Voz, many cooperatives that sell a portion of their coffee at fair-trade prices and the rest to the conventional market may pay members in one lump sum without fully explaining the price premiums earned in the fair-trade market. For example, in interviews I conducted with the managers of four recently established cooperatives in Guatemala each indicated that he was more concerned with establishing loyalty to the group itself than with explaining the intricacies of the international fair-trade market. Additionally, many newer cooperatives have high initial operating and administrative costs, forcing them to return only a small percentage of the fair-trade premium to their members as the rest is reinvested in the group. It is difficult to explain the benefits of fair trade to producers who are not actually earning a significant amount of extra money.

Although employees of Elan and Green Mountain Coffee Roasters regularly visited San Juan, the cooperative had little contact with fair-trade certifiers before and during the research period. However, a certifier arrived in August 2002 (and presumably began annual inspections thereafter). After the visit I spoke with my landlord, José, who at the time was a member of the board of directors. José and the board members, along with a handpicked group of what the manager described as the "twenty most active members of the cooperative" met with the certifier during her visit. I asked José whether the certifier visited to complete an inspection for fair-trade certification. He replied: "No. She is just here to see how everything is going with us." Clearly the certifier had failed to adequately explain her presence to the group and to engage them in a meaningful discussion of the cooperative's and fair trade's successes and failures from their vantage point. Because FLO does not advocate a participatory social auditing process, this "snapshot" or "checklist" form of auditing (Barrientos, Dolan, and Tallontire 2003; Smith and Dolan 2006) potentially not only hinders the inspector's ability to clearly understand the variety of problems cooperative members face but also curtails the knowledge and participation of the excluded members.

The certification process itself is potentially disempowering in its form: producer organizations are investigated and assessed by outsiders who often are unfamiliar with local culture, history, and politics; have little local agricultural knowledge or expertise; and have class and ethnic backgrounds starkly different from those of producers. Although it was not the case for La Voz, primarily because the cooperative was so rarely visited by fair-trade certifiers, there is evidence that fair-trade certifiers and development agencies assisting fair-trade cooperatives can exert undue influence on the internal politics and functioning of local organizations (Murray,

Raynolds, and Taylor 2003:21). For example, multiple sources shared a rumor surrounding the events that occurred in a fair-trade coffee cooperative located in Huehuetenango, Guatemala. According to sources, the local director of the Canadian development agency Center for International Studies and Cooperation (CECI) developed a personality conflict with the organization's respected, long-term manager. The CECI employee reportedly forced the cooperative to fire the manager by threatening to rescind all of the financial and technical assistance the group received from CECI and other organizations.

Because of their lack of contextual knowledge and familiarity with local histories and customs, certifiers may also be unduly influenced by rumors and allegations of corruption. For example, in 1999 the Majomut cooperative in Chiapas, Mexico, reportedly fell victim to false rumors and anonymous e-mails, circulated around FLO, that stated that the cooperative was involved in paramilitary activities and should therefore be expelled from the fair-trade system (Perezgrovas Garza 2002). Similarly, the Mexican cooperative La Selva was decertified because of its "administrative deficiencies" when the organization failed to complete a contract with a Dutch buyer during the 1998–1999 harvest. However, the group's board of directors maintained the FLO auditor had failed to submit a written report of his work, had questioned the honesty of the organization's trusted manager, and effectively had handed control of the organization to an unelected group of cooperative advisors and employees (Gonzalez Cabanas 2002). These cases demonstrate how through the certification process cooperatives can become vulnerable to surveillance and the power of external administrators who command discursive procedures and institutions. They also lend support to the argument that the differential access to knowledge enjoyed by fair-trade administrators and producers creates a system of inequality and neocolonialism. In examining certification practices the altruistic leanings of fair trade seem to be trumped by neoliberalism because of these gaps in understanding. As a result, the well-intentioned motives replicate a colonial dynamic that impedes a more relational form of governance and ultimately a more equitable economy.

The hierarchical relationships characterizing fair-trade coffee networks are reinforced by the mandate for transparency enacted through the written reports produced by certifiers. For example, one interviewed cooperative manager described his unhappiness with a fair-trade inspector who refused to provide the group a copy of his written report. The inspector reportedly claimed it would be useless to the manager because it was written in English. The manager explained that he asked the inspector, "How is it that you do this audit of our cooperative and don't give us the information?" The manager understood the importance of this document and that the words contained within it would determine the future of his cooperative. At a more practical level, he believed the assessment it contained might potentially help him improve the cooperative's operations. Additionally, because the manager did not know what problems the inspector reported, he was unable to contest his assessment of the cooperative. These written assessments and the certification process amount to a ritual of control that effectively maintains the hierarchical relations limiting producer influence within fair-trade networks and hinders the formation of truly equitable trade relations.

Although a necessary part of the fair-trade model, the certification process is also about the "control of control," with the consequence that the auditing or certification process tends to make organizations more opaque rather than more transparent; in adding another layer of control, certification creates the very sense of loss of trust that it is intended to counteract (Miller 1998:202). The paradoxical impact of the combination of hierarchical power relations and the mandate for transparency through written documents is also evident within the organic certification process. For example, Carlos once complained that organic inspectors do not provide copies of the forms they complete nor do they offer advice to the coffee cooperatives they certify. He said, "The agency simply sends the cooperative a letter saying, 'you have to fix this, this and that' without telling them how they can go about fixing it." After translating several communiqués from OCIA for the cooperative's former manager, I know from experience that organic certifiers do not always provide cooperatives with documents and instructions written in Spanish. By refusing to provide written reports in a language understood by the producers being certified, the agency added yet another level of opacity to the process. Creating documents but not sharing them or producing them in forms that farmers understand effectively obscures the knowledge that could empower small-scale coffee producers to understand fair-trade certification and market relations.

Because the supply of potentially certifiable fair-trade coffee is significantly larger than the current market demand, it is difficult for coffee associations to assert authority during the certification process. If cooperatives are unwilling to submit to the demands of inspectors, they will lose their certification and their market and, most likely, plenty of small-scale producer associations will happily take their place. As a result, certified markets are often paradoxically perceived as unfair by the smallholder coffee farmers they work to support (Mutersbaugh 2003). In general, coffee producers demonstrate a lack of clarity and uncertainty within the fair-trade system over how decisions are made, the applicability of different rules, and who participates at different organizational levels. Some producers question whether the same rules, philosophies, and moral values apply to importers and roasters. For example, Taylor reports that one Mexican cooperative member questioned whether "[t]hey ask for the history of the importers like they ask for certain requirements from us, and like we are monitored, is it the same for them?" (2002:17). In reality, the mandate for transparency applies solely to producers within fair-trade coffee networks. For example, in an attempt to counteract the corporate cooptation of fair-trade coffee retailing in the United States, in 2004 a group of small-scale roasters initiated a movement to have TransFair USA list all licensees by pounds of fair-trade coffee sold and by the percentage of their total sales that number represented. However, TransFair USA refused to provide the information or even to ask the licensees to reveal it, citing "corporate confidentiality." As one of the fair-trade movement's leaders, Dean Cycon (founder of the Massachusetts-based fair-trade roaster Dean's Beans) reported, "It seems incongruous that in a movement that demands transparency by the farmers, a similar demand is not made of the companies—especially when those figures would give consumers a fair and complete picture of a company's commitment to fair trade, thereby strengthening their capacity to make a reasoned choice" (Cycon 2005).[7]

Paradoxically, although auditing processes, such as fair-trade certification, are ostensibly designed to make the inner workings of organizations more visible, in reality these processes are positioned as an increasingly private and invisible expert activity (Power 1996). As a result, certification disrupts the culture of "communicative interactions" among producers, certifiers, labelers, and consumers that fair trade should ideally foster (Mutersbaugh 2002). Together, fair-trade certification standards and practices constitute an "audit culture" that fosters social change as certifiers become catalysts for improving performance, not simply ensuring compliance with standards. Auditing institutions, such as FLO International, are often framed in terms of quality, accountability, and empowerment, suggesting processes of emancipation and self-actualization (Shore and Wright 2004). However, as auditing becomes more widely promoted, individuals and organizations, such as small-scale coffee producers, begin to think of themselves as "auditees" and subtly (and perhaps unwittingly) contribute to a growing audit mentality (Power 2003; Campbell, Lawrence, and Smith 2006:73). As we consumers sip our fair-trade coffee, our minds wander to the liberated coffee growers in distant locations who are actively engaged in democratic organizations and sustainable production methods. Although we like to imagine that the connectivity linking us to these producers is part of a new economic reality rooted in socially embedded equitable exchanges, in reality the connectivity forged by fair-trade networks emerges from the scientific audits and the false promise of transparency characterizing the certification process.[8] This process is a "global assemblage" (Collier and Ong 2005) linking technologies of production, such as seemingly objective regulations and certification practices with the forms of social life, political identities, and ethical orientations that we hope fair trade will foster. The monitoring that fair-trade producer organizations are subjected to and the power inequities that make it possible for certifiers to withhold information from them are part of the "fixing" process through which coffee growers are transformed into neoliberal capitalist subjects who more closely resemble the consumers who drink their coffee. The opacity helps maintain the hierarchical nature of this economic system and functions similarly to the neoliberal multiculturalism of Guatemala analyzed by Hale (2006). Fair trade makes small concessions (such as higher prices) to keep farmers behaving well but to date has provided few substantive openings in the economic system for them to permanently improve their structurally weak position in the commodity network.

Fair trade is predicated on the formation of equitable economic partnerships between producers and consumers. However, because of the low level of producer participation in the international realm of decision making and standard setting, it has yet to radically transform these trade relationships into vehicles for social justice. Many have noted the lack of democratic procedures in establishing agricultural commodity certification standards (including fair trade, organic, and ethical) and the lack of mechanisms ensuring the inclusion of developing nation stakeholders in the design of standards, monitoring, and the evaluation process (Busch and Bain 2004). For example, in his summary of a comparative, multi-sited research project on fair-trade coffee cooperatives, Taylor maintains that the majority of the organizations' experience of fair-trade networks has occurred at the regional and national levels, and interviewees "[c]onsistently report that their access to information about fair trade and conventional market chains beyond their borders has been inadequate" (Taylor 2002:5). As a result, fair-trade certification standards have been criticized for lacking sufficient transparency, failing to ensure that benefits reach local communities, and destabilizing notions of trust and partnership.[9] Developing countries and the producers within them have a great deal to lose if they are not party to negotiations regarding standards. Without this input, certification systems are more likely to be paternalistic reflections of the values and concerns of northern companies and consumers that could potentially do great harm to producers (Blowfield 1999; Busch and Bain 2004:339). Furthermore, standards and certifications effectively serve as barriers to entry (Guthman 2004, 2007). This is particularly evident in fair-trade coffee networks where younger and less successful cooperatives may be blocked from certification and, as a result, market participation, because they cannot afford the cost of registration and inspection (up to $3,500 per cooperative) and cannot demonstrate evidence of a preexisting market (buyer) for their coffee (Lockie and Goodman 2006:108). To FLO's credit, in 2004 the organization began to charge other actors in the system, including exporters, importers, and processors, an annual registration fee and per pound fee (Nicholls and Opal 2005:127).

To successfully foster equitable international trading partnerships and relational governance within fair-trade coffee networks, producers must contribute to the formation of standards, certification requirements, and agreed upon levels of just compensation as well as the establishment of future collective goals. In response to criticism, FLO added four producer representatives to its twelve-member board of directors (FLO 2003) and established a producer business unit in 2005 to assist producer groups. In addition, the Latin American Coordinating Committee of fair-trade producer organizations was created to negotiate participation and specific demands. However, in a global economy, human social and economic rights must extend beyond local, isolated spheres. Therefore, to be a true vehicle for social justice fair-trade markets need to further address this power imbalance. Democratic participation that is both inclusive and international is necessary for fair trade to avoid the objectifying gaze common to more conventional development institutions that create clients and categories (such as the small-scale coffee producer) to control (Escobar 1995:155–156). There are few signs in the contemporary global economy that indicate this democratization process will unfold painlessly over time. Skeptics argue that in fact the organization of our current world system systematically prevents this from happening. However, fair trade serves as a powerful vehicle for educating both consumers and producers, and as discussed in the book's conclusion, this process may provide critical openings for substantive global change. Even with this internationalization and more inclusive participation, individuals within fair-trade networks still will assume new managerial roles and in the process adopt practices that dramatically change self-concepts of agrarian identity and personhood. Part of "managing the Maya" in the cooperative will always entail the transformation of people through the reorganization of relationships, auditing, standardization, and other practices.

CONTROLLING COFFEE QUALITY

In the United States, fair-trade products tend to be premium-priced, and therefore, they need to be premium quality to stay competitive. Quality is assessed along the coffee network at various junctures and according to various attributes. Daviron and Ponte distinguish between material attributes of products, which are usually seen as objective, existing independently of the identity of sellers and buyers, and symbolic quality attributes, which are based on reputation. The ability to measure material quality attributes depends on the existence of measurement operations and devices, which can include human senses and technological devices. Symbolic quality attributes are signaled through trademarks, geographical indications, and sustainability labels (2005:127). Among producers quality is mainly assessed in terms of material attributes, and the symbolic attributes generated through branding, packaging, retailing, and consumption do not play an important role. However, the exception is when quality is embedded in a geographical origin, such as La Voz's coffee, which, under the Anacafé appellation system, is a "Traditional Atitlán" coffee characterized as "delightfully aromatic, with a bright citrus acidity and a full body." In this case it is not only the material coffee that is sold but also a place, a story, sometimes a sense of exoticism (Daviron and Ponte 2005:129). These symbolic attributes are clearly evident in Anacafé's description of "Traditional Atitlán" coffees, which encompasses much more than a pure flavor profile:

> Of Guatemala's five volcanic coffee regions, Atitlán's soil is the richest in organic matter. Ninety percent of Traditional Atitlán is cultivated along the slopes of the dramatic volcanoes that dominate the shores of Lake Atitlán, the largest and most famous of Guatemala's many crater lakes. The daily winds (called Xocomil) that stir the cold lake water are an important influence on the microclimate. The culture's highly developed artisan tradition is reflected in the small producer's skilled cultivation and processing. Although some take their coffee to nearby farms for milling, many belong to cooperatives with their own mill, or process their harvest at home.[10]

Furthermore, the organic, fair-trade, and shade-grown certifications provide additional symbolic quality attributes to La Voz's coffee. These symbolic quality attributes can come to outweigh the material quality attributes of the coffee in the minds of some coffee buyers and even of the producers themselves. Anacafé has worked diligently to improve the actual and perceived quality of Guatemalan coffees. The country ranks second behind Colombia in terms of coffee quality and first in the percentage of its crop classified as highest quality (the latter is partially attributable to the large percentage of Guatemalan coffee classified as strictly hard bean [SHB] because of the high altitudes at which it is produced) (Jordan 2004).

Coffee quality is evaluated through physical parameters such as color, size, and defects and inherent, external factors including the genetic type of the coffee tree, the cultivar, the agro-climatic conditions, farm practices, harvesting procedures, primary processing, export preparation, and handling and storage during the passage from one stage to the next in the marketing chain (Daviron and Ponte 2005:130). La Voz's coffee is *Arabica* and a mixture of cultivars, although primarily members own *Bourbon* trees. It is grown organically at high altitudes. Cooperative members are expected to harvest only ripe cherries clear of foreign matter and the coffee is processed in a beneficio. This primary processing at the beneficio does not improve material quality—it can only maintain the original quality of the bean; therefore, quality control at every stage of processing is critical to the final level of coffee quality. Poor handling, pulping, fermentation, drying, storage, or shipping can negatively affect the appearance of the bean and the coffee's flavor. Because they do not tend to drink their own coffee, or comparable high-quality coffee, the members of La Voz (and other smallholder coffee producers in Latin America) primarily understand quality in relation to farm practices and primary processing rather than their own consumption experiences.

In an effort to ensure their access to high-quality coffee a small number of companies in the specialty industry are promoting "relationship coffees" in which they formulate multi-year fixed-price contracts with their suppliers and base prices on quality and production costs rather than the New York futures market. Relationship coffees allow roasters to know the price at the beginning of the year, so that they can concentrate on roasting instead of dedicating too much time and energy to sourcing. They hold obvious advantages for producers as well: they can minimize risk, upgrade their production and processing methods, and invest in achieving supply reliability. Currently Green Mountain Coffee Roasters annually buys about 35 percent of its approximate 100,000 bags of green coffee through relationship coffees on the basis of long-term, fixed-price contracts (Daviron and Ponte 2005:156).

For close to a decade Green Mountain Coffee Roasters (GCMR) has promoted La Voz as one of its relationship coffees. The roaster uses the coffee produced by members in its Fair Trade Organic French Roast and Heifer Hope Blend coffees. Over the years, GMCR (with the help of the importer Elan Organic Coffees in the past) has worked closely with La Voz to

FIGURE 6.2. *A photo of a coffee picker adorns the walls of the employee computer center at a GMCR roasting facility.*

improve and maintain coffee quality. The desire to maintain this long-term relationship with its buyer served as an incentive for the cooperative to improve its product quality by investing in infrastructural and production improvements. In addition to Carlos's regular visits to the cooperative, over the course of my research La Voz was visited monthly, or every other month, by GMCR employees. Through this steady contact, cooperative members honed their communication skills, enhanced their business practices, and learned valuable information about quality and certification demands. This ongoing close contact with the buyers helped some members and the management to learn international standards for price, quality, and the delivery of export products. Pedro, the agricultural monitor, directly linked the improved coffee quality to the group's close relationships with its northern buyers. He explained: "We are in contact with the foreigners that bring us information about coffee and new techniques. They are teaching us, for example, how to improve the quality for the consumers."

If the fair-trade market is going to expand beyond its charitable roots and broaden its potential impact, it must convince consumers to buy fair-trade coffee not because the producers are poor but because the quality of their coffee is excellent. Research on small firm clusters suggests that by dealing directly with buyers, producers can discover the true value of their work and what they can legitimately ask for in payment (Tendler 1983:51, in Cohen 1999:155). The demand-driven assistance provided by Elan and Green Mountain Coffee Roasters outperforms the supply-driven assistance the cooperative previously received from organizations such as Anacafé. Demand-driven assistance fashions customized assistance around production for a specific contract while supply-driven assistance delivers standardized service to as many participants as necessary. Although some view small-scale producers as "pathetic" recipients of aid, when they are held to strict quality standards and provided demand-driven assistance, they can succeed (Tendler and Amorim 1996:421). For example, Bacon's research among small-scale coffee producers in Nicaragua indicates that demands for quality coupled with producer education effectively instilled a pride in craftsmanship and a motivation toward improvement (2005).

Coffee quality is not something to be achieved and then forgotten. It instead must be consistently monitored, season after season. In the case of fair-trade coffees produced cooperatively, this quality monitoring is complicated by the fact that rather than a centralized operations system, the coffee quality is determined by the actions of 100 or more individual producers in their own fields and during their rotating shifts in the beneficio. During an interview, one coffee importer described coffee quality as "[a] custom, a routine that you have to maintain everyday and it is the responsibility of the cooperatives to fulfill their commitments and to provide this quality coffee." In short, the importer implied that high-quality coffee cannot be produced without a shift in personhood among growers—a shift away from the natural rhythms of agrarian life toward a detail-oriented practice of monitoring and hard work. Through his regular contact and conversations with La Voz's exporter, importer, and roasters, Guillermo, the former manager, understood that La Voz is "[s]ucceeding in the market because of the quality of our coffee." I overheard him tell a group of visiting coffee farmers one afternoon, "If we lose our quality then Elan is going to lose its reputation at the national level." However, during an interview, one U.S. coffee importer suggested that cooperatives with secure fair-trade markets are slowly losing sight of the importance of quality control. He explained, "Maybe they have too much confidence after working so many years and they've lost the rhythm of constant maintenance." However, Miguel, the San Pedro–based Anacafé extension agent, expressed a very different opinion. Over coffee in his office one afternoon, Miguel vehemently argued that fair-trade coffee was declining in quality because buyers inconsistently apply quality standards. He theorized, "This year the growers will cut a few corners in their mill and the buyers don't say anything and next year they are even lazier in the mill and the quality of their coffee gets worse and worse."

Miguel was referring to quality control in the mill itself, which at La Voz is monitored by the agricultural monitor, a handful of full-time employees, and the rotating shifts of cooperative members who work there during the harvest. However, coffee quality can also be negatively impacted as a result of poor dry-mill processing, contamination during shipping (coffee easily absorbs the scent of surrounding products), and mistakes during roasting, none of which is controlled by the cooperative. Furthermore, the quality of the coffee we drink is also determined by roasting techniques, packaging, proper storage, and brewing. Recently roasted, fresh-ground beans combined with distilled water in the proper proportions and brewed using a preferred method will certainly produce a higher quality cup of coffee than what is served in the average university cafeteria.

In interviews conducted with managers of various fair-trade coffee cooperatives across the western highlands, several expressed frustration over the difficulty of explaining quality demands to their members in an understandable fashion. They subtly argued that the smallholders' mentalities needed to be "fixed" or reoriented toward the market—a move that is integral to standardization and quality control. For example, one stated: "You have to think in the logic of the market. It's clear what the market wants, it's clear that organic [and fair-trade] coffee has the best market on the basis of its quality. Putting the concept of quality in their [the members'] heads is hard." Another argued, "It is hard to convince people that the only way to survive in this market is to sell your very best product because the intermediaries [coyotes] pay for trash."

A significant factor hindering the farmers' ability to fully understand the international market's quality standards is the subjectivity of taste. Taste is determined by social position (Bourdieu 1984). Guatemalans prefer heavily sugared, weak coffee, which they drink throughout the day. This form of coffee consumption tends to obscure the distinct flavor profiles that roasters work so diligently to enhance in U.S. markets. I found that the managers of many coffee cooperatives held an overrated opinion of their coffee's quality. Because they produce high-altitude coffee, some believe they can afford to ignore the technical factors of production and quality control in the mill. For example, the manager of the newly formed coffee cooperative in San Juan (part of the World Vision–funded organization Cotz'ija's development efforts) told me: "The coffee we have is one of the best in the world in its characteristics due to its altitude. Our coffee is specialty coffee and organic and with our coffee alone we should find higher prices." However, this manager also admitted that he had never met a coffee importer or roaster and had never tasted specialty coffee. At the time of this conversation (2002), the organization's beneficio's drying "patios" consisted of sheets of black nylon laid on the bare ground (which can negatively impact coffee flavor). Because the cooperative lacked the experience gleaned through regular contact with northern roasters, his firm belief in the superior quality of his cooperative's coffee was not necessarily warranted (e.g., his coffee had never been cupped or classified) but instead generated through conversations with Anacafé representatives and the directors of the development agency funding his organization.

TACKLING THE WINEY FERMENT: A CASE STUDY IN QUALITY IMPROVEMENT

In his 2001 review of La Voz's coffee (roasted by Kaladi Brothers Coffee, based in Anchorage, Alaska), coffee cupper extraordinaire Ken Davids remarks on the characteristic winey ferment of La Voz's coffee. He writes: "Clear, sweet ferment tones are turned cherryish chocolate by the darkish roast. The winey ferment tones, giddy and buoyant when the cup is hot, flatten just a bit as the cup cools." He argues that this is not a coffee for "coffee purists. The winey ferment tones make this a coffee for the exuberantly open palate."[11] In an earlier review (2000), Davids romanticizes this winey ferment: he recalls watching farmers haul in their ripe fruit on their own backs or on the backs of horses, from their "remote" farms located on the "[r]ugged volcanic slopes above the mill and Lake Atitlan." He concludes that the "[l]ong, laborious trip down the mountainside obviously could allow plenty of time for a slight ferment to develop in some of the ripe, red fruit" (Davids 2000). In essence, Davids transforms La Voz's production practices into a marketable trait, one to which he assigns a new meaning—quality resulting from the combination of a rugged landscape and manual labor. He argues that many Guatemalan farms are located in remote places on harsh terrain, and therefore, we should excuse the quality defects of their coffee—for example, those caused by preprocessing fermentation—because these farmers are authentic small-scale producers. However, as a guarantor of La Voz's product and its quality, Green Mountain Coffee Roasters did not agree.

In January 2002, Green Mountain Coffee Roasters' vice president visited the cooperative with the owner of the group's then exporter, Excagua. During lunch at a restaurant in neighboring San Pedro, the vice president turned to Juan, then president of the cooperative, to explain in heavily accented Spanish: "We love the flavor of your coffee but the most important

FIGURE 6.3. *The new drying patios, built in the cooperative's wet mill, with a donation from GMCR.*

thing is the coffee quality. Some people like a fruity flavor but others don't. So we don't want to have it. Therefore you have to be careful of the quality." Juan hastily replied that he understood this well and that the cooperative was working hard to improve the coffee's quality. This fruity, or winey, undertone was the exact flavor characteristic GMCR was hoping to eliminate from La Voz's coffee when it donated US$15,000 to the cooperative for the construction of additional drying patios. The GMCR vice president traveled to San Juan to inaugurate the new patios and further discuss the necessary quality improvements. At 10:00 AM the morning of the visit I arrived at the beneficio only to find the members of the board of directors joking with one another as they waited (for more than an hour) for the vice president and his tour guides from Excagua to arrive. I joined the board members as they languidly sorted through a large pile of drying coffee beans on the patio. They were separating the brownish coffee beans, which had not been adequately depulped by the beneficio machinery (which was not working optimally at that point in time) from the pale beige beans, each of which was covered by a dry, translucent skin called parchment. This rather tedious quality control was interrupted by a shout of "They're coming" as the visitors entered the beneficio's gates.

The owner of Excagua began by walking GMCR's vice president around the new patios and explaining in English how they had been built. However, the vice president was much more interested in gathering the board members together for a photo, establishing early the general tenor of the day, which was lighthearted, ceremonial, and heavily photographed. I envisioned a framed copy of this photo hanging on both the water-stained, cement-block walls of the cooperative's office and the tidy, painted ones of the executive's office in Vermont. As a physical representation of the business relationships underlying transnational fair-trade coffee networks, these photographs constitute one tool used by participants to help craft the relationships of mutual dependence, cooperation, and trust on which fair trade's future depends. Before the awkward ribbon-cutting ceremony, Juan, as president, made a short speech: "The people of San Juan are very happy. There are people who destroy a lot like what we saw happen in the United States [9/11] but there are also people who construct. We at the cooperative are sorry to hear what happened in the United States. In the name of the 116 families we are thankful for the help you gave us for the patios and the bodegas so that we can produce *coffee of good quality*" (emphasis added). This statement demonstrates that Juan, and by extension the cooperative, understood the symbolic weight that the word "quality" carried with GMCR, even if they had never had the opportunity to cup their own coffee and most likely did not fully understand what characterized a winey/fruity flavor, why it is undesirable, and how it can be eliminated. In response to Juan, GMCR's vice president stated: "Speaking for the people of my company, I am very happy to be here with you. It's an investment in the quality of the coffee, your lives and the coffee business." The vice president then cut the ribbon and each member of the board of directors in turn cut a small piece for themselves.

After the ribbon was cut and the beneficio was toured the manager, Guillermo, asked the group to sit down so that he could present an accounting of the patio construction to the vice president. He began by handing the visitors manila folders with several sheets of paper in them and explained, "I want to explain how we spent all of the money that Elan and Green Mountain gave to us." This statement is interesting in that it signals the important mediating role occupied by the coffee importer in the initial years of GMCR's and La Voz's fair-trade coffee relationship. Theoretically, fair trade shortens the commodity chain and eliminates middlemen. However, this is a difficult goal to achieve, and at this point in time, both Elan and Excagua stood between the producer and the roaster as intermediaries and translators (literally, in the sense that the exporter was present to translate for the

GMCR vice president, but also symbolically). Today La Voz has its own export license and no longer sells its coffee through Excagua. However, coffee roasters with a minimal commitment to fair trade have been criticized for eschewing the opportunity to form close working relationships with cooperatives and relying instead on a chain of intermediaries to purchase the coffee for them.

Fair-trade coffee networks are increasingly being shaped by an audit culture that encompasses compliance with standards and social change in the form of "fixing" producers and the creation of new forms of personhood. The manila folders that Guillermo handed to the visitors are an example of how individuals and organizations come to think of themselves as "auditees" and subtly contribute to the growing audit mentality. In addition to the manila folder, Guillermo had handwritten the figures on large sheets of paper that he taped to the beneficio's walls. With the money provided by GMCR La Voz purchased materials and hired skilled masons. According to the manager's calculations, the cooperative contributed a nearly equal amount to the project in the form of sand and rocks (for the construction), the purchase of land, and unskilled labor (each cooperative member donated fifteen days of his own or a paid employee's labor to the project). After constructing the patios, the cooperative used the remaining funds and voluntary labor to build a large room to store coffee in parchment before it is transported to the dry mill in Guatemala City. After explaining the accounts Guillermo said: "I want you to have this information to present to your company. The work was completed in one month's time: it began on November twelfth and was finished on December fifteenth. I have photos, but only the negatives. I haven't had time to develop the film. I will send the photos to the United States with a final report." Although I cannot say this without a doubt, I intuitively felt that the GMCR vice president was not expecting such a precise record of the construction expenses (presumably, US$15,000 is a negligible donation for GMCR, the country's second-largest specialty coffee roaster and a publicly traded corporation). Instead, what GMCR hoped for was an improvement in the coffee quality and the erasure of the fermented flavor characteristics. The fact that GMCR continues to purchase La Voz's coffee indicates that the company remains pleased with the coffee. However, despite their quality-control efforts a more recent (2005) review of the Heifer Hope Blend (roasted by GMCR) echoes earlier reviews in describing the coffee as "dominated by a sweetly fermented fruit that reads as a rich, brandy-toned, cherryish chocolate. This lush flavor complex is heady in the aroma and sweetly refreshing in the cup. As the coffee cools, however, the ferment reveals a slight bitter edge." In a celebration of the symbolic over the material coffee attributes, the reviewer suggests that the coffee should be drunk by *"social idealists* who are lovers of the wilder and fruitier side of the coffee flavor spectrum."[12] The willingness of GMCR to continue roasting this coffee despite the ongoing presence of the undesirable flavor characteristics indicates that the company itself, which has chosen to firmly root its brand identity within the framework of social responsibility, recognizes the power of symbolic quality attributes and the good story that photographs of indigenous coffee farmers tell.

As fair-trade coffees become more firmly integrated into the specialty coffee market, it is highly likely that quality demands will continue to increase. Despite the fact that fair-trade detractors routinely complain that the coffees are poor quality, in a 2004 review of coffee cuppings, Ken Davids and GMCR's Lindsey Bolger found that fair-trade coffees "[a]re on average very good, but . . . may not offer quite the number of peak sensory experiences as non–fair trade coffees do." The average rating for all fair-trade coffees reviewed in 2004 was 87.3 out of 100 against 86.8, the average rating for all reviewed coffees (Davids and Bolger 2004). FLO certification standards require an existing demand for the producers' product, indicating that at least minimal quality control is enforced and the administrators possess commercialization experience. However, as Taylor points out, this conversely means that "[c]ooperatives lacking advisors and leaders with the language and other skills to be effective international interlocutors . . . [find] entry into fair trade markets much more difficult" (2002:3). When fair trade conforms to the dictates of the market and demands for quality, those growers with the highest quality product benefit the most, even if they are not the most vulnerable (Shreck 2002). This points to the often-repeated contradiction inherent to the fair-trade model: should the market be a charitable one designed to assist the most disenfranchised small-scale farmers, even if their products do not meet quality standards, or should the market instead provide the necessary training and development to those organizations already producing quality products and simply lacking a market? In an ideal world fair trade would accomplish both.

BUILDING RELATIONS OF TRUST AND DEPENDENCE: THE FUTURE OF FAIR-TRADE COFFEE NETWORKS

The relationships within fair-trade networks are strongly influenced by the fair-trade certification process, which is marked by a low degree of producer understanding and low levels of producer participation in the collective establishment of standards, and movement goals and processes of quality control, which entail surveillance of production and processing. These limitations are offset, however, by the market access and information that fair-trade coffee networks provide to small producers. Furthermore, without accepting the discipline required for participation in fair-trade coffee networks, producers cannot reap the benefits of working closely with agents in more advanced segments of the network, which is necessary to move into higher skill and higher value-added positions; for example, La Voz was able to acquire its own export license after working closely with an exporter and importer for many years. GMCR and La Voz have slowly built an increasingly strong working relationship that is not threatened by the demands of transnational commerce, language barriers, and cultural differences. For more than a decade more than 20 percent of GMCR employees from all segments of the business have traveled to Central America for Coffee Source Trips. Steve Sabol, who planned and hosted many of these trips, observed: "The effect is profound. I have seen it bring people to tears. The knowledge of the care that goes into the coffee is important, but when they see the social part of it, and how dependent these growers are on us being a quality partner it hits right home, the obligation we have to do well" (Pendergrast 2004). Although GMCR's relationship with La Voz is not without its flaws, the experience indicates that it is possible to work within fair-trade networks to promote exchange relationships rooted in cooperation and mutual dependence, thereby contributing to the movement's long-term goal of crafting a viable alternative to the neoliberal economic paradigm.

The cooperative members' understandings of the fair-trade coffee network for the most part begin and end with their relationships with certifiers, importers, and roasters. These relationships form the core of the network and without fully investigating them; we cannot truly understand the impact of fair trade on local communities nor can we adequately assess larger movement goals. However, many academics researching fair trade have systematically underemphasized the enduring importance of mediating actors within the commodity networks, such as certifiers, importers and roasters, preferring instead to analytically privilege the vague, and largely theoretical, links uniting producers and consumers.[13]

In multiple studies, market access and information is identified as a primary benefit of fair trade for producer participants (Shreck 2002; Moore 2004; Paul 2005; Lyon 2006, 2007). Key actors in commodity chains—in this case, Elan's agricultural monitor, Carlos, and various GMCR employees—manage the interfirm division of labor and support the capacities of producers in their efforts to upgrade their activities. The certification process and quality demands discussed above require a stronger form of coordination between roasters and producers in fair-trade coffee networks. This coordination is shaped by the long-term relations promoted by fair-trade organizations and the structural supply-and-demand mismatch, which provides considerable power to roasters to decide which coffee farmers should have access to fair-trade markets and which should be excluded from the system. Despite these power asymmetries, strong coordination entails considerable upgrading opportunities for those producers who are able to participate (Muradian and Pelupessy 2005). La Voz capitalized on this when it applied for, and was granted, its own exporting license.

Through the steady visits from the roaster, importer, and exporter the employees and members of La Voz honed their communication skills, improved their business practices, and learned valuable information about quality and certification demands. Cooperatives can gain a competitive advantage by actively fostering ongoing close contact with northern buyers and teaching their members foreign market preferences and international standards for price, quality, and delivery of export merchandise. Additionally, the desire to maintain long-term relationships with buyers can provide an incentive for cooperatives to improve their product quality by investing in infrastructural and production improvements. These direct trade relationships allow fair-trade producers to bypass the often exploitative local buyers and enable groups to bargain more effectively with large buyers such as Starbucks and Walmart. In summary, fair trade's close alliance with coffee roasters, retailers, and consumers and its focus on supporting access to new markets facilitate a wider distribution of benefits to small-scale producers (Taylor 2002, 2004).

The close working relationship that some fair-trade coffee roasters, such as GMCR, maintain with producers is not entirely altruistic. These relationships can help secure roasters' long-term access to superior coffee while improving the quality of the product they are already buying. The frequent visits provide opportunities to gather information about groups and take photos of members that are both used for marketing purposes. Fair-trade consumption in the North is predicated on consumers' access to information regarding the conditions of production and increasingly the social circumstances and cultural traditions of producers themselves (Lyon 2006). This gathering and sharing of information helps strengthen the networks of connectivity linking southern producers and northern consumers. Roasters use descriptions of these relationships with the producers they buy from as a signal to consumers of their commitment to equitable trade, human rights, and development in producer communities.

Over the course of research in San Juan, I witnessed the cooperative's attempts to establish strong working relationships with their buyers and present themselves as business partners rather than charitable recipients of foreign aid and technical assistance. One of the most frequent tactics the cooperative management and board used to express their appreciation for their northern buyers was presenting them with ceremonial gifts and *recuerdos* (mementos) in the form of local weavings and paintings of lake vistas. For example, after the manager presented the visitors with a thorough accounting of the patio construction, Juan, the cooperative's president, stood to say: "It's a pleasure to meet you, and this coffee work, this international friendship, is very important in our organization. There aren't words enough to thank you for your help. We prepared a small painting for the company and we want you to receive this." Another member of the board of directors, Alberto, added: "You should take this message back to your company: that we are proud and thankful for everything we've received. It's important to us that you trust us and it's important to us that you came here to see how we lived." After ceremonial photos were taken of the GMCR vice president holding the painting, a member of the internal committee in charge of the construction project stood and presented him with another painting, explaining, "The other painting was for the company but this one is for you."

In light of the corruption so pervasive in Guatemalan business and politics, it is understandable that cooperative members place a high degree of importance on trust and mutuality. Despite the signing of Guatemala's Peace Accords in 1996, rural Guatemala remains, at times, a dangerous and uncertain place. In 2000, a truck filled with La Voz's coffee was stolen on its way to the Guatemala City dry mill owned by Excagua. For the cooperative, this represented a substantial financial loss. In light of the corruption and inefficiency plaguing the judicial system within the country, the group felt powerless to recoup their coffee. They were therefore surprised when the owner of Excagua presented them with a check for the value of the stolen coffee. Although they had known the coffee was insured, they never expected to receive any of this money. The exporter told me that when he visited months later, the board of directors and management celebrated their partnership by forcing him to visit a local *cantina*, or bar, after signing the next year's contract. Guatemala's class and ethnic boundaries are firmly established and dictate that wealthy, urban businessmen rarely share liminal moments with rural, indigenous farmers. While telling the story to me and a group of cooperative members over lunch, the owner of Excagua entertained us by mimicking his own drunkenness, making fun of his wobbly attempts to board a waiting boat after the celebration.

The cooperative's attempts to cultivate relational governance based on relationships of trust and mutual dependence are also strategic attempts to secure a long-term market within the notoriously volatile international coffee market while potentially strengthening their own power within the coffee network. This strategy resembles that employed by the Maine lobstermen analyzed by Acheson (1985), who contends that because lobstermen have little idea where their lobsters actually go or how many hands they pass through on their way to the consumer, they suspect the worst. Lobstermen traditionally manage these uncertainties and market risks by forming long-term relationships and ties with one particular dealer. The risk-management strategy employed by the lobstermen and cooperative members supports Plattner's assertion that reciprocal economic relationships are instrumental responses to social constraints and reduce risk in transactions that would otherwise be too uncertain or expensive to undertake (1985). Analyses such as this challenge the popular image of markets populated by autonomous actors. Economic anthropologists and sociologists have long argued that when firms deal with each other over any significant length of time, they commonly abandon the impersonality and autonomy of the market and instead establish relatively durable relationships with a clear moral component, criteria of fairness, and expectations of trust (Dore 1983; Granovetter 1985; Carrier 1997).

Although these emergent relationships rooted in trust and mutual dependence help to counteract the "fixing" of fair-trade producers that the certification process seems to inevitably entail, more concrete steps could be taken within fair-trade organizations to help curtail the negative impacts of standardization and auditing. One way to potentially ameliorate the negative impacts of fair-trade certification is to adopt a participatory social-auditing model that emphasizes the involvement of workers and workers' organizations in the process of code implementation and assessment (Auret and Barrientos 2006). Participatory social auditing works to develop partnerships between different actors (such as management, members, and auditors) and a locally suitable approach to improving conditions and addressing weaknesses. Auret and Barrientos explain: "Snapshot audits tend to focus on formal management compliance rather than helping to support genuine improvement . . . They tend to pick up 'visible' issues, such as health and safety, but often fail to pick up issues that are not easily verified . . . They are often insensitive to issues of concern to women workers" (2006:129). On the other hand, participatory social auditing, where workers are integrated within every stage of the auditing process, including (and especially) during feedback decisions is one way of improving the effectiveness of certification codes (Smith and Dolan 2006).

Ironically I have more faith in the future ability of producer/roaster relationships to empower smallholders in the global economy than I do in the fair-trade certification process. However, FLO and fair-trade certification itself could be transformed into a useful tool for producers if it were more participatory and helped groups identify problems and areas for future growth. These possibilities for change are discussed in the book's conclusion.

7

Marketing the Maya:
Fair Trade's Producer/Consumer Relationships

Beginning in May and lasting through October, Guatemala's rainy season was so ferocious that it forced me to rearrange my daily activities. I am not an overly religious person; however, while making a late afternoon return from an interview in Panajachel during a particularly strong storm, I found myself praying with the elderly Kaqchikel woman who clutched at my raincoat as wave after wave of water soaked us. After that day I began to limit afternoon appointments and instead generally stayed close to home. When possible, I conducted interviews in my neighborhood and always kept an umbrella close. Sometimes I spent the stormy hours catching up on transcribing interviews and typing field notes. But more often than I care to admit, I succumbed to laziness and spent many an hour watching the storms roll in over the peaks of the looming volcanoes while thumbing through the used paperback mysteries I bought cheaply from a gringo who owned a mail service in Panajachel. One of these afternoons my neighbor's eight-year-old son, Miguel, came to visit. We lay sprawled on my bed, idly flipping through the glossy coffee-trade magazines I had brought with me from the United States. The near deafening noise of the torrential rain on my tin roof left us to our own thoughts. Suddenly, my drowsy reverie was disrupted by Miguel, who excitedly began exclaiming, "Look! Look! It's my grandfather." I laughed at his foolishness—of course his grandfather was not in the *Tea and Coffee Trade Journal*: he had never left Guatemala, and despite the fact that he was on the cooperative's board of directors, he could barely speak Spanish. Miguel shoved the magazine into my lap and pointed to a full-page advertisement for a U.S. coffee importer. It featured a color photograph of a *camepsino* using a wooden rake to spread coffee on a concrete patio for drying. I stared intently at the photograph—only the man's profile was shown and at first I was sure Miguel was mistaken. However, upon close inspection I recognized Don José's lined face and his trademark fedora, the same hat he had me painstakingly take a picture of months earlier so I could buy a similar one for him when I traveled to California for the Specialty Coffee Association of America's annual meeting. Miguel and I ripped the advertisement out of the magazine and scurried across the footpath to find Don José, who was relaxing in his house. He was surprised (and pleased) to see his photo in this U.S. advertisement. However, he had no idea how it came to appear there. The importer did not purchase coffee from La Voz and had no economic or advisory relationship with the cooperative, and clearly Don José was never asked whether he wanted his photograph used. Although Don José was (perhaps surprisingly) not offended by this unauthorized use of his image, I found it troubling and reminiscent of the foreign tourists who flock to Guatemala in search of authentic culture, weavings, and colorful photographs.[1] As Little explains, some tourists are under the impression that literally everything in Guatemala is for sale—they believe that they can purchase anything or take a picture of anyone, that this is their right (Little 2004).[2]

This advertisement is representative of the ways in which producer and consumer relationships are mediated within the fair-trade coffee market. Don José's image was used to signal the symbolic attributes of the coffee sold by the importer: an unidentified, "everyman" campesino, his labor is representative of attention to detail and the authenticity of the coffee's source of origin. Of course, there is no reciprocity here: small-scale coffee producers such as Don José are never handed glossy magazines depicting the consumers who sip their coffee. In contrast with producers, fair-trade consumers are well-educated by retailers and roasters regarding their role in the market. Unlike the place-bound coffee producers, they are free to travel both metaphorically, through their coffee consumption, and literally, as a result of their high incomes and unrestricted access to Guatemala. However, in general, the producer/consumer relationship in fair-trade coffee networks is heavily mediated by advertising material and the roaster and importer liaisons who celebrate symbolic quality attributes and shape consumer preferences. Attempts to understand fair-trade producer/consumer relationships are generally framed by fair-trade advocates and researchers by two common discourses: first, that fair-trade consumption emerges from the political choices and conscious reflexivity of northern consumers, and second, that it defetishizes coffee by revealing the social and environmental conditions of coffee production. There is some validity to each of these arguments; however, they fail to fully capture the complexity of producers' relationships with northern consumers. They cannot explain what it means to be Maya in the world market (versus in the cooperative and the community). Nor do they explore the "identity economy" (Comaroff and Comaroff 2009) of fair trade in which market relationships are structured by the reinforcement of differences and northern impressions of community, small-scale farmer poverty, and in some cases indigeneity.

This chapter delves into these complex questions to demonstrate that despite fair trade's claims to shorten the commodity chain, the relationships between fair-trade producers and consumers are strongly regulated by intermediaries. In the case I analyze here, important intermediaries include the employees of Green Mountain Coffee Roasters who regularly visit La Voz to monitor the coffee's quality. In addition, advertising materials, such as the educational videos displayed on the GMCR website, shape the nature of producer/consumer relationships in fair-trade coffee networks and also the motivations of the fair-trade advocates who work to grow the market. This focus on the "middlemen" of the fair-trade coffee networks challenges the supposedly clean dichotomy between producer and consumer spheres. Many advocates who celebrate fair trade as a social movement uniting dispersed producers and consumers are blind to these undercurrents within fair-trade coffee networks. However, the role of roaster and importer intermediaries must be central to our debates over the future of the movement for without them there are no fair-trade coffee networks.

Rather than forging equitable producer/consumer relationships rooted in trust and participation, fair trade creates an "imaginary community" that unevenly unites producers and consumers and is nurtured by advertising and the fair-trade mirror in which consumers' fantasies about producers' lives are reflected back to them in their coffee cups. Anderson first coined the term "imagined community" to describe contemporary nations that are imagined "because the members of even the smallest nation will never know most of their fellow-members, meet them, or even hear of them, yet in the minds of each lives the image of their communion" (1983:6). According to Anderson, among the most powerful domains or arenas in which these imagined connections were forged was in the print media. Clearly fair-trade coffee networks are not akin to nation-states. However, they are similar in the sense that consumers are motivated to participate in these transnational economic relationships by images of the impoverished small-scale farmers who are struggling to survive in a volatile and fundamentally unjust market. These images are circulated among consumers via print capitalism (advertising, journalism, and informational websites). The fair-trade imaginary community is by necessity uneven in the sense that producers by and large do not participate in the circulation of these images nor do they consume them. However, there are instances in which the members of La Voz actively shape their own imaginary by foregrounding their indigenous identity and the symbolic quality attributes of their coffee. In critically assessing the nature of the producer/consumer relationships I am not suggesting that we should attempt to distinguish the falsity or genuineness of this transnational community but instead the style in which it is imagined (Anderson 1983:6). I am critical of fair trade's "political ecological imaginary" and the ways in which images and descriptions of farmers are used to develop a moral economy between fair-trade producers and consumers. However, without doubt this is preferable to the current shift in the "imagineering" of fair trade (Routledge 1997)—from poor farmers to touristic landscapes of quality and, more recently, to movie, television, and music celebrity endorsers—which signals a parallel shift in the cultural politics of fair trade itself (Goodman 2010).

The meaning of commodities and markets is not solely created by consumers but also by producers. However, there is a conceptual flaw in the study of global commodities that is increasingly shaped by a de facto acceptance of a division of global labor into "producers" and "consumers" in which consumers are the privileged subjects who shape their own destinies through their actions. As Weiss points out, the flaw in this model is that it grants consumers the "luxury of giving value to things of their world, while producers are enchained to the dictates of an overarching system" (2003:6). Although members of La Voz cannot control how their coffee is advertised, they do actively influence how both their coffee and they themselves are perceived by northern consumers. They help shape the meaning of their coffee in the marketplace by strategically foregrounding their indigenous identity and stressing their own authenticity as Maya coffee producers. In essence, in a globalizing economy, cooperative members are slowly transforming their marginality and cultural identity into a means of communicating with the world while simultaneously reinscribing significance in the local (Little 2004; Canessa 2005).

FAIR-TRADE CONSUMPTION: POLITICS AND REFLEXIVITY

Much of the academic literature on fair-trade consumption argues that it is motivated by the political choices and conscious reflexivity of northern consumers. This conscious decision making is represented as a radical departure from previous consumption patterns as fair-trade consumers are said to use their purchasing power to express ethical or political assessments of favorable and unfavorable business and government practices. Like other forms of ethical and environmental consumption, fair-trade consumption is argued to reflect the trends of globalization and individualization that prompt citizens to "create new arenas for responsibility-taking" (Micheletti 2003:5) while forging political and ethical identities. However, they are not simply protesting at a symbolic level but instead are hoping to transform economic exchanges into vehicles for the promotion of human rights, environmental conservation, and trade equity.

In recent years, U.S. fair-trade advocates followed the lead of other consumer campaigns and advocacy groups and employed the rhetoric of globalization as a symbolic resource (Cunningham 1999:599). The success of this strategy is summed up by a *New York Times* reporter who described fair-trade coffee as "a pet project of the anti-globalization movement" (Bendheim 2002). As anthropologists have pointed out, globalizing discourses have proven useful to both movements of resistance and projects of governance.[3] Fair-trade market advocates at Global Exchange and TransFair USA consciously framed fair trade as a means to channel consumer anti-globalization sentiment into concrete action. Keck and Sikkink argue, "[A]n effective frame must show that a given state of affairs is neither natural nor accidental, identify the responsible party or parties, and propose credible solutions" (1999:96). Fair-trade advocates, roasters, and organizers did exactly this. The framing included concise press releases and activist kits that explained to consumers the effects of the coffee crisis, the disadvantaged position of small-scale coffee producers within the market, and the small ways individual consumers could make a difference. For example, the director of Global Exchange's fair-trade coffee campaign published an article strategically framing fair trade as an alternative to free trade: "As this country's first product with an independent monitoring system to ensure against sweatshop-style labor abuses, coffee represents an important alternative model to the free trade practices advocated by the iron triangle of the global sweatshop economy: the World Bank, the IMF, and the WTO" (James 2000). Similarly, a flyer distributed by activists in fall 2001 in Seattle described five ways "consumers can help change the world": "Buy only fair trade certified coffee, ask for fair trade coffee at your local café and grocery store, make sure that your local workplace or place of worship serves fair trade certified coffee, encourage your community organization or church to purchase fair trade products for fundraisers [and] write a letter to the editor about your concern for coffee farmers and your commitment to seeing more fair trade coffee in supermarkets and local cafes." Talking points such as these gained such widespread currency that the misleading "fact" that coffee is the second-most valuable commodity in the world was repeated again and again by advocates and journalists.

This successful framing of fair-trade coffee involved leveraging consumer power against coffee roasters reluctant to embrace fair trade. With its launch in 1998, TransFair USA identified roasters as the key link in the fair-trade coffee networks they hoped to create and promptly initiated a consumer campaign targeting the specialty coffee industry. It is important to stress that this campaign was created by a certifying agency rather than concerned citizens. Because of its high profile as a publicly traded corporation, Starbucks became the first, and most influential, target. The specialty coffee giant had already faced consumer protests in 1994, when the United States–Guatemala Labor Education Project picketed outlets, distributing brochures informing customers that the retail price of one pound of Starbucks roasted coffee was equivalent to a Guatemalan coffee plantation laborer's weekly wage. Although some Guatemalan coffee also ends up in the blends sold by the "can" coffee companies, Starbucks was the most visible high-volume Guatemalan coffee customer and therefore an ideal target for activists protesting labor conditions in the Guatemalan industry.

Capitalizing on a publicity wave initiated by KGO San Francisco's February 2000 investigative report of the low wages and child labor found on Guatemalan coffee plantations, Global Exchange petitioned Starbucks stockholders at their 2000 general meeting in Seattle, urging them to roast fair-trade coffee. That week Starbucks announced a onetime shipment of 75,000 pounds, derisively labeled by Global Exchange as a mere "drop in the cup." In April 2000, Starbucks agreed to offer fair-trade coffee in each of its outlets three days before Global Exchange planned to launch its large-scale consumer campaign (James 2000). During a 2001 interview, the vice-president of corporate social responsibility for Starbucks recalled that one fair-trade campaign leader told her, "You're not public enemy number one but your customers care about these types of issues." As an indisputable industry leader, Starbucks opened the fair-trade floodgates with this decision. In short, the consumer campaign against Starbucks was an influential factor in the decisions made by many smaller specialty roasters to enter the fair-trade market. For example, one smaller coffee roaster told me, "I feel strongly that fair trade would not be where it is today if it weren't for Global Exchange taking Starbucks to the mat."

Fair-trade advocates also employed paid forms of advertising to spread their message, for example, TransFair's commercial featuring the actor Martin Sheen and Oxfam's "Make Trade Fair" campaign, which featured photos of musicians and actors doused in fair-trade agricultural products, such as milk, chocolate, coffee, and wheat. This trend toward celebrity fair-trade endorsements by global stars has grown more pronounced in recent years; for example, Coldplay's lead singer, Chris Martin, visits certified cooperatives on press junkets and scrawls "Make Trade Fair" on his body during performances (Goodman 2010). Increasingly the subaltern speaks through the globally recognized megastar and this trend toward celebrity endorsements presents the danger of transforming fair trade into a virtual house of mirrors where our own consumerist subjectivities are simply reflected in the newly embodied cultural politics of the celebrity spectacle (Goodman 2010).

Fair trade's current glossy and polished advertising campaigns mask a history of true grassroots promotional efforts, which in the United States date back decades to the early efforts of 100 percent fair-trade roasters, such as Equal Exchange.[4] During my research in Seattle, local advertising and educational efforts included tables at community markets, radio spots, and event sponsoring. Advocates also urged community organizations, such as the Church Council of Greater Seattle and local labor unions, to brew only certified fair-trade coffee during meetings. In 2001, the Northwest Sustainable Coffee Campaign (discussed in Chapter 5), initiated through a partnership between TransFair USA, Seattle Audubon, and the Songbird Foundation, sponsored concerts across Seattle to publicize fair-trade and shade-grown coffee. During an interview in 2001, one of the campaign directors explained: "Culture is moved largely by icons and the nature of communication is fundamental. This fall we'll have . . . community coffee house concerts. We want to show you these iconic photographs of the birds [and] the people who grow coffee for you and why they are important to you." These marketing tactics attempted to imprint on consumers the transnational links between themselves and the locales where their coffee is produced—to encourage them to acknowledge their own subject position in a globalizing world. Fair-trade advocates also enlist college students across the country to assist their campaign. TransFair USA and Oxfam International published a fair-trade resource and action guide for campus organizers and the United Students for Fair Trade (USFT) was founded in 2003. As Kimberly Easson, TransFair's former marketing director, told a *Seattle Times* reporter shortly thereafter, "I think it's a natural fit, when they understand the situation of farmers, for students to want to do something" (Bastell 2004). By 2004, the organization had affiliates on more than 100 college campuses, and more than 200 colleges and universities were offering fair-trade coffee and at least 15 were solely brewing it (Capone 2004).

As stated above, many scholars maintain that fair-trade market expansion is a direct result of the political choices and reflexivity of consumers. However, a more nuanced understanding of how specialty coffee roasters and fair-trade advocates influence the market problematizes this assumed correlation. Although fair-trade coffee advocates are also consumers, not all fair-trade consumers are well-educated activists. In light of the influence of advocacy groups and coffee roasters, fair trade is perhaps better understood as a "consumer-dependent" movement for change rather than a consumer-led movement (Goodman 2004:901). However, this does not discount the probability that some fair-trade consumers *are* engaged in a consciously political project. It is critical to treat consumer motivations as an empirical question, not something that can be determined a priori.

Fair-trade coffee forms part of the "visible part" of culture (Douglas and Isherwood 1979:66). It reflects cultural assumptions and anxieties surrounding free trade, corporate globalization, and economic injustices and in the process politicizes everyday consumption practices. The strategic framing of fair-trade coffee described above provides consumers with a relatively simple, concrete course of action. This framing is firmly situated within discourses of globalization and human rights that are predicated on the strategic goal of making us recognize that global poverty is everyone's responsibility. In other words, the modes of connectivity that fair-trade networks foster do not occur in a vacuum but instead operate within a matrix of emergent discourses of global connectivity. In the experience-based economy,[5] consumers can purchase fair-trade coffee to combat their feelings of political fatalism and chronic insecurity that many argue result from the sheer scale of contemporary social and economic change and the inability of national governments to control or resist it (Beck 1992). This sentiment was repeatedly expressed during my interviews with roasters and advocates. For example, during an interview, one fair-trade coffee roaster contextualized his business decisions within national political concerns. He stated: "Where do you recruit terrorist cells from? It's all part of better world security." Similarly, an interviewed advocate explained how she came to channel her anti-WTO sentiment into fair-trade coffee, "I think I could have gone a lot of different directions but . . . it was a concrete issue, it [was] tangible, everybody drinks coffee in Seattle and it also encompasses a lot of things I care about."

The political nature of fair-trade consumption is predicated on a novel combination of what Giddens (1991) terms life politics and emancipatory politics. Giddens maintains that lifestyles—which he defines as "a more or less integrated set of practices which an individual embraces, not only because such practices fulfill utilitarian needs, but because they give material form to a particular narrative of self-identity" (1991:81)—have gained primary importance in projecting, understanding, and experiencing local conceptions of modernity. Consumers who consciously purchase fair-trade coffee are engaging in a form of self-directed life politics. Their political decisions flow from their freedom of choice and their ability to self-actualize while constructing a morally justifiable form of life in the context of global interdependence (Giddens 1991:215). However, they are also engaging in emancipatory politics by focusing their attention on the divisions between human beings and international power differentials. Emancipatory political projects center on the reduction or elimination of exploitation, inequality, or oppression and attempt to address the inequitable distribution of power and resources (Giddens 1991:211, 215).

This combination of life politics and emancipatory politics characterizing fair-trade consumption is evident in the ways that interviewed advocates situated their interest in fair trade within their lifestyle choices, their sense of self, and their vision of the world. Several interviewed advocates identified with specific religious traditions. For example, one explained: "I really identify with my faith. It's part of my purpose in the world—service to correct injustices. Economic injustices seem to be the worst injustices in the world." Other interviewed advocates described fair-trade coffee as one of many causes they support. One described himself as "a New Left conservative." He explained: "I try to take all Left positions. In other words, if I'm at a party I'm to the left of everybody there but I am a conservative because I utilize conservative methodologies to get to my position. I really want to be political but I'm just sort of in retreat right now. But that's the thing that really interested me in coffee."

Access to the means of self-actualization and the ability to pursue life politics is informed by class divisions and the inequitable distribution of resources. Fair-trade consumers are able to engage in life politics while their producer counterparts, struggling against political and economic inequalities, do not enjoy that luxury. Several interviewed advocates struggled with this aspect of fair trade. One described her occasional doubts: "Coffee is such a luxury. Coffee is something you don't even need. And, sometimes I think that maybe it's kind of petty. I'd remind myself that no it's not because it's the second highest traded commodity next to oil, and that's huge." The disjuncture between consumer life politics and producer livelihoods reflects the questions raised by critics of fair trade who maintain that fair trade normalizes global inequalities, reenacts colonial trade relationships, and relegates southern participants to mono-crop export production.[6]

Ethical consumption enables consumers to conceptually reconcile the gap between the haves and have-nots by re-embedding affective ties and equitable economic relationships in abstract exchange relations (Dolan 2005b). However, as Giddens points out, virtually all questions of life politics also raise problems of an emancipatory sort and "struggles to emancipate oppressed groups can help liberate others by promoting attitudes of mutual tolerance which in the end could benefit everyone" (1991:230). Therefore, to the extent that the life politics of fair-trade consumption can foster an understanding of and appreciation for cultural differences through more equitable international trade relationships, it will prove to be a worthwhile project.

DEFETISHIZATION AND MODES OF CONNECTIVITY

At the end of February 2002, Guillermo, La Voz's then manager, called me into his office. He met me at the door with a bewildered look, telling me that two U.S. university students had arrived that morning and he needed my translation help because he could not understand their Spanish. I observed the students tell Guillermo, in relatively clear Spanish, their desire to "help out" the coffee farmers they had heard so much about during a fair-trade campaign on their campus. In English, the students explained that through their activist work and the promotional pamphlets they distributed across their community, they had developed a deep sense of solidarity with the cooperative members they thought of as poverty stricken and wanted to help them pick coffee during this period of crisis. It occurred to me that the manager was confused not so much by the students' Spanish but more by their very presence. Not only did their disheveled clothing, dirty hands, and straggly hair offend local notions of personal grooming and appropriate dress but their unannounced arrival from abroad and lack of a formal letter of introduction from an entity known to the cooperative made it difficult for Guillermo to categorically place these visitors. Did they deserve the respect granted to coffee buyers or the disdain directed toward the thousands of wandering adolescent gringos that visited the lakeshores of this tourist region each year? Not surprisingly the students were quickly placed in the latter category by cooperative members. They did pick coffee—for all of two days. I bumped into them nearly a week later at an Internet café in neighboring San Pedro where they explained that the demanding physical nature of the skilled manual labor and the indifferent local welcome was not what they had expected and so they quickly found other diversions. Without doubt these students had felt a true connection with these distant coffee producers; why else would they have traveled so far in search of authentic small-scale farmer poverty? However, the bewildered, and even cold, reception they received indicates that the supposed "modes of connectivity" (Whatmore and Thorne 1997) linking producers and consumers in fair-trade networks are figurative. In fact, their physical presence in San Juan disrupted the balance of the fair-trade imaginary community and laid bare the tenacious nature of these connections.

It is often argued that the true counter-hegemonic power of fair trade lies in its ability to connect northern consumers and southern producers within commodity networks (e.g., see Raynolds 2002). However, there is little empirical research on the exact nature of these modes of connectivity: *how* are the relationships formed by fair-trade producers and consumers nurtured? In fact, these modes of connectivity are similar to Anderson's "imagined communities," maintained largely by print media and coffee experts such as fair-trade institutional representatives, exporters, importers, and roasters. It is undeniably the case that in the United States, Global Exchange, TransFair, United Students for Fair Trade, and individual roasters have performed an exceptional task of educating consumers about fair-trade coffee producers, the poverty they face, and the necessity of fairer market relations. The success of this effort is evidenced in the ease with which these passionate undergraduates packed their bags and showed up at the cooperative's doorstep: they were motivated not only by an adolescent sense of adventure and expanding frontiers of possibilities but also by a genuine desire to "help out" while experiencing the lives of bona fide small-scale coffee farmers. However, the view from the opposite end of the fair-trade coffee network is not quite as crystal clear: members of La Voz had great difficulty imagining the consumers who ultimately drank their coffee. In their eyes, the fair-trade network by and large begins and ends with the importers and roasters who buy their coffee.

The management of knowledge—or what different actors connected in spatially extensive networks of production, exchange, and consumption know about their place in the network and their connections to other actors—is a constitutive feature of the fair-trade coffee network and a significant source of value creation (Foster 2002, 2008). It is not so much intrinsic features of fair-trade coffee that distinguish it from the growing crowd of uncertified specialty coffees but instead the trust consumers place in its symbolic value—its *fairness*. Therefore, fair-trade products are given significance and gain value because they are more than just food. Knowledge of where the products are produced and how they are connected to wider cultural and political trends is a critical component of consumer choice and participation. It is the consumers who create fair-trade coffee's value through their meaningful use of the product in their daily lives and social relationships.

The fair-trade market is celebrated for creating modes of connectivity and re-embedding producer-consumer relationships through humanized market mechanisms. Through this process, commodities such as coffee are arguably defetishized as the hidden layers of information are peeled away to reveal the social and environmental conditions of the commodity's production.[7] In other words, the fair-trade certification process and market exchange provide consumers with an unprecedented degree of information about commodity production and presumably producer identities.[8] However, although northern roasters, retailers, and advocates may attempt to personalize products by offering consumers limited information about their production, they also engage in the commodification of difference (Goodman 2004) and the recuperation of "familiar discourses of 'self' and 'other'" (Dolan 2005b). Consumers purchase fair-trade coffee in order to assist southern producers, who are fundamentally different from these consumers. The social relations signified when fair-trade coffee is defetishized are those of charity at a distance.[9] Despite their successful participation in the global coffee market, fair-trade producers will always be conceived of as just that, producers, and although consumers might think of them as part of our daily lives, it is a part that is partitioned and discontinuous from our domestic concerns.

Douglas and Isherwood suggest that instead of accepting the premise that goods are primarily needed for subsistence and competitive display, "let us assume that they are needed for making visible and stable the categories of culture they write" (1979:59). Consumption has long offered one of the most palpable realms for the West to distinguish itself from the Rest (Colloredo-Mansfeld 2005), and fair-trade consumers are called to ethical action through demonstrations of cultural difference, not sameness (Dolan 2005:370b). Cosmopolitan fair-trade consumers seek to immerse themselves in other cultures and engage with the "other" through their coffee consumption. Like other forms of ethical consumption, consumers purchasing fair-trade coffee mark themselves as savvy members of an informed transnational community, concerned with the lives of disenfranchised coffee producers in exotic locales. In doing so, they make visible categorical differences between the consuming self and the producing other.

Embedded economic relationships are rooted in proximate contact, familiarity, and trust (Polanyi 1985). However, within the fair-trade market, coffee consumers and producers rarely, if ever, enjoy actual proximate interaction. Therefore, the modes of connectivity linking producers and consumers are largely symbolic ones formed in the North through marketing, and fair-trade coffee networks are imaginary rather than actual communities. The rare face-to-face meetings of producers and consumers are sponsored and mediated by organizations such as Global Exchange and TransFair USA, which periodically organize tours of the United States for fair-trade cooperative members during which they visit coffee shops, universities, and churches across the country. These events provide consumers with the opportunity to shake producers' hands and hear their stories. Although there is no quantifiable data demonstrating their impact on fair-trade consumption patterns, several interviewed advocates found them highly motivating. For example, one recalled how encouraged she was by a visiting cooperative manager who spoke about the clinic and school the group was building with its fair-trade profits.

These symbolic modes of connectivity linking consumers and producers seem relatively strong when interpreted by scholars who stress the ways in which fair trade is understood by consumers and activists in the North (Shreck 2002). However, although consumers are provided with images and descriptions of fair-trade producers, the members of La Voz had little knowledge of the consumers who bought their coffee. Despite their ongoing participation in fair-trade coffee networks, cooperative members held, at best, a confused fantasy of U.S. consumers, informed largely by U.S. television programs and contact with anthropologists, Peace Corps volunteers, and the hordes of tourists, on the whole, young, budget-conscious travelers in search of adventure, "authentic" Maya culture, and cheap drugs. At times, interviewed cooperative members exhibited an almost antagonistic attitude toward their consumers. For example, La Voz's former manager attended the 2002 Specialty Coffee Association of America's annual conference. Upon his return Guillermo regaled members with stories of the coffee shop he visited, where cups of the cooperative's coffee sold for US$3.00 each. During interviews, several members recounted this price in disbelief. One incredulously demanded of me, "How many cups of coffee can be made from one pound?" In asking this question, he acknowledged the vast differences between himself and the wealthy consumers in the North. Similar findings are reported by Fisher, who writes that the young male beekeepers she researched "[s]pent hours examining Oxfam, Traidcraft [a UK-based fair trade retailer], and Body Shop advertising leaflets, to [her] extreme embarrassment and their incredulity. Widely held images of Europe as the land of milk and honey were confirmed" (1997:132).

It is crucial to remember that the marketing and educational materials provided to fair-trade consumers are designed primarily with the goal of increasing their purchases. However, capitalist intentions aside, it is reasonable to assume that coffee roasters also hope to foster connections between the consumers and producers that they themselves unite by revealing the social and environmental conditions of production. It is arguable whether this translates into a truly defetishized coffee product. Furthermore, even if the product was completely defetishized, meaning there were no gaps or middlemen in the commodity network and consumers purchased the coffee directly from producers (the way that consumers buy directly from local producers at farmers' markets), "Maya culture" or another aspect of producer identity would most likely remain fetishized. As distances between consumers and producers increase, the negotiation of the tension between knowledge and ignorance becomes a critical determinant in the flow of commodities (Appadurai 1986). Even with the best intentions, most people do not have access to all of the information they need to make moral choices about their consumption. Fetishism in the Marxist sense does not refer simply to the masking of the production of particular commodities; it also encapsulates the process through which commodities are possessed of a "mystical character" through the objectifying effect of the system of exchange (Gottdiener 2000, in Goss 2004). In foregrounding producer identities and other symbolic quality attributes, fair-trade marketing deepens this "mystical character," turning commodities such as coffee and the rural labor that produces it into a yet another spectacle for northern consumers (Bryant and Goodman 2004).[10]

Fair-trade consumption—and the re-embedded economic relationships and modes of connectivity it arguably fosters—is rife with contradictions. This becomes even more evident when we take a closer look at fair-trade coffee marketing. For example, a behind-the-scenes examination of how promotional videos are conceived demonstrates the ways in which producer cultures are fetishized as strategic images are used and daily reality is eschewed.

FAIR-TRADE MARKETING

According to Whatmore and Thorne, within the modes of connectivity structuring fair-trade market relationships, "stories are told of partnership, alliance, and fairness" (1997:295). In their study of a fair-trade coffee commodity network, they cite the Cafédirect freeze-dried coffee label, which states: "[T]his is a fair trade product . . . more of the money you pay . . . goes directly to the small-scale coffee farmers . . . Fair trade means coffee growing communities can afford to invest in healthcare, education and agriculture." The authors argue, *"These words* establish a connection between those who grow and those who buy Cafédirect coffee" (1997:298, emphasis added). In fact, because fair-trade coffee consumers and producers rarely, if ever, enjoy actual physical interaction, by and large it is exactly these words printed on coffee labels and roasters' web pages combined with the strategically essentialized images of coffee producers found in promotional materials that form the backbone of the consumers' relations with fair-trade coffee producers. Merchandise in many product categories easily becomes more valuable if retailers are able to provide a story about its producers and/or the cultural traditions from which the objects originate. It is in the transmission of these stories that the important mediating role occupied by importers and roasters (middlemen) in fair-trade networks is laid bare. Not only do middlemen build capital based on their knowledge of product authenticity, but they also reinforce their cultural capital by creating or controlling the narratives that may help to sell their merchandise better (Esperanza 2008).

In the North, fair-trade marketing mirrors consumers' attachment to far-off places and traditions, infusing products with information regarding the peoples, places, and cultures engaged in the production of particular commodities (Raynolds 2002). The information provided by retailers presents consumers with an avenue for virtual engagement with the "other" through their consumption. This is primarily achieved through advertisements that pair testimonies and stories about coffee producers with colorful photographs. These stories are simply framed because their singular purpose is to persuade consumers to take action by purchasing specific products. Fair-trade coffee advertising relies heavily on structures of common difference (Wilk 1995) and strategically essentialized identities (Warren 1998; Brosius 1999). Roasters market their fair-trade coffee through one-dimensional representations of fair-trade producers as small-scale farmers, celebrating some kinds of difference while submerging others. For example, advertisements often include information about a cooperative's age, location, ethnic identity, and how it benefits from fair trade. They often contain inspirational quotes. For example, each TransFair brochure features a sentence or two from a cooperative representative, such as "We know that if we did not sell at fair-trade prices, we would not break even in our coffee production" (Manrique Lopez Castillo, ASOBAGRI, in TransFair n.d.) or "Prior to fair trade we did not have any chance to survive, now we see the light at the end of the tunnel" (Marcos M. Perez, FEDECOCAGUA, in TransFair n.d.). Similarly, on the Green Mountain Coffee Roasters website the page advertising La Voz's coffee long-featured a quote from the former manager, Guillermo, which read: "Every single child of the members of La Voz is in school . . . The children come back to work to help their parents in whatever way they can. The best inheritance parents can give their children is education."[11] The images and descriptions are used with a particular end in mind—branding fair-trade coffees to attract additional consumers, increase the fair-trade market, and expand the benefits of fair trade.

This marketing strategy is not the result of happenstance. Instead, it reflects an industry-wide privileging of the symbolic quality attributes of specialty coffee (discussed in Chapter 6). Even a cursory analysis of one of the industry's leading publications, *Tea and Coffee Trade Journal*, reveals a remarkable proliferation of articles celebrating symbolic quality attributes, such as producer identities, origin, and environmentally sustainable production methods. For example, as early as 1994, one writer advocated for the importance of roaster interest in small-scale farms and origin coffees, arguing that small-scale coffee farmers "[m]ay be exactly what the gourmet market is looking for—excellent coffee from clearly identifiable regions produced in relatively limited quantities by interesting people with colorful stories to tell" (*Tea and Coffee Trade Journal* 1994:20). Over the past decade, as the specialty coffee market in the United States expanded and became more firmly established, it consciously began to model itself on the wine appellation system—one that pays close attention to the details of origin and flavor characteristics. Although commonplace today, this trend first dates to the 1800s, when much Latin American quality coffee was exported "[n]ot as Colombian or Costa Rican coffee but, like 'French wines,' under the mark of a particular Costa Rican processor or Colombian hacienda" (Roseberry 1995:12).

As the sophistication of the U.S. specialty coffee palette increased, growing numbers of roasters began to routinely visit coffee producers to expand their coffee knowledge and seek new sources of higher quality coffees. These trips may also have been inspired by trade journals, which regularly highlight exotic origins and idyllic travel opportunities. While providing detailed information of origin characteristics and local coffee history, these articles are filled with the flowery language of glossy travel brochures, clearly aimed at furthering the mystique of specialty coffee. For example, one reads: "Here, in this forgotten corner of paradise, a hummingbird hovers between lush green coffee trees while, nearby, a bright blue butterfly lazily flutters here and there through a group of orange trees and wild yellow orchids. Welcome to Finca Irlanda, an organic coffee farm in the southern state of Chiapas" (Wallengren 2000:40). Others focus on the adventurous aspects of coffee sourcing. For example, one begins: "Coffee buyers know the scenario . . . there are the long hours of difficult travel through rugged landscape to remote coffee growing regions" (Lorenzetti 1999). Because of the rapid growth of the specialty coffee industry, a few smaller roasters told me they entered the market propelled simply by a entrepreneurial spirit, not necessarily a deep passion for coffee. For these relative coffee novices, trips to origin can prove enlightening. One stated: "Well, personally, when I came into coffee, I didn't know how coffee was grown, and who does know that it comes from a tree? I think generally everybody is just blown away by all the labor involved." The increasing popularity of origin coffees within the specialty market encouraged a heightened awareness among roasters of the cultural, economic, and environmental contexts of coffee production. Several roasters explained how in the past they focused on buying the best-quality coffee at the lowest price. They claimed that visiting coffee farmers, especially small producer cooperatives, caused them to rethink this business strategy. For example, one told me: "There are a number of issues morally there. Number one, we don't do that with any other supplier . . . our copy paper? Here's our core product [coffee] that we've seen and know and we've seen how people live and can we feel good about doing that [ignoring their poverty]? I don't think so."

Roaster trips to coffee-producing regions, during which they create and nurture relationships based on proximate contact with producers, are also conveniently translatable into marketing tools. A powerful way for retailers to market this vicarious travel is through the prominent display of the photos and profiles of the producers who grow the coffee they serve. Starbucks once marketed the vicarious travel experience with the coffee "passports" they issued to consumers detailing the origins and unique, place-based characteristics of different coffees. More recently (in 2007), Starbucks' retail outlets featured a coffee wheel emblazoned with the phrase "Geography is a Flavor." Consumers spin the wheel to a specific geographic location, such as Latin America, and then narrow their choice to a particular Starbucks blend. Each blend is paired with a flowery description. For example, the Colombia Nariño Supremo is described as "balanced and nutty" whereas the Guatemala Antigua is "elegant and intriguing" and the Organic Shade Grown Mexico is "crisp and refreshing" (Starbucks n.d.).

Many specialty coffee roasters have marketed organic coffees to natural foods consumers for years and therefore found it relatively simple to integrate fair-trade offerings into this preexisting "alternative" niche market. In fact, the fair-trade certified label itself is a form of marketing: it provides coffee roasters with a ready-made way for them to communicate their social responsibility and the symbolic quality attributes of the coffee they are selling. For example, one roaster told me: "The fact is, to explain what fair trade is on the supermarket shelf is complicated. If we have our own program that's not even tied into a seal on the front of the bag that people can research, how are our customers going to learn about it?" However, not every roaster jumped at the chance to occupy this niche; another argued: "All these certified coffees are still niche players, there just isn't enough volume. But for some companies, that niche becomes their marketing strategy . . . if you're a small player and only need a container or so of coffee a year to do that . . . you can build a brand around this." Today's consumer market is characterized by product standardization, meaning products now require signs, such as brand names, that add value to them (Goldman and Papson 1996:3). Communicating product attributes other than use-value has always been the goal of advertising; however, during the recent years of post-Fordist flexible production and increasing levels of consumption, advertising and sign values have become constitutive features of products, not simply descriptors of them.

Many specialty coffee companies built their image and definition of quality around taste combined with environmental responsibility or social justice issues. This strategic coupling of ideology and more conventional marketing tools was reflected in the statements of many interviewed roasters, such as the GMCR employee who explained, "It's not necessarily just promoting your product, but promoting a cause and then also your product." This ideological marketing has also been noted by industry writers, such as Easson, who notes, "Their [roasters'] success has been based on making quality coffees 'with a conscience' more accessible to consumers, and then educating consumers about these issues" (2000:33). Although some roasters readily acknowledged the fact that fair-trade coffee makes for good advertising copy, others claimed promoting fair-trade coffee to consumers poses a distinct challenge, especially in light of the widespread tragedies resulting from the coffee crisis. For example, Michael Optiz, director of Neumann's (one of the two largest coffee brokers) sustainability branch, remarked: "The image of coffee is endangered due to the oversupply on world markets and campaigns by non-profit groups. It is becoming a product where the farmers are dying and birds are being denied habitats" (Silver 2003). However, the discursive framing of fair trade as an alternative to globalization resting on individual choice and action provides a direct means of combating these negative associations. For example, the director of marketing at GMCR recalled: "The copywriter said, 'Oh it's just so tragic.' She didn't want to put a tragic message out there. So how do you take a tragic situation and flip it so it's more embraceable? What we try and do is say: 'The coffee you buy can make a difference.'" Several years later Green Mountain continues to promote this line of thinking with the current tagline "Brewing a Better World."[12]

CAPTURING AUTHENTICITY:
FILMING MAYA COFFEE PRODUCERS

In 2003 the CEO and several employees of Green Mountain Coffee Roasters visited La Voz to meet with the cooperative members who supply coffee for several of the company's blends. The visiting group also included a film crew from *Frontline*, broadcast by the Public Broadcasting System in the United States, and the trip coincided with the launch of the Green Mountain and Newman's Own co-branded (meaning both company trademarks are on the label) fair-trade and organic coffee blends.[13] Nell Newman travelled with the group in order to meet the producers growing the coffee that bore her family's name. *Frontline* filmed the whole visit as part of a piece on the coffee crisis, broadcast in spring 2003. The resulting program was educational and emotionally moving, and it provided free publicity for Green Mountain, Newman's Own, and the cooperative. At the same time, the program and the filming experience worked to bridge the geographic distance separating the coffee producers and their northern buyers.

In addition to the high quality of its coffee, the cooperative is attractive to coffee importers and retailers because its members have a cohesive ethnic identity easily marketed as authentic Tz'utujil Maya Indians. Their language, artisan traditions, and the presence of women who continue to wear *huipils* and *cortes* (traditional blouses and wrap skirts, respectively) serve as symbolic markers of "Mayaness" for outsiders searching for signs of Guatemala's cultural heritage. Cooperative members are aware of this and consistently stress their Maya identity in their interactions with visitors. In preparation for the Green Mountain visit, men dressed in *traje*, the community-specific Maya outfits they rarely wear in daily activities. In fact, several men without the necessary clothing borrowed it from others. They repeatedly expressed their excitement over the opportunity to demonstrate their distinctive cultural traditions. The cooperative's management and board of directors chose to use their Tz'utujil culture to demonstrate the quality of their coffee and the stringent production guidelines they followed. In effect, they claimed that their coffee is high quality and organic *because* they are traditional Tz'utujil. The *Frontline* producers followed that lead. They distilled cooperative members' identity into a package of ethnic and cultural traits identified in terms of "structures of common difference" (Wilk 1995). These celebrated particular kinds of diversity, such as Maya traje and environmentally sensitive production methods, while suppressing others, such as the structural inequality shaping the producers' life opportunities. In short, in the way it celebrates selected symbolic attributes of the producers' coffee and their lives, the film is a mechanism through which economic and social participation in the market makes difference manifest (Little 2004).

Cooperative members might have chosen to highlight something other than their distinctive culture. They could, for instance, have stressed the group's modernity: the strict guidelines members follow when making organic fertilizer or tending their coffee, the large loans from international lenders they collectively manage, or their plans to construct a dry mill and training center. One of the traje-clad coffee harvesters might have pointed out the similarities between his own life and the lives of consumers by explaining that he is a physician who rarely performs agricultural labor but instead monitors his day laborers' work during his free time. Another might have mentioned how two of his children are office workers in Guatemala City who are finishing their college degrees on the weekends. However, they chose to represent the group as the "small farmer cooperative rich in Indian tradition" described in Green Mountain Coffee Roasters' promotional materials. This sort of representation subsumes their sophisticated organic production practices and community development efforts under the veneer of an image of the time- and place-bound "other." At the same time it is a strategic use of indigenous identity that furthers the members' economic interests and helps the group resist processes of financial domination.

This foregrounding of community identity and indigenous authenticity is also evident in the coffee tour the cooperative developed with the assistance of Anacafé. For example, the script read by the cooperative members who serve as tour guides begins by pointing out that "[o]ur culture is

FIGURE 7.1. *A cooperative founder, dressed in traje, speaking to visiting GMCR employees about the group's coffee.*

FIGURE 7.2. *A cooperative member's wife and children, dressed in traje, demonstrate coffee picking for the GMCR film crews.*

Tz'utujil Maya, one of the most important populations in the development of Lake Atitlan." The tour guides then describe the history of the name of the cooperative, signalling the key role that Catholicism plays in the community: "As you see around you, we are not in a desert. It is for the patron of our community, the apostle St. John, who preached in the desert. For him, to have his blessing." The tour guides describe the importance of maize in Tz'utujil culture, explaining how "[n]ow . . . we can't speak about our culture if we don't talk a little about maize . . . our Tz'utujil culture is very related to maize. The *tzuhuj* is the flower of corn; the word Tz'utujil comes from it." Finally, the tour ends with an introduction to the community's artisan tradition: the guides point out, "For more than two centuries, Maya clothing and weavings have served as an artistic expression and have facilitated communication." The guides describe the clothing and explain, "This clothing isn't imported; we make it ourselves." These cultural explanations are interspersed throughout the longer tour script, which is primarily devoted to an explanation of the organic production methods utilized by the cooperative and their environmental goals.

Photographs taken that day are still on Green Mountain's website, including one placed front and center on the Corporate Social Responsibility page, which features the company's CEO with his arm around the traje-clad son of a cooperative member.[14] GMCR also used some of the footage to create a short (3:11) digital video for online consumption.[15] The film, titled *Heifer Hope Blend: Brew up a Cup of Hope*, intersperses sweeping landscape panoramas with scenes of cooperative members and their wives dressed in traje as they contentedly pick coffee and transport it to the beneficio. Rather than interviews with cooperative members, there is a female voice-over who explains: "In Central America, right below Mexico, in a country with only two seasons, wet and dry, lives the antiquity of Guatemala. In this country of ancient ruin and highland climate many people live in poverty and despair." The voice explains how the partnership between GMCR and Heifer International "focuses on bringing assistance to these farmers, providing sustainable solutions for income and nutrition and a market for their high quality coffee." There are two short clips from an interview with an individual whose affiliation is undecipherable (because of the poor quality of the film). He explains in halting English that "people should buy Heifer Hope Blend because it is a contribution to resolve a problem that doesn't belong just to Guatemalan people, it's a problem of everybody." The voice-over then explains: "Now you too can contribute to the solution when you buy Heifer Hope Blend. For every bag purchased GMCR will donate forty cents to Heifer International in support of coffee growing families around the world." All of this is set to Andean-flavored pipe music quietly playing in the background, used to signal indigeneity and cultural authenticity.[16]

What is interesting about this film is that the day the footage was shot, it was clear that members of La Voz were active subjects in the project—through their self-depiction they concretely shaped the meaning of their coffee and the message of the marketing materials. However, this short film clip effectively turns them into objects for consumption. Again, this highlights the fact that in the process of defetishizing fair-trade coffee, Maya culture itself is refetishized. When we purchase the Heifer Hope Blend, we are also buying a bit of Maya culture—we are helping to keep the "antiquity of Guatemala" alive. In the film, the cooperative members' voices are never heard (as opposed to the longer *Frontline* piece, which includes several clips from interviews with cooperative members), and in fact, the low quality of the film makes their faces difficult to distinguish. Their bright traje and the Andean music are signs used to evoke their cultural identity and authenticity. However, the fact that the film includes a still photo of a woman sitting next to a goat (whereas the Heifer program in San Juan primarily involves chickens) and dressed in traje from a community other than San Juan indicates that the producers' subjectivity is not a key concern here.

The film is not prominently placed on the company's website. In fact, I simply stumbled upon it one day when researching La Voz's coffee profiles. Beneath the summary of critics' comments on the Heifer Hope Blend, in small type it reads, "Watch this film to learn more about the results of our partnership with Heifer." This placement is strategic and reflects the delicate balance companies such as GMCR must make among marketing their products, educating consumers, and over-celebrating their own social responsibility. During an interview in 2003, GMCR's marketing director explained: "What we're struggling with is the words and what the right tone is. And it's a tricky thing, especially when you want to convey your social and environmental initiatives. You really don't want it to sound like you're puffing your chest and patting yourself on the back. You'd like it to be more of a discovery—that someone discovers you do this as a company."

The need for generic and easily digestible images of fair-trade farmers to disseminate to northern consumers can create definite disjuncture between reality and representation. One afternoon I waited with some members of the coffee cooperative organized by the local World Vision–sponsored development program Cotz'ija. The members were told to assemble that afternoon to await a Dutch filmmaker who was coming to film footage for a video to be shown to consumers in Holland. After two hours, he arrived and immediately got down to business. The cooperative's manager had prepped the members in advance, instructing them to show the filmmaker how they made organic fertilizer and cared for their coffee plants. However, the film-maker interrupted their discussion and gruffly stated: "We need ten men to carry sacks of coffee down that path by the mill. Even if they are sacks of paper or plastic, I don't mind because we want it to look like they are carry-ing coffee." The cooperative's president didn't quite understand this order and replied, "What a shame that we are not in the harvest season right now." Undeterred, the filmmaker responded, "For that reason we have to invent it because that is what is interesting." While filling their coffee sacks and baskets with organic fertilizer (as a substitute for coffee cherries), a coopera-tive member asked if their wives and children should also participate. The filmmaker responded that the women should carry their baskets on their heads but the children should not be filmed, "[b]ecause they [the Dutch con-sumers] will think the children are forced to work and that is a bad thing." A cooperative member confusedly replied, "But here it is a reality that the children work with us." In his whirlwind visit, the visitor filmed forty-five minutes of footage and left without asking the names of the participants or their cooperative. However, before scurrying off he was kind enough to purchase us all cold orange sodas from a nearby *tienda*.

On the surface, both of these films employ strategic essentialisms of Maya culture to influence the purchasing habits of northern consumers. However, a deeper probing reveals stark differences in the subjective experi-ences and relative agency of the participants. For example, the Dutch film-maker's refusal to film laboring children is ironic because fair-trade coffee is, by definition, produced by *family* farmers who rely on the labor of their loved ones instead of hired help. In addition, according to the International Labor Organization, more than 70 percent of the world's working children work in agriculture. In Central America, more than 2.6 million child labor-ers work in agriculture and half of these do not receive a salary because the tasks are carried out on family farms (Rodriguez 2004).[17] Reflecting this real-ity, in the footage captured by the *Frontline* and GMCR crews, cooperative members proudly included their traje-dressed children in the production: their mothers and fathers encouraged them to pick coffee and help load it onto the waiting mule. The children eagerly complied and every few min-utes they looked directly at the cameras and giggled.

However, the Dutch filmmaker wanted to portray a generic Maya cof-fee farmer. Although this farmer might be recognizably Guatemalan, all dis-tinguishing cultural features, such as community identity marked through the traje, were blurred. The participating members of Cotz'ija had no con-nection with the filmmaker and little familiarity with the directors of the

FIGURE 7.3. *The Dutch filmmaker filming members of a coffee cooperative carrying fertilizer down a mountain path.*

sponsoring development organization, World Vision. Nor was their creative input sought. In contrast, the members of La Voz were given little direction and worked independently, prior to the filmmakers' arrival, to craft their own vision of authentic coffee harvesting and processing. Although they may have strategically reduced Juanero identity to a few essential components, such *as traje*, woven baskets, and family labor, these components directly reflected the vision of San Juan *they* chose to proudly share with northern consumers.

CONCLUSION: HUMAN RIGHTS AND GLOBAL MARKETS

As noted in the introduction, coffee has been called the beverage of post-modernism (Roseberry 1996), not to suggest that coffee exists in a unique relationship with capitalism but that it provides a window through which we can view a range of relationships and social transformations. This includes the critical links between the consumption habits of northern consumers and the daily lives of producers, such as the members of La Voz. These links constitute an uneven imaginary community in which producers and consumers are united through print capitalism and marketing. Producers and consumers are not members of an actual face-to-face community, and as a result it is not entirely accurate to depict the market transactions as the embedded exchange of a defetishized product. However, this imaginary community still plays a critical role in shaping local realities and promoting human rights within countries that consistently threaten individual freedoms, such as Guatemala. This process does not occur through direct producer-consumer contact. Instead, it is channelled through two distinct avenues: first, the certification system, which requires producer groups to be democratic, transparent, and accountable, and second, the relationships between producers and coffee roasters, who, within fair-trade coffee networks, act as conduits for consumer actions and intentions. These two facets of the fair-trade coffee market, both dependent on consumer support, promote and protect the secure organizational space that is necessary for cooperation and producer-initiated community development.

This freedom to identify and fulfil economic and social development goals through cooperation also reaffirms existing cultural traditions of community service and mutual aid within San Juan. The freedom to organize and respect for cultural practices are key components of human-rights compliance and are critically important in countries such as Guatemala with its history of violent repression, structural inequality, and cultural discrimination against indigenous populations and community organizers. Cooperative members' successful participation in the global economy through their coffee sales is predicated upon remaining in their community and maintaining the competitive advantage they gain through their distinct Tz'utujil identity. Therefore, the relationship between market success and local processes of cultural identification is reciprocal. Although their Mayaness may be a distinct market advantage, participation in fair-trade coffee networks can also play an important role in the preservation and promotion of cultural traditions. Rather than a simple contradiction between a timeless indigeneity and modern market demands, it is perhaps better to understand the cooperative and its actions as a process of modernization grounded in tradition.[18]

Although some fear that global economic integration will result in cultural homogenization or a significant crisis of both collective and individual identity (Jameson 1991; Friedman 1994), contemporary markets are also marked by consumers who seek exotic and unique third-world objects, and as a result, authenticity and indigenous identity are rewarded. This increasing market value of indigenous identity challenges historic associations of indigenous populations with underdevelopment, poverty, and tradition-bound cultural practices (Levi and Dean 2003; Garcia 2005). Therefore, within fair-trade coffee networks some of the forces commonly associated with globalization, such as increased flows of information and capital, also result in the reaffirmation of indigenous identity and permit the reinforcement of translocal spaces of resistance (Harvey 1989). Cooperative members foreground their indigenous identity to foreign coffee buyers to gain competitive advantage, thereby resisting the postmodern condition and its characteristics of cultural homogenization and financial domination (Nigh 1997). In turn, roasters market their coffee through the calculated use of Maya identity as a commodity sign contributing to the reverse commodity flows of exotic and unique objects produced in third-world countries (Nash 1993a).

Although cooperative members do not actively support the pan-Maya movement and its political project,[19] like other indigenous people who embrace the use of strategically essentialized representations of cultural authenticity to facilitate tourism and artisan sales rather than political or cultural goals, they are active agents in the construction and presentation of their identity (Stephen 1993, 2005; Little 2004; Zorn 2004). The relationship between market success and Maya identity is dialogical. Although their identity may be a distinct market advantage, participation in the fair-trade market and a cooperative that combines cultural norms of reciprocity and contemporary business practices contributes to the preservation and promotion of local cultural traditions. Furthermore, market participation provides international validation of Maya cultural traditions, historically denigrated within the Guatemalan nation-state.

Conclusion: A Fairer Future

When I first began this research, nearly a decade ago, few people I encountered were familiar with fair trade. I was forced to continuously explain the then-novel idea to my friends, family members, and colleagues. Today this is no longer the case as fair-trade coffee has entered the mainstream of North American culture. No longer do you have to buy your fair-trade coffee at fund-raisers held in church basements. Rather than scooping your (inevitably stale) fair-trade coffee out of the bulk bins at natural foods cooperatives, you can now grab vacuum-sealed bags of it off your local grocery store's shelf or, depending on where in the United States you live, you can buy a steaming cup of it at your corner McDonald's or Dunkin' Donuts. However, this mainstreaming has had the unintended effect of ushering in public doubts and criticisms of fair trade. Fair trade has been criticized in the popular press as a "misguided attempt to make up for market failures" (Economist 2006) and for encouraging market inefficiencies and overproduction (Lindsey 2004;

Hartford 2007). Furthermore, several media exposés have questioned exactly how "fair" fair trade is (Stecklow and White 2004; O'Neil 2007), suggesting that it is an inefficient channel for improving economic opportunities while hinting that retailers unfairly mark-up fair-trade products and that certified producers do not earn substantially higher incomes.

In writing this book I have attempted to move beyond the rhetoric surrounding fair trade and to use ethnographic research to illuminate the reality of fair-trade coffee networks. Despite the many interviews and the hours of observation, like all anthropology (and, for that matter, all research regardless of disciplinary origin) this book can offer only partial truths. I have highlighted the ways in which I think fair trade is truly "fair" (or fairer) for the members of La Voz. Yes, cooperative members earn higher incomes than their nonmember neighbors; however, they are certainly not getting rich. On the other hand, there are other benefits of fair trade that are rarely discussed in the popular press. In addition to price premiums, cooperative members have access to new markets, credit, training, and information. Perhaps more importantly, their participation in this transnational commodity network provides them with a secure organizational space and an affirmation of their indigenous identity that is a stark reversal from the centuries of inequality, oppression, and violence that they and their forebears endured.

However, these benefits do not necessarily negate what some view as a critical flaw limiting the development potential of contemporary certified coffee networks—that the vast majority of coffee produced by these farmers is exported. Pinning the hopes for prosperity onto foreign markets undeniably continues the region's historical dependence on agro-export markets. Indeed, fair trade is not a quick fix for the myriad problems facing small-scale producers in underdeveloped countries. However, although participation in the fair-trade commodity network might not radically alter the daily reality and grinding poverty of the members of La Voz, it is providing new life opportunities for the next generation. As demonstrated in Chapter 3, the members of La Voz are investing their fair-trade coffee profits heavily in their children's education, and as a result many of their offspring have escaped the agrarian dependency on foreign export markets for the shade and comfort of a professional career. Moreover, some cooperative members have invested their fair-trade profits in diverse economic pursuits. For example, the cooperative's former president, Juan, runs a bakery with his wife and bought a machine to seal purified water into small plastic bags to sell on street corners. Similarly, the former agricultural monitor, Santiago, invested his profits in the general store he owned with his children. The store, San

Juan's answer to Walmart, sold farming implements and food next to computer disks and printer cartridges. I discussed in Chapter 4 how Santiago resigned from the cooperative because of the members' collective refusal to sanction the manager. At the time, I suspected that Santiago's decision was not necessarily a reflection of his moral convictions but instead emerged from his desire to devote more of his time to his family's growing business. When I returned to San Juan in 2006, Santiago and his children had moved their store from the front room of the family house to a shining white, two-story building in the center of town. Their offerings at the store, now called "Super Perez" (after the family's last name), had expanded even more, and Santiago was devoting diminishing energy to his agrarian pursuits. As a cooperative founder, Santiago belonged to the cooperative for close to three decades, during which he used the proceeds from his coffee sales to educate his children and diversify his economic livelihood.

Despite the benefits of fair trade, the case of La Voz illuminates a number of ways in which it falls far short of its promises. For example, to access certified coffee markets, the members of La Voz have consistently improved the quality of their coffee while working to meet the required standards for organic and shade-grown certification. As the market for certified coffees expands, certification systems—and the rules, experts, and paperwork they generate—play a growing role within the commodity network and increasingly determine the nature of connections between participants and within producer associations such as La Voz. Supply-chain governance forms a critical component of the certification system and quality standards. However, certification requirements, combined with the mandate for quality, contribute to a culture of managerialism and growing systems of external governance in which cooperative members are observed, evaluated, and instructed. The growing role of the management within the cooperative threatens the bonds of solidarity that are the cooperative's true strength. Advertisers sell us an image of fair-trade farmers who work together harmoniously and innately, and as consumers we are more than eager to buy this vision and the product behind it. However, the members' collective struggle over issues such as overdue credit accounts and managerial corruption demonstrate that cooperation is in fact an ongoing process of negotiation and conflict resolution rather than an intrinsic and static value of third-world farming communities.

Chapters 5 and 6 explore the ways in which certification demands shape production practices and daily life among cooperative members. Although in theory fair-trade coffee networks are marked by mutual dependence, cooperation, and trust, in practice, the members of La Voz are subjected to high levels of governance and external surveillance as a result of their hierarchical relationships with northern buyers and certifying agencies. This external governance contributes to emerging tensions between the cooperative's currents of solidarity and equality and market demands. For example, the strong relationships that bind the members of the group to one another also make it difficult to punish one another for quality infringements in their production practices. Moreover, certification standards developed in the North often lack the flexibility necessary to accommodate local livelihood needs (e.g., the local need for fast-growing shade trees whose limbs can be used as firewood) and promote secondary goals, such as gender equity.

When I discuss the benefits and limitations of fair-trade coffee in my undergraduate classes, predictably a student asks me how she should spend her money. In light of these problems, is fair trade worth it? Is she really helping the producers by going out of her way to seek the fair-trade label? Generally my answer is self-reflexive—I point out that despite the problems I have uncovered through my research, I still try to buy fair-trade products when possible. Chin eloquently points out that scholars, even scholars of consumption, "are no less free than anyone else from commodity fetishism, keeping up with the Joneses and all the other illnesses that come with contemporary consumer culture . . . knowing about these things only makes the pain that much greater" (2007:336). Like many U.S. consumers, my shopping habits are schizophrenic, my grocery cart crowded with twelve-packs of Diet Coke, overpriced organic vegetables, fair-trade tea, and multi-packs of toilet paper—the soft and squishy brands, not the environmentally friendly recycled one. I might teach a class in the morning on the environmental and labor abuses of the banana industry and then, caught up in the evening rush, place a bunch of non-organic, non-fair-trade bananas in my shopping cart. I am much more likely to purchase a bar of fair-trade, organic chocolate in a sleek wrapper than I am to buy unbranded, fair-trade, organic sugar from the bulk bins at the natural food store.

Many scholars researching fair trade argue that its true counter-hegemonic power results from its ability to link northern consumers and southern producers within commodity networks, thereby re-embedding their relationships and creating modes of connectivity. They argue that fair-trade market expansion is a direct result of the political choices and reflexivity of consumers. However, *Coffee and Community* presents a more nuanced understanding of how specialty coffee roasters and fair-trade advocates influence the market, thereby problematizing this assumed correlation. Although fair-trade coffee advocates are also consumers, not all fair-trade consumers are well-educated activists. Furthermore, in coming out of the politically correct consumption closet I have demonstrated that even informed shoppers like me are not guided 100 percent of the time by their ethical convictions. In light of the influence of advocacy groups and coffee roasters, fair trade is perhaps better understood as a "consumer-dependent" movement for change rather than a consumer-led movement (Goodman 2004:901). However, this does not discount the probability that some fair-trade consumers *are* engaged in a consciously political project. Future research on the topic needs to be conducted, research that treats consumer motivations as an empirical question, not something that can be determined a priori.

In writing this book I have attempted to dramatize both the promise and inherent contradictions of fair trade's attempt to build collaborative networks across national, economic, and cultural borders by nurturing relationships between southern producers and northern consumers. Embedded economic relationships are traditionally understood as those that are rooted in proximate contact, familiarity, and trust. Polanyi (1985) argued that as relations of production are increasingly obscured within a capitalist system, economic relationships become disembedded. As demonstrated in Chapter 7, in their current manifestation, the modes of connectivity linking consumers and producers are symbolic ones and we cannot truly label these relationships "embedded." On the other hand, the material modes of connectivity that fair trade fosters among participants, such as the members of La Voz and the employees of Green Mountain Coffee Roasters who visit them, are increasingly rooted in familiarity and reciprocity. *Coffee and Community* presents a more critical and nuanced view of embeddedness, acknowledging that economic concerns and self-interest are found amid even the strongest of social ties.

Although there is little evidence to support the argument that fair trade fosters embedded producer / consumer relations in the traditional Polanyian sense, the symbolic connectivity linking these participants in the network is an integral component of fair trade's material consequences. Anthropologists have long acknowledged the power of symbolism, and it does not require a leap of faith to envision a future in which this connectivity is based on more than the words printed on the side of a bag of coffee. The commodity network framework employed in this book links the members of La Voz to the consumers of fair-trade coffee. This approach illustrates the ways in which fair trade can potentially challenge the logic of the expanding free market by promoting a "critical consumer culture" that challenges the individualistic, competitive, and ethically impoverished culture of capitalism (Simpson and Rapone 2000:54). Nurturing this "critical consumer culture" lays the groundwork for fair trade's attempt to build collaborative networks across national, economic, and cultural borders by nurturing relationships between southern producers and northern consumers. Fair-trade advocates and consumers are not simply contributing to the financial well-being of a distant coffee grower but are also seeking a relationship with the individuals who produce the commodities we consume. The fact that this relationship is not maintained through proximate contact does not necessarily lessen its impact and may, on the contrary, represent a pioneering approach to effecting change in an increasingly interconnected world. Moreover, with our multi-faceted understanding of the "local" and our disciplinary awareness of markets as political constructions, anthropologists could help to ensure that disadvantaged producers have the opportunity to participate in fair trade's international decision making and agenda setting. The members of La Voz are active participants in the fair-trade moral economy—they are contributing to it and creating it but yet their voices are appropriated and commoditized by TransFair, FLO, and other northern participants. Coffee producers need to be allowed to have a level of international institutional participation in fair-trade networks that mirrors their practical engagement.

Like many academic disciplines, millennial anthropology was swept up in the rhetoric of globalization as we celebrated its transnational flows and networks. Our analyses often seemed to unquestioningly accept the premises and inevitability of contemporary economic globalization. While we rushed to affirm the imperatives of the new discourses of globalization, we tended to sideline the projects of resistance and protest enacted by the people who were confronting its more insidious processes (Nash 2005). More recently, globalization has become a passé theoretical trope, and an intellectual backlash to such heady concepts as chaos, flows, and hybridites has emerged. Critics warn that in our rush to celebrate the demise of totalizing frameworks, we ignore current attempts to impose the most universalized framework of all, the world market. They argue that previous disciplinary attempts to model global cultural change, such as unilineal evolutionism and modernization theories, were not particularly successful, and they question the wisdom of employing the language of globalization to construct our problems in terms of local loyalties versus deterritorialized flows (Graeber 2002; Wilk 2006).

However, the list of malaises grouped under currently popular concepts such as neoliberalism or imperialism resemble those once attributed to globalization. Regardless of how we label the problem, as anthropologists and as citizens many of us search for ways to disprove pundits such as the *New York Times* columnist and champion of globalization, Thomas Friedman, who argues, "People can talk about alternatives to the free market and globalization, they can demand alternatives, they can insist on a 'Third Way' but for now none is apparent" (Friedman 2000:101). With the global proliferation of free-trade agreements and the exponentially expanding power of the World Trade Organization, international trade continues a long tradition of penalizing the citizens of less-developed nations and benefiting world powers. More than 200 million Latin Americans live below the poverty level, representing an increase of more than 20 million in just one decade (Grandin 2006:198). Furthermore, despite political rhetoric, there is little reason to hope that the implementation of CAFTA (Central American Free Trade Agreement) will significantly improve the living conditions of the 60 percent of Maya Guatemalans who live in conditions of extreme poverty (Fischer 2001:5–6).

So can fair-trade coffee truly give us "a taste of a different world"? In their current guise, fair-trade coffee networks do not represent a fundamental challenge to the neoliberal market model. However, fair trade's contradictory emphasis on the transformation of conventional markets from within differentiates it from development programs that are not rooted in explicit social and economic justice goals. A reinvigorated fair-trade movement, one that joins together the imperatives of expanding fair-trade markets *and* challenging global trade inequities, could potentially challenge the hegemony of neoliberal economic policies and help usher in a new global order of trade equality and sustainable development. In conclusion, rather than chastising fair trade for not single-handedly transforming our global economy, we should consider the spaces it opens and the possibilities it creates for ordinary people—like you, me, and the members of La Voz—to participate in larger projects of radical social and economic change.

CHAPTER 1

1. For example, Gledhill (2003:214) argues that the mission of many NGOs is directly supportive of agendas premised on the idea of individual self-help and empowerment rooted in a "determined pursuit of utopias of 'alternative development' conceived outside the region and not systematically adapted to its people's own perceived needs and aspirations." Similarly, Roper, Perreault, and Wilson (2003:19) argue that by forging links between indigenous communities and the market, NGOs and indigenous organizations are contributing to the state goal of economic integration. They urge us to consider whether this focus on community development has deflected the attention of indigenous leaders away from agendas or forms of protest more threatening to state domination and whether this has weakened the position of indigenous groups vis-à-vis the state.

CHAPTER 2

1. This story echoes Brintnall's account of the psychological and physical domination the indigenous population of

Aguacatan experienced at the hands of Ladinos. He writes: "Mayas were afraid of Ladinos, even in casual encounters . . . Many of their stories tell about the misery of carrying heavy burdens over long and difficult trails. One story, for example, tells of how a man carrying a burden was driven so hard that blood began to stream from his nose but the Ladino taskmaster would not let him rest" (1979:103).

2. Similarly, Maya living in San Andres Semetebaj, across Lake Atitlan from San Juan, recall the years of Ubico as a time in which rights were protected by legislation universally applied to Maya and Ladinos alike (Warren 1978:148).

3. A cuerda is an inconsistent measurement that varies from region to region in Guatemala. In San Juan, residents defined a cuerda as twenty-five by twenty-five varas (twenty-five varas is equivalent to approximately twenty-one meters, or sixty-nine feet).

4. His 1952 Ley de Reforma Agraria was inspired by Mexico's *ejido* (communal property) program and emerged from concerns about poverty and the unequal distribution of resources to both the Maya and poor Ladinos.

5. The agrarian reform sought to advance capitalist relations of production through the extension of democracy in the countryside. The reform created an administrative structure designed to "weaken the ironclad grip planters had over rural life," thereby empowering peasants to demand higher wages, which would in turn transform rural laborers into consumers of manufactured goods while simultaneously forcing planters to invest in new technologies and the rationalization of production to increase profits (Grandin 2004:54).

6. While it might appear that the local indigenous leadership squandered in factional rivalry the opportunity to take greater charge of their local affairs, Wasserstrom (1975) argues that the goals of the reform government never converged with those imagined to exist in native communities. While Arbenz hoped to develop a strong system of smallholder capitalist production, he did not present an alternative social order to free the semi-proletarianized workforce from the throes of the exploitative plantation economy. Support for Arbenz's reforms among the rural peasantry was scattered, and many smallholders, sharecroppers, and tenants (more than half the total population) remained unaffected by the benefits of collective bargaining and the eighty-cent minimum wage that Arbenz's reforms allotted for rural laborers (Wasserstrom 1975:457). For example, there is little evidence that the agrarian reforms directly impacted landholdings within San Juan, a community generally lacking (at the time) in a local, wealthy elite and removed from both urban centers and large plantation holdings. Another factor contributing to the inconsistent application of Arbenz's policies in rural areas was the complex maneuverings of local political factions. Nash's 1958 ethnography of Cantel documents how successful landowners and factory employees were quick to join Arbenz's governing political party, thereby placing their own interests above those of the poorer local *campesinos* and manipulating the reforms to their own advantage. As a result, national and regional officials frequently confronted the difficult choice of whether to support peasant leagues against their own local partisans or abandon the poorest people in rural areas (Nash 1958:133; Wasserstrom 1975:470). Similarly, in his

historical ethnography of Quetzaltenango, Grandin contends that class cleavages within the indigenous communities themselves contributed to the uneven application of the agrarian reforms across the countryside. Within the municipality of Quetzaltenango poor, rural K'iche' attempted to use the Ley de Reforma Agraria to claim unused communal land and convert it into agricultural plots. However, use of this communal land was traditionally administered by the urban elite and represented a source of their continued class power. Grandin argues that by the middle of the century, the political power and cultural identity of urban K'iche' elites rested on their claims to represent the interests of all Mayas. Through attempts to strengthen the class-consciousness of the rural poor, Ladino and Maya alike, the revolution potentially undermined this foundation. Therefore, elites "initiated a campaign of intimidation and repression against rural indigenous campesinos organizing under agrarian reform" and maintained their own allegiance to the municipal administration (Grandin 2000:15).

7. While Operation Success has long been interpreted by many as a gross example of private interest influencing governmental policy, more recently, historians have stressed the growing threat posed by the increasing power of the PGT (the Communist Party) over Guatemalan society and over Jacobo Arbenz himself (Grandin 2004:52). The U.S. State Department labeled the "Ten Years of Spring" as Communist (LaFeber 1983:113) and indeed the 1944 Revolution represented a limited rejection of the nation's domination by external capital (primarily the United Fruit Company) on behalf of the nation-state, represented by both the coffee and non-coffee business elite. As Grandin points out, Operation Success would not have achieved its durability and strength if it had not connected with oppositional currents within Guatemala at the time (2004:77).

8. This finding is corroborated by Smith's research, which demonstrates that during the 1970s less than 10 percent of the agricultural workers from many municipalities in Chimaltenango traveled to coastal fincas (Smith 1990).

9. Based on 1950 and 1964 average census figures.

10. At this time 188 coffee farms larger than 2,200 acres accounted for 20 percent of Guatemala's coffee production nationwide and 3,463 farms with more than 110 acres accounted for 64 percent (Williams 1994:171).

11. The Kennedy administration's Alliance for Progress aimed to create a "prosperous, stable middle class inoculated against Castroism" (Grandin 2004:10). However, at the same time that the United States was promoting modernization, it was also funding Latin American militaries and intelligence agencies in an effort to counter real and perceived insurgent threats. Grandin convincingly documents that although Washington promised to transform Guatemala into a "showcase for democracy" after the successful implementation of Operation Success and the overthrow of Arbenz in 1954, it instead created a "laboratory for repression" managed by a highly skilled and brutal military (2006:109). The Carter administration cut military funding to Guatemala as human rights violations dramatically increased in the late 1970s. While it was politically impossible for the United States to openly support the Guatemalan army's counterinsurgency campaign, the Reagan administration

continued to provide covert CIA assistance and funds (LaFeber 1983; Handy 1984; Jonas 2000; Grandin 2006). This was true across the region, and during the height of the Guatemalan genocide U.S. military aid to Central America grew from US$10 million in 1980 to US$283.2 million in 1984 with the number of troops in Central America rising from around 48,000 at the end of the 1970s to more than 200,000 in 1985 (declining to 179,000 in 1991) (Pearce 1998:594).

12. Several key events fueled support for the insurgency and the corresponding government repression, including the deaths of thirty-four Maya farmers at the Panzos massacre of 1978; the deaths of thirty-nine highland Maya killed in the Spanish Embassy in 1980 while protesting military repression in El Quiché; the ongoing occupation of Nebaj and the formation of an effective coalition of Maya and Ladino peasants represented by the Comité de Unidad Campesina (CUC). These events, especially the Panzos massacre, mobilized the nation's left and provided a focal point for unification. The events merged both the city and the country while also transforming isolated land conflicts into a single movement with a common enemy (Grandin 2004:165).

13. The most visible manifestation of the civil war within San Juan was the formation of the civil patrols. In 1983 and 1984, 1.3 million indigenous men between the ages of fifteen and sixty, approximately 17 percent of the population, were members of the civil patrols (Schirmer 1998:82). The official functions of the civil patrols included patrolling crops and villages, acting as the army's ears and eyes, and fighting guerrillas, if necessary. An estimated 20,000 military commissioners were in charge of the civil patrols at the local level, and depending on the number of eligible local men, periods of service ranged from several hours to an entire twenty-four-hour shift from once every four days to once a month (Sexton 1985:427). Civil patrols were highly variable in their attitudes and compliance with the law. In some areas they were heavily armed and closely supervised by the regional military supervisor, whereas in other communities they were much more casual about service. San Juan seemed, for the most part, to have fallen in the latter category. Many civil patrols committed brutal acts of violence that ruptured community and family ties. It was reportedly common to settle old scores through the patrols, and they frequently became vehicles for extortion and corruption. For example, in neighboring San Pedro, the army recruited agents and spies within the community, effectively exploiting existing cleavages (Paul and Demarest 1988:153–154).

14. The most commonly cited story of violence in San Juan involves the brutal nighttime murder of a local woman who worked with the directors of a Santiago Atitlan radio station, established by the priests of the Oklahoma Catholic Mission to promote adult education in the local Maya language (two other Juaneros were also targeted because of their participation; however, they survived their torture). This victim had also built a successful business buying and selling local weavings. Multiple sources told me she was shot to death for her economic activity, and this version of the story is corroborated by Paul and Demarest (1988:124), who report that "[s]he was fingered by a [Pedrano] commissioner who had asked the woman, a seamstress by trade, to sell him on credit two fine skirts for his daughter's wed-

ding. She delivered the skirts and repeatedly asked for payment. Her payment was death." Paul and Demarest (1988:123) argue that the Pedrano military commissioners played a duplicitous game, doing their dirty work by night and posing as protectors by day—"knowing who were responsible was not enough to dispel the darkness of what became, in one Pedrano's words, an endless *noche negra*." This brutal murder was a highly public event in San Juan that, at the time, no one reportedly spoke about or questioned beyond the intimate confines of their nuclear families. There were no authorities to ask for help and therefore no recourse for the event. Perhaps for this reason, for many Juaneros, it has become emblematic of the civil war itself.

15. The size, strength, and sophistication of the gangs in Guatemala have increased dramatically since the implementation of the U.S. 1996 Illegal Immigration Reform and Immigrant Responsibility Act, which mandates the deportation of illegal immigrants convicted of even the most minor offenses. Today it is estimated that upwards of 14 percent of the nation's homicides are committed by the more than 14,000 members of the nation's 434 gangs (UN 2007). While there are only 180,000 legally registered firearms in the nation, United Nations Verification Mission in Guatemala (MINUGUA) estimates that there are approximately 1.8 million illegal weapons (only 1,500 weapons were collected during the 1996 disarmament during the Peace Accords) (UN 2007).

16. See Li (2000), Clifford (2001), and Dove (2006) for a more thorough analysis of the articulation of indigeneity.

CHAPTER 3

1. Similar to the Chimaltecos studied by Watanabe, Juaneros are reluctant to divulge the exact amount of land they own because they fear, among other things, government taxation and the envy of their neighbors (Watanabe 1992:136). Therefore, even after cross-checking my own findings with cooperative records, it is impossible to verify, without doubt, the extent of individual holdings. However, I include these figures to provide the reader with a general idea of the proportion of land used for each crop.

2. For example, Barlett's research in rural Costa Rica in the 1970s indicates that as more land is devoted toward a specific agricultural commodity (in the Costa Rican case, cattle; in the San Juan case, coffee), the insecurity of tenure and the overall scarcity of land increase as all households hope to purchase more land (1982:40). See also Ortiz (1973) and Sick (1999).

3. In his analysis of fair-trade coffee producers in Costa Rica, Luetchford (2007:121) argues that milpa acts as a site of resistance to the power of the market and its character is therefore as much political as economic. He writes: "It represents producing food por el gasto—it suggests a time before market domination and a symbolic space outside exchange and monetary value. Whereas the market is often associated with supplements and luxuries, subsistence agriculture is symbolic of the serious business of family reproduction and guaranteed access to the bare necessities of life (Scott 1976)."

4. For example, see Wagley (1941:31), Fischer (2001:239), and Green (2003:60).

5. See Sick (1997) for a discussion of how Costa Rican coffee farmers coped with an earlier coffee crisis. Luetchford argues that although the most obvious solution to low prices is to cut down coffee bushes, "the consensus is that it is a mistake to destroy a cafetal, and many who had done this expressed regret at their decision. One less radical option is to temporarily abandon all inputs, concentrate on other economic activities, and await better times" (2007:63).

6. On average, cooperative members have six children.

7. For example, Pendergrast (1999:34–35) describes the credit and debt problems of coffee farmers during the 1800s when European and North American banks would loan to coffee import houses at 6 percent. The import houses would, in turn, lend to export houses at 8 percent, who then loaned to large-scale growers, or *beneficios*, at 12 percent. The smaller producer would have to pay the *beneficio* between 14 and 25 percent, depending on the perceived risk. Therefore, most coffee entrepreneurs were deep in debt by the time their first crop matured four years after the initial planting. Wolf argues that debt distinguishes peasants from independent cultivators since this is how political control is effected and it is what makes the peasants part of a hierarchical social order. He argues, "The peasant's loss was the power holder's gain" (1966:10).

8. The average debt load of all cooperative members was calculated using records provided by the cooperative on the basis of an exchange rate of Q7.9/US$1.

9. See http://www.langlink.com/guatemala-general-info (accessed 10/28/09).

10. Furthermore, it is likely that Mendoza and Bastiaensen's argument is more applicable to larger groups and second-tier organizations linking numerous small-scale producer cooperatives.

CHAPTER 4

1. Hacker and Elcorobairutia, for example, argue that in the case of the Mondragon cooperative, workers increasingly elected members of the professional university-trained elite to make important decisions, which ultimately weakened workplace democracy (1987:372).

2. Diagnóstico de la Situación ante el Desastre del 5 de Octubre del 2005, Municipalidad de San Juan La Laguna, Departamento Solota, Guatemala (Municipalidad 2005).

3. This section refers to research conducted in 2002. Regrettably, the former manager passed in 2006. His death resulted in an upheaval in the cooperative. At the time of my last research trip in June 2006 the former accountant (assistant manager) had been hired to replace him. For this reason this section is written in the past tense and should be understood as a case study of managerial conflicts rather than an accurate portrayal of ongoing difficulties.

4. See www.transparency.org (accessed 12/20/07).

5. In January 2003, the Bush administration "decertified" Guatemala as a cooperative partner in the antidrug effort, jeopardizing millions of dollars in foreign

aid and further tarnishing Guatemala's image among foreign investors. Manuel Orozco, the Central American project director at the Inter-American Dialogue, a Washington policy group, stated that Guatemala was "[t]he most corrupt country right now," while Elfidio Cano, a member of Guatemala's anti-corruption commission, stated, "Corruption in Guatemala is a type of social pathology that should be analyzed by a sociologist or psychiatrist" (New York Times 2003).

6. As Hansen points out, within systems of mutual aid, failing to ask for help is considered "[a]s serious a violation of the group norm as failure to give help when requested" (1981:74, in Smart 1993:396).

7. For similar arguments see Gluckman (1963), Handelman (1973), Wilson (1974), and Merry (1984).

8. This parallels the basis of traditional stratification in Maya communities more broadly, which, as Carmack describes, results from a complex combination of ascribed and achieved factors: "Age, sex, ritual condition, and kinship affiliation are all necessary for the attainment of the highest-grade status" (1995:307).

9. Juana's father was a *principal* of the highest grade in the community, a male who had passed through the graded ranks of the religious hierarchy. Principales are traditionally addressed as "father" and lower-status people usually bow their heads in greeting. Men and women from lower grades defer to them in public meetings and they command the right to speak when and as often as they wish, sit in the front chairs, and remain active in decision making (Carmack 1995:306).

10. This is consistent with research on community authority and power in Maya communities. For example, Carmack argues (1995:307) that women and children are excluded from many public affairs; when present they must remain silent or take part only as directed by men.

11. See www.fairtrade.net (accessed 10/2/07).

12. Furthermore, the traditional agricultural exports rely on the "housewivization" of Mayan women's labor in various ways (Nelson 2001). For example, labor on coffee, sugar, and cotton plantations is often not waged but instead paid by the amount harvested, so entire families will work together for one payment. In cases where men alone undertake seasonal migration to the coast, women's labor in maintaining crops, raising children, and household production is also unpaid.

13. An FLO representative explains, "Our development approach means that we set entry standards which are not too high, so that poor producers can enter Fair Trade but then use progress standards to foster improvements" (Raynolds, Murray, and Heller 2007).

14. See www.fairtrade.net (accessed 10/20/06).

15. For example, see Mayoux (2001); Redfern and Snedker (2002); Ronchi (2002); Shreck (2002); Utting-Chamarro (2005); and Fridell (2007).

16. The producer profiles are available at www.fairtrade.net (accessed 10/20/06).

17. As in the stories that circulate about coffee cooperatives in Latin America, allegations of corruption (and actual corruption) also plague weaving associations across Guatemala (Ehlers 1990; Hendrickson 1995; Little 2004). Ehlers provides insight into one case of corruption in her analysis of the San Antonio Palopo weaving

cooperative. The officers were caught embezzling thousands of quetzals of the group's working capital; the founder threatened to blow the whistle and was quickly kicked out of the cooperative. Members then left to work for the expelled founder who ran his new business like the cooperative. Ironically, several years later the founder's weavers deserted him after he was found to be embezzling money from the new business and six new middlemen picked up the slack. Ehlers argues that corruption actually spread entrepreneurship in this community and fostered local competition (1993:188).

18. This is consistent with the consensus of the international development community that strengthening women's empowerment is an effective way to promote children's educational achievement (UNDP 2002, in Bacon 2010).

19. As Gill details, the Alliance for Progress prodded the U.S. Congress to exert greater control over foreign aid through the creation of the "New Directions" guidelines for aid allocation in 1973, which directed the U.S. Agency for International Development to devote a larger percentage of development assistance to rural areas (1985).

20. For example, see Galjart (1975); Nash, Dandler, and Hopkins (1976); deJanvry (1981); Gill (1985); and Cohen (2000).

21. See www.fairtrade.net (accessed 12/20/07).

CHAPTER 5

1. I have outlined the specific requirements of the Organic Crop Improvement Association (OCIA), the agency certifying the cooperative during the research period (OCIA 2004). All information regarding OCIA certification standards is from the Organic Crop Improvement Association International Inc. 2004 International Certification Standards (effective July 6, 2004).

2. It is important to note that interviewed members of Seattle Audubon consistently stressed that their organizational activities and goals are independent of the National Audubon Society, an organization many of the interviewees held in great contempt because they disagreed with the organization's mission and practices.

3. Available at www.si.edu/smbc (accessed 10/01/06). Institutions such as the Rainforest Alliance have since developed competing certification systems.

4. The service defines a birder as an individual who travels a mile or more from home for the primary purpose of watching birds or closely observes or tries to identify them around the home.

5. A Blueprint for the Future of Migratory Birds: Migratory Bird Program Strategic Plan 2004–2014, available at http://www.fws.gov/migratorybirds/mbstrat plan/finalmbstratplan.pdf (accessed 6/3/07).

6. This price is significantly less than the current price paid to producers of certified organic, fair-trade coffee. However, this oft-cited minimum price is for green coffee (which has been processed up to the point of roasting), whereas cooperative members are paid for their coffee cherries, prior to coffee processing. The minimum price also does not take into account operating expenses, including cooperative ad-

ministration, transportation, fees paid for processing, and any assessed taxes, which are all deducted from the final price paid to individual cooperative members.

7. On the other hand, in an interesting parallel to the above argument for the coupling of organic certification with market access, Plaza Sanchez maintains that although organic production does not necessarily compensate for production costs, one argument for continued certification is that the price of organic products will resist market downturns more readily, thereby providing protection against market fluctuations (1998:313).

8. See www.organicstyle.com (accessed 6/7/07).

9. See www.footprintnetwork.org (accessed 6/7/07).

CHAPTER 6

1. This "fixing" was succinctly described to Taylor by a Mexican coffee cooperative manager: "It is expected that [fair trade] serves to get producers to make a series of changes that increasingly will make them look more like the consumers that buy their products. This desire isn't meant negatively. On the contrary, consumers are convinced that they are doing this for the good of the producers since they are the best mirror. The idea could be summed up as 'nice neocolonialism'" (Taylor 2002:17).

2. For a more detailed explanation of governance relations in network commodity analysis please see Kaplinsky (2000), Barrientos (2002), and Raynolds (2004). Recent studies have employed similar approaches to investigate segments of the agro-food sector, demonstrating how powerful buyers increasingly govern enterprise participation, production processes, and product specifications in international supply chains (Dolan and Humphrey 2000; Ponte 2002; Talbot 2002; Raynolds 2004).

3. Foucault defines governmentality as the art of defining the appropriate conduct of conduct (1979). It is the means by which an individual becomes a subject capable of governing him- or herself through self-regulation—someone who is both subject to someone else by control and dependence, and tied to his own identity by a conscience or self-knowledge (1979).

4. Mutersbaugh (2002, 2003) argues that organic coffee certification systems exert the power of governmentality over participating Mexican cooperative members. Similarly, in his study of Michoacan small-scale dairy farmers, McDonald (1999) demonstrates that the practices of governmentality are driven by the introduction of new concepts of production associated with the globalization process and neoliberal ideals (such as quality, efficiency, and productivity).

5. Raynolds and her colleagues argue that fair trade stands out as having the strongest democratic NGO base of all the major coffee certifications. Yet, participation in fair trade is limited by the character of certification since it is a fundamentally private strategy that limits democratic participation (2007).

6. This finding is supported by research in diverse locales, indicating that producers understand fair trade in terms of market access (Tallontire 2000:175) or

international aid (Shreck 2002) and not as an equitable trade relationship in which they are actively participating. Still other researchers maintain that fair-trade producer groups are "passive suppliers of product" dependent on higher order groups (Utting-Chamorro 2005)—that fair trade is an "intervention" rather than a partnership and that producers do not fully understand the market's benefits (Paul 2005:135).

7. It is important to note here, however, that fair trade is the only coffee initiative that specifies standards for coffee importers—requiring adherence to established prices, commitment to long-term contracts, and pre-financing—beyond importer and chain-of-custody documentation (Raynolds, Murray, and Heller 2007).

8. Fair-trade certification is rooted in an approach to auditing that supposedly produces scientifically validated knowledge based on universally accepted methods and the presumption of a common culture. Strathern points out that while the instruments of measurement have to be held stable, ethically and socially validated knowledge is the outcome of internal negotiations between interest groups in a pluralistic population where one may not be able to, and may not want to, invoke a moral consensus (2005:477).

9. For examples of these arguments please see Raynolds (2002), Calo and Wise (2005), Giovannucci and Ponte (2005), and Lyon (2006).

10. See www.guatemalancoffees.com (accessed 1/25/08).

11. Guatemalan Atitlan "La Voz," August 2001, www.coffeereview.com (accessed 1/28/08).

12. Heifer Hope Blend, November 2005, www.coffeereview.com (accessed 1/28/08).

13. This is not unique to analyses of fair trade. For example, Schmitz (2000) argues that in the small-firm cluster literature, relations between buyers and producers have been more part of an ideological debate than the subject of thorough research. This may be partially explained by the influence of traditional neoclassical economic theory, in which buyers are generally defined as passive intermediaries who form the physical link between demand and supply (Schmitz 2000). Furthermore, social scientists have generally shied away from studying the "cultures of expertise" characterizing the operations of experts such as coffee roasters (Holmes and Marcus 2005).

CHAPTER 7

1. Berlan describes the misrepresentation of coffee farmers in fair-trade promotional materials writing, "One of my local supermarkets currently displays a large poster advertisement for Fair Trade bearing a farmer carrying a large bunch of bananas. The small print beneath the photograph reads: 'Photography is representational and may not depict or relate to the actual Fairtrade farms or farmers who supplied this product. This photograph has been supplied courtesy of the Fairtrade Foundation.' Whereas no one would assume that the characters in mainstream advertising, be it a happy family whose life has been 'transformed' by a particular

brand of washing powder or the purchase of a particular car, were real people, consumers expect that Fair Trade advertisements literally capture the lives of individuals. This results from consumers' preexisting expectations of Fair Trade and from the explicit emphasis in many campaigns on 'meeting' and 'knowing' the farmers" (Berlan 2008:176).

2. Little describes a particularly troublesome incident in which a tourist continued to film his daughter who was playing with several young Maya friends, despite the fact that the children clearly did not want to be filmed. He told the tourist repeatedly to stop filming, and in response she swore at him, only putting away her camera when Little took out his own to take her picture (2004:49–50).

3. For example, see Brysk (2000), Edelman (2005), and Garcia (2005).

4. Goodman argues that the current advertising is a direct reaction to this early history. As an interviewee explained to him, past images and descriptions of farmers and their livelihoods became too ethical and fair trade, thus maintaining early perceptions of poor quality that plagued the fair-trade market (2010).

5. Pine and Gilmore explain, "While prior economic offerings—commodities, goods, and series—are external to the buyer, experiences are inherently personal, existing only in the mind of an individual who has been engaged on an emotional, physical, intellectual, or even spiritual level" (Pine and Gilmore 1998:99, in Foster 2008).

6. For example, see Johnston (2002), Shreck (2002), and Starr and Adams (2003).

7. For variations on this argument see Whatmore and Thorne (1997), Raynolds (2000), Barham (2002:350), Hudson and Hudson (2003), Bryant and Goodman (2004), Goodman (2004), Goodman and Cohen (2004), and Moberg (2005).

8. Allen and Kovach make a similar argument for the organic market—that its greatest potential "lies less in some objective 'truth' of ecological sustainability, and more in its potential to demystify the commodity form of food" (2000:225).

9. These relations of difference are signs and social constructs defined by categories of thought and the products of society and history (Taussig 1980:9, in Castree 2001:1520). Malkki maintains that the world of national spaces is conceived as one of partitionings and discontinuities naturalized in such a way that people and place are permanently territorialized (1990).

10. As Pratt argues (2008:68), the labels and the conversations about product and producer authenticity provide a variable and tenuous connection to the world of rural labor. They may continue to reify that labor and they certainly do not achieve an end to commodity fetishism per se if the labor is alienated.

11. See www.greenmountaincoffee.com (accessed 6/28/06).

12. See www.greenmountaincoffee.com (accessed 10/1/09).

13. This partnership has flourished in recent years and Newman's Own Organics now advertises that "[i]t seems only natural that two companies with a shared vision of a better world would unite to bring you exceptional coffee and the chance to make a difference"; www.newmansownorganicscoffee.com (accessed 10/1/09).

14. See http://www.gmcr.com/csr (accessed 10/1/09).

15. See http://www.greenmountaincoffee/com/prdCoffee.aspx?Name=Heif erHopeBlend (accessed 2/27/08).

16. This use of Andean music to authenticate the film's representation of Maya culture is reminiscent of the "outsourcing of otherness" that occurs in artisan production. Esperanza explains, "[T]he outsourcing of otherness does not imply that the Balinese have been hired to reproduce traditional objects by the cultural groups from which the objects originate, but rather, they have been contracted to continue the work of imagining Otherness; to continue the simulacrum of subaltern culture imagined by those who hold the economic and political influence" (2008:150; see M'Closkey [2010] for an examination of the economic costs to Navajo artisans when their otherness is outsourced by middlemen to Mexico).

17. See http://www.ilo.org (accessed 6/01/06).

18. As Bebbington (1996:1163) explains, modernized forms of indigenous organizations, such as the cooperative, can enact strategies of modernization that are grounded in their ethnic and regional identity and organization, and so have a potential to be sustainable, accountable, and locally adaptive.

19. See Fischer and Brown (1996), Warren (1998), Nelson (1999, 2004), Warren and Jackson (2002), Fischer (2004), and Postero and Zamosc (2004) for more information on the pan-Maya movement.

Works Cited

Acheson, James
  1985   "Social Organization of the Maine Lobster Market."
          In *Markets and Marketing: Monographs in Economic
          Anthropology*, ed. S. Plattner, 4:105–132. New York:
          University Press of America.

Adams, Abigail
  2001   "The Transformation of the Tzuultaq'a: Jorge Ubico,
          Protestants and Other Verapaz Maya at the Cross-
          roads of Community, State and Transnational In-
          terests." *Journal of Latin American Anthropology* 6(2):
          198–233.

Adams, Dale W.
  1992   "Microenterprise Credit Programs: Deja Vu." *World
          Development* 20(10): 1463–1470.

Alcorn, Janis B., and Victor M. Toledo
  1998   "Resilient Resource Management in Mexico's For-
          est Ecosystems: The Contributions of Property
          Rights." In *Linking Social and Ecological Systems:
          Management Practices and Social Mechanisms for Build-*

ing Resilience, ed. F. Berkes and C. Folke, 216–249. Cambridge: Cambridge University Press.

Allen, P., and M. Kovach
2000   "The Capitalist Composition of Organic: The Potential of Markets in Fulfilling the Promise of Organic Agriculture." *Agriculture and Human Values* 17(3): 221–232.

Anderson, Benedict
1983   *Imagined Communities: Reflections on the Origin and Spread of Nationalism.* London: Verso.

Annis, Sheldon
1970   "Land of Our Ancestors: A Study of Land Tenure and Inheritance in the Highlands of Guatemala." PhD dissertation, Social Anthropology, Harvard University, Cambridge, MA.
1987   *God and Production in a Guatemalan Town.* Austin: University of Texas Press.

Appadurai, Arjun
1986   "Introduction: Commodities and the Politics of Value." In *The Social Life of Things: Commodities in Cultural Perspective*, ed. A. Appadurai, 3–63. New York: Cambridge University Press.

Arce, Alberto
2009   "Living in Times of Solidarity: Fair Trade and the Fractured Life Worlds of Guatemalan Coffee Farmers." *Journal of International Development* 21: 1031–1041.

Auret, Diane, and Stephanie Barrientos
2006   "Participatory Social Auditing: Developing a Worker-Focused Approach." In *Ethical Sourcing in the Global Food System*, ed. Barrientos, S. and C. Dolan, 129–148. London: Earthscan Press.

Bacon, Christopher
2005   "Confronting the Coffee Crisis: Can Fair Trade, Organic, and Specialty Coffees Reduce Small-Scale Farmer Vulnerability in Northern Nicaragua?" *World Development* 33(3): 497–511.
2010   "A Spot of Coffee in Crisis: Nicaraguan Smallholder Cooperatives, Fair Trade Networks, and Gendered Empowerment." *Journal of Latin American Perspectives* 37(2): 50–71.

Barham, Elizabeth
2002   "Towards a Theory of Value-Based Labeling." *Agriculture and Human Values* 19: 349–360.

Barlett, Peggy F.
1982   *Agricultural Choice and Change: Decision Making in a Costa Rican Community.* New Brunswick, NJ: Rutgers University Press.

Barrientos, Stephanie
  2002   "Mapping Codes through the Value Chain: From Researcher to Detective." In *Corporate Responsibility and Labour Rights: Codes of Conduct in the Global Economy*, ed. R. Jenkins, R. Pearson, and G. Seyfant, 61–78. Sterling, VA: Earthscan Publications Ltd.

Barrientos, Stephanie, Catherine Dolan, and Anne Tallontire
  2003   "A Gendered Value Chain Approach to Codes of Conduct in African Horticulture." *World Development* 31(9): 1511–1526.

Bartley, Tim
  2005   "Corporate Accountability and the Privatization of Labor Standards: Struggles over Codes of Conduct in the Apparel Industry." *Research in Political Sociology* 14: 213–247.

Bastell, Jake
  2004   "Coffee in Good Conscience: Students Campaign for Roasters to Provide Only 'Fair-Trade' Beans." *Seattle Times*, March 17. http://community.seattletimes.nwsource.com/archive/?date=20020317&slug=collegecoffee17 (accessed 1/6/09).

Bebbington, Anthony
  1996   "Organizations and Intensifications: Campesino Federations, Rural Livelihoods and Agricultural Technology in the Andes and Amazonia." *World Development* 24(7): 1161–1177.

Beck, Ulrich
  1992   *Risk Society: Towards a New Modernity*. London: Sage.

Bendheim, KIim
  2002   "Global Issues Flow into America's Coffee." *New York Times*, November 3.

Berlan, Amanda
  2008   "Making or Marketing a Difference? An Anthropological Examination of the Marketing of Fair Trade Cocoa from Ghana." *Research in Economic Anthropology* 28: 171–194.

Berlo, Janet Catherine
  1991   "Beyond Bricolage: Women and Aesthetic Strategies in Latin American Textiles." In *Textile Traditions of Mesoamerica and the Andes*, ed. M. B. Schevill, J. C. Berlo, and E. B. Dwyer, 437–479. Cambridge: Cambridge University Press.

Blowfield, Michael
  1999   "Ethical Trade: A Review of Developments and Issues." *Third World Quarterly* 20: 753–770.

Bossen, Laurel
  1984   *The Redivision of Labor: Women and Economic Choice in Four Guatemalan Communities*. Albany: State University of New York Press.

Works Cited

Bourdieu, Pierre
    1984   *Distinction: A Social Critique of the Judgment of Taste.* Trans. R. Nice. Cambridge, MA: Harvard University Press.

Bray, David Barton, Jose Luis Plaza Sanchez, and Ellen Contreras Murphy
    2002   "Social Dimensions of Organic Coffee Production in Mexico: Lessons for Eco-labeling Initiatives." *Society and Natural Resources* 14: 429–446.

Brintnall, Douglas
    1979   *Revolt against the Dead: The Modernization of a Mayan Community in the Highlands of Guatemala.* New York: Gordon and Breach.

Brockett, Charles D.
    1998   *Land, Power and Poverty: Agrarian Transformation and Political Conflict in Central America.* Boulder: Westview Press.

Brosius, Peter
    1999   "Green Dots, Pink Hearts: Displacing Politics from the Malaysian Rain Forest." *American Anthropologist* 101(1): 36–57.

Browne, A. W., P.J.C. Harris, A. H. Hofny-Collins, N. Pasiecznik, and R. R. Wallace
    2000   "Organic Production and Ethical Trade: Definition, Practice and Links." *Food Policy* 25: 69–89.

Bryant, Raymond L., and Michael K. Goodman
    2004   "Consuming Narratives: The Political Ecology of 'Alternative' Consumption." *Transactions of the Institute of British Geographers* 29: 344–366.

Brysk, Allison
    2000   *From Tribal Village to Global Village: Indian Rights and International Relations in Latin America.* Stanford, CA: Stanford University Press.

Busch, Lawrence, and Carmen Bain
    2004   "New! Improved? The Transformation of the Global Agrifood System." *Rural Sociology* 69(3): 321–346.

Cabrera, R., and A. D. Cifuentes
    1997   *El Proceso de Negociaciones de Paz en Guatemala.* Guatemala: Ediciones Nueva Era.

Calo, Muriel, and Timothy A. Wise
    2005   *Revaluing Peasant Coffee Production: Organic and Fair Trade Markets in Mexico.* Medford, MA: Global Development and Environment Institute Tufts University.

Cambranes, Julio Castellano
    1985   *Coffee and Peasants in Guatemala.* South Woodstock, VT: CIRMA.

Campbell, Hugh, Geoffrey Lawrence, and Kiah Smith
    2006   "Audit Cultures and the Antipodes: The Implications of EurepGAP for New Zealand and Australian Agri-Food Industries." In *Between the Local*

and the Global: Confronting Complexity in the Contemporary Agri-Food Sector, ed. T. Marsden and J. Murdoch, 69–94. New York: Elsevier.

Cancian, Frank

1965   *Economics and Prestige in a Maya Community: The Religious Cargo System in Zinacantan.* Stanford, CA: Stanford University Press.

1992   *The Decline of Community in Zinacantan: Economy, Public Life, and Social Stratification, 1960–1987.* Stanford, CA: Stanford University Press.

Canessa, Andrew

2005   *Introduction: Making the Nation on the Margins. In Natives Making Nation: Gender, Indigeneity, and the State in the Andes,* ed. A. Canessa, 3–31. Tucson: University of Arizona Press.

Capone, Lisa

2004   "There's a New Cause Brewing on Campuses." *Boston Globe.* February 2. http://www.boston.com/news/globe/living/articles/2004/02/02/theres_a_new_cause_brewing_on_campuses/ (accessed 1/7/09).

Carey, David, Jr.

2001   *Our Elders Teach Us: Maya-Kaqchikel Historical Perspectives.* Tuscaloosa: University of Alabama Press.

2006   *Engendering Mayan History: Kaqchikel Women as Agents and Conduits of the Past, 1875–1970.* New York: Routledge.

Carmack, Robert M.

1995   *Rebels of Highland Guatemala: The Quiché-Mayas of Momostenango.* Norman: University of Oklahoma Press.

Carrier, James G.

1997   "Introduction." In *The Meanings of the Market: Free Market in Western Culture,* ed. J. G. Carrier, 1–68. Oxford: Berg Publishers.

Castree, Noel

2001   "Commodity Fetishism, Geographical Imaginations and Imaginative Geographies." *Environment and Planning* A 33: 1519–1525.

CEH

1999   *Guatemala Memoria del Silencio: Conclusions and Recommendations.* Guatemala City: Comision para el Esclarecimiento Historico, United Nations.

Chance, John K.

1990   "Changes in Twentieth-Century Mesoamerican Cargo Systems." In *Class, Politics and Popular Religion in Mexico and Central America,* ed. Lynn Stephen, James Dow, and Leigh Binford, 27–42. Washington, DC: Society for Latin American Anthropology.

Chin, Elizabeth

2007   "The Consumer Diaries, or, Autoethnography in the Inverted World." *Journal of Consumer Culture* 7(3): 335–353.

Works Cited

Clifford, James

    2001   "Indigenous Articulations." *The Contemporary Pacific* 13(2): 468–490.

Cohen, Jeffrey H.

    1999   *Cooperation and Community: Economy and Society in Oaxaca*. Austin: University of Texas Press.

    2000   "Textile Production in Rural Mexico: The Complexities of the Global Market for Handmade Crafts." In *Artisans and Cooperatives: Developing Alternative Trade for the Global Economy*, ed. K. Grimes and L. Milgram, 129–142. Tucson: University of Arizona Press.

Collier, Robert

    2001   "Mourning Coffee: World's Leading Java Companies are Raking in High Profits, But Growers Worldwide Face Ruin as Prices Sink to Historic Low." *San Francisco Chronicle*, May 20. http://articles.sfgate.com/2001-05-20/news/17600679_1_arabica-coffee-farm-la-reforma (accessed 10/17/10).

Collier, Stephen J., and Aihwa Ong

    2005   "Global Assemblages, Anthropological Problems." In *Global Assemblages*, ed. Aihwa Ong and Stephen J. Collier, 3–21. Malden, MA: Blackwell.

Collins, Jane L.

    2003   *Threads: Gender, Labor, and Power in the Global Apparel Industry*. Chicago: University of Chicago Press.

Colloredo-Mansfeld, Rudolf

    1994   "Architectural Conspicuous Consumption and Economic Change in the Andes." *American Anthropologist* 96(4): 845–865.

    1999   *The Native Leisure Class: Consumption and Cultural Creativity in the Andes*. Chicago: University of Chicago Press.

    2005   "Consumption." In *A Handbook of Economic Anthropology*, ed. J. G. Carrier, 23–45. Oxford: Edward Elgar.

Comaroff, John L., and Jean Comaroff

    2009   *Ethnicity, Inc.* Chicago: University of Chicago Press.

Conroy, Michael E.

    2001   "Can Advocacy-Led Certification Systems Transform Global Corporate Practices? Evidence and Some Theory." In Working Paper 21, Political Economy Research Institute. Amherst: University of Massachusetts–Amherst.

Crewe, Emma, and Elizabeth Harrison

    1998   *Whose Development? An Ethnography of Aid*. London: Zed Books.

Cunningham, Hilary

    1999   "The Ethnography of Transnational Social Activism: Understanding the Global as Local Practice." *American Ethnologist* 26(3): 583–604.

Cycon, Dean
　2005　"Confessions of a Fair Trader." *Cultural Survival Quarterly* 29(3). http://www.culturalsurvival.org/ourpublications/csq/article/confessions-a-fair-trader (accessed 4/13/10).

Danford, Natalie
　2003　"The Call of the Wild." *Publishers Weekly*. April 28, p. 36.

Davids, Kenneth
　2000　"Organically Grown Coffees." *Coffee Review*. www.coffeereview.com (accessed 1/28/08).
　2001　"Guatemalan Atitlan 'La Voz.'" *Coffee Review* (August 2001). www.coffeereview.com (accessed 1/28/08).
　2005　"Heifer Hope Blend." *Coffee Review* (November 2005). www.coffeereview.com (accessed 1/28/08).

Davids, Kenneth, and Lindsey Bolger
　2004　"The Fair-Trade Cup: Quality and Controversy." *Coffee Review*. www.coffeereview.com (accessed 1/28/08).

Daviron, Benoit, and Stefano Ponte
　2005　*The Coffee Paradox: Global Markets, Commodity Trade and the Elusive Promise of Development*. London: Zed Books.

Dearlove, Des
　1999　"Built on Ethical Grounds." *The Times London*, September 2.

DeJanvry, Alain
　1981　*The Agrarian Question and Reform in Latin America*. Baltimore: Johns Hopkins University Press.

DeJanvry, Alain, and Elisabeth Sadoulet
　2000　"Rural Poverty in Latin America: Determinants and Exit Paths." *Food Policy* 25: 389–409.

Desmarais, Annette-Aurelie
　2002　"The Via Campesina: Consolidating an International Peasant and Farm Movement." *The Journal of Peasant Studies* 29(2): 91–124.

Devereaux, Leslie
　1987　"Gender Differences and the Relations of Inequality in Zinacantan." In *Dealing with Inequality*, ed. M. Strathern, 89–111. Cambridge: Cambridge University Press.

Dewalt, Billie R.
　1975　"Changes in the Cargo Systems of Mesoamerica." *Anthropological Quarterly* 48(2): 87–105.

Dolan, Catherine S.
　2005a　"Benevolent Intent? The Development Encounter in Kenya's Horticulture Industry." *Journal of Asian and African Studies* 40(6): 411–437.

2005b   "Fields of Obligation: Rooting Ethical Sourcing in Kenyan Horticulture." *Journal of Consumer Culture* 5(3): 365–389.

Dolan, Catherine S., and John Humphrey
2000   "Governance and Trade in Fresh Vegetables: The Impact of UK Supermarkets on the African Horticulture Industry." *Journal of Development Studies* 37(2): 147–177.

Dore, Ronald
1983   "Goodwill and the Spirit of Market Capitalism." *British Journal of Sociology* 34: 459–482.

Douglas, Mary, and Baron Isherwood
1979   *The World of Goods*. New York: Basic Books.

Dove, Michael R.
2006   "Indigenous People and Environmental Politics." *Annual Review of Anthropology* 35: 191–208.

Durham, William H.
1995   "Political Ecology and Environmental Destruction in Latin America." In *The Social Causes of Environmental Destruction in Latin America*, ed. M. Painter and W. Durham, 249–264. Ann Arbor: University of Michigan Press.

Easson, Kimberly
2000   "The Revolution of Quality." *Tea and Coffee Trade Journal* 172(2): 33.

Economist
2006   "Food Politics." *Economist* (December 7).

Edelman, Marc
1992   *The Logic of the Latifundio: The Large Estates of Northwestern Costa Rica since the Late Nineteenth Century*. Stanford, CA: Stanford University Press.
1995   "Rethinking the Hamburger Thesis: Deforestation and the Crisis of Central America's Beef Exports." In *The Social Causes of Environmental Destruction in Latin America*, ed. M. Painter and W. Durham, 25–61. Ann Arbor: University of Michigan.
2005   "Bringing the Moral Economy Back in . . . to the Study of 21st Century Transnational Peasant Movements." *American Anthropologist* 107(3): 331–345.

Ehlers, Tracy Bachrach
1990   *Silent Looms: Women and Production in a Guatemalan Town*. Boulder, CO: Westview Press.
1991   "Debunking Marianismo: Economic Vulnerability and Survival Strategies among Guatemalan Wives." *Ethnology* 31(1): 1–16.
1993   "Belts, Business, and Bloomingdale's: An Alternative Model for Guatemalan Artisan Development." In *Crafts in the World Market*, ed. J. Nash, 181–198. Albany: SUNY Press.

Escobar, Arturo
1995   *Encountering Development: The Making and Unmaking of the Third World.*
        Princeton, NJ: Princeton University Press.
1996   "Construction Nature: Elements for a Poststructural Political Ecology."
        In *Liberation Ecologies: Environment, Development and Social Movements*,
        ed. R. Peet and M. Watts, 47–68. New York: Routledge.
1999   "After Nature: Steps to an Antiessentialist Political Ecology." *Current An-
        thropology* 40(1): 1–30.

Esperanza, Jennifer S.
2008   "Outsourcing Otherness: Crafting and Marketing Culture in the Global
        Handicrafts Market." *Research in Economic Anthropology* 28: 143–169.

Esteva, Gustavo, and Madhu Suri Prakash
1998   *Grassroots Postmodernism: Remaking the Soil of Cultures.* New York: Zed
        Books.

Euraque, Dario A., Jeffrey R. Gould, and Charles R. Hale, eds.
2005   *Cultura Política en Centroamérica de 1920 al Presente.* Guatemala City:
        CIRMA.

Ferguson, James, and Akhil Gupta
2002   "Spatializing States: Towards an Ethnography of Neoliberal Govern-
        mentality." *American Ethnologist* 29(4): 981–1002.

Fischer, Edward
2001   *Cultural Logics and Global Economies: Maya Identity in Thought and Prac-
        tice.* Austin: University of Texas Press.
2004   "Beyond Victimization: Maya Movements in Post-War Guatemala." In
        Indigenous Movements and the Indian Question in Latin America, ed. N. Pos-
        tero and L. Zamosc, 81–104. Portland, OR: Sussex Academic Press.

Fischer, Edward F., and Peter Benson
2006   *Broccoli and Desire: Global Connections and Maya Struggles in Postwar Gua-
        temala.* Stanford, CA: Stanford University Press.

Fischer, Edward F., and Carol Hendrickson
2003   *Tecpán, Guatemala: A Modern Maya Town in Global and Local Context.*
        Boulder, CO: Westview.

Fischer, Edward F., and R. McKenna Brown
1996   "Introduction: Maya Cultural Activism in Guatemala." In *Maya Cultural
        Activism in Guatemala*, ed. E. F. Fischer and R. M. Brown, 1–18. Austin:
        University of Texas Press.

Fisher, Eleanor
1997   "Beekeepers in the Global 'Fair Trade' Market: A Case from Tabora
        Region, Tanzania." *International Journal of Sociology of Agriculture and
        Food* 6: 109–259.

Works Cited

FLO

2003   "Generic Fairtrade Standards for Small Farmers' Organizations." www.
        fairtrade.net.

2006   "Explanatory Document for the Generic Fairtrade Standard for Small
        Farmers' Organizations." Bonn, Germany: Fairtrade Labelling Organi-
        zations International. www.fairtrade.net.

2007a   "Generic Fairtrade Standards for Smallholder Organizations." Bonn,
        Germany. www.fairtrade.net.

2007b   "Consultation Document: FLO Draft Generic Fairtrade Standard for
        Small Producers' Organizations." Bonn, Germany. www.fairtrade.net.

2009   "Coffee." http://www.fairtrade.net/coffee.html (accessed 1/27/09).

Folke, Carl, Fikret Berkes, and Johan Colding

1998   "Ecological Practices and Social Mechanisms for Building Resilience
        and Sustainability." In *Linking Social and Ecological Systems: Management
        Practices and Social Mechanisms for Building Resilience*, ed. F. Berkes and C.
        Folke, 414–436. Cambridge: Cambridge University Press.

Foster, George

1967   *Tzintzuntzan: Mexican Peasants in a Changing World*. New York: Little,
        Brown and Company.

1972   "The Anatomy of Envy: A Study in Symbolic Behavior." *Current Anthro-
        pology* 13(2): 165–202.

Foster, Robert J.

2002   "Labor and Love: An Anthropological Approach to Value Chain Analy-
        sis." Paper presented at the American Anthropology Association An-
        nual Meeting, New Orleans, LA.

2008   "Commodities, Brands, Love and Kula: Comparative Notes on Value
        Creation." *Anthropological Theory* 8(1): 9–25.

Foucault, Michel

1979   *Discipline and Punish*. New York: Vintage Books.

Fox, Jonathan

1996   "How Does Civil Society Thicken? The Political Construction of Social
        Capital in Rural Mexico." *World Development* 24(6): 1089–1103.

Fox, Tom, and Bill Vorley

2006   "Small Producers: Constraints and Challenges in the Global Food Sys-
        tem." In *Ethical Sourcing in the Global Food System*, ed. S. Barrientos and
        C. Dolan, 163–178. London: Earthscan.

2007   *Fair Trade Coffee: The Prospects and Pitfalls of Market-Driven Social Justice*.
        Toronto: University of Toronto Press.

Friedman, Jonathan

1994   *Cultural Identity and Global Processes*. Thousand Oaks, CA: Sage.

Friedman, Thomas
   2000   *The Lexus and the Olive Tree: Understanding Globalization.* New York: Farrar, Strauss and Giroux.

Galeano, Eduardo
   1967   *Guatemala, Pais Ocupado.* Mexico City: Editorial Nuestro Tiempo.

Galjart, Benno
   1975   "Peasant Consciousness, Cooperation and Solidarity." *Development and Change* 6:75–83.

Garcia, Maria Elena
   2005   *Making Indigenous Citizens: Identity, Development and Multicultural Activism in Peru.* Stanford, CA: Stanford University Press.

Garzon, S.
   1998   "Conclusion." In *The Life of Our Language: Kaqchikel Maya Maintenance Shift and Revitalization*, ed. S. Garzon, R. M. Brown, J. B. Richards, and W. Ajpub', 188–198. Austin: University of Texas Press.

Gereffi, Gary
   1994   "The Organization of Buyer-Driven Global Commodity Chains: How US Retailers Shape Overseas Production Networks." In *Commodity Chains and Global Capitalism*, ed. G. Gereffi and M. Korzeniewicz, 95–122. Westport, CT: Greenwood Press.

Gereffi, Gary, John Humphrey, and Timothy Sturgeon
   2005   "The Governance of Global Value Chains." *Review of International Political Economy* 12(1): 78–104.

Giddens, Anthony
   1991   *Modernity and Self-Identity: Self and Society in the Late Modern Age.* Stanford, CA: Stanford University Press.

Gill, Lesley
   1985   "Rural Cooperatives and Peasant Differences." *Research in Economic Anthropology* 7: 225–249.

Giovannucci, Daniele
   2002   "Who Shall We Blame? The Politics of Coffee." *Tea and Coffee Trade Journal* (January): 30–35.

Giovannucci, Daniele, and Freek Jan Koekoek
   2003   *The State of Sustainable Coffee: A Study of Twelve Major Markets.* London and Winnipeg: ICO and IISD.

Giovannucci, D., and S. Ponte
   2005   "Standards as a New Form of Social Contract? Sustainability Initiatives in the Coffee Industry." *Food Policy* 284–301.

Works Cited

Giovannucci, Daniele, and Andres Villalobos
  2007   *The State of Organic Coffee: 2007 U.S. Update.* Costa Rica: CMS (Sustainable Markets Intelligence Center.

Gledhill, John
  2003   "Rights and the Poor." In *Human Rights in Global Perspective: Anthropological Studies of Rights, Claims and Entitlements,* ed. Richard Ashby Wilson and Jon P. Mitchell, 209–228. New York: Routledge.

Gluckman, Max
  1963   "Papers in Honor of Melville J. Herskovits: Gossip and Scandal." *Current Anthropology* 4(3): 307–316.

Goldman, Robert, and Stephen Papson
  1996   *Sign Wars.* New York: Guilford.

Gonzalez Cabanas, Alma Amalia
  2002   *Evaluation of the Current and Potential Poverty Alleviation Benefits of Participation in the Fair Trade Market: The Case of Union La Selva.* Chiapas, Mexico: Fair Trade Research Working Group.

Goodman, Douglas, and Mirelle Cohen
  2004   *Consumer Culture: A Reference Handbook.* Santa Barbara, CA: ABC-CLIO.

Goodman, Michael
  2004   "Reading Fair Trade: Political Ecological Imaginary and the Moral Economy of Fair Trade Foods." *Political Geography* 23: 891–915.
  2010   "The Mirror of Consumption: Celebritization, Developmental Consumption and the Shifting Cultural Politics of Fair Trade." *GeoForum* 41(1): 104–116.

Goss, Jon
  2004   "Geography of Consumption I." *Progress in Human Geography* 28(3): 369–380.

Gottdiener, Mark
  2000   *New Forms of Consumption: Consumers, Culture and Commodification.* Lanham, MD: Rowman and Littlefield.

Graeber, David
  2002   "The Anthropology of Globalization (with Notes on Neomedievalism, and the End of the Chinese Model of the Nation-State)." *American Anthropologist* 104(4): 1222–1227.

Grandin, Greg
  2000   *The Blood of Guatemala: A History of Race and Nation.* Durham, NC: Duke University Press.
  2004   *The Last Colonial Massacre: Latin America in the Cold War.* Chicago: University of Chicago Press.
  2006   *Empire's Workshop: Latin America, the United States, and the Rise of the New Imperialism.* New York: Metropolitan Books, Henry Holt and Company.

Granovetter, Mark
1985   "Economic Action and Social Structure: The Problem of Embeddedness." *American Journal of Sociology* 91: 481–510.

Green, Linda
1999   *Fear as a Way of Life: Mayan Widows in Rural Guatemala.* New York: Columbia University Press.
2003   "Notes on Mayan Youth and Rural Industrialization in Guatemala." *Critique of Anthropology* 23(1): 51–73.

Greenberg, James B.
1995   "Capital, Ritual and Boundaries of the Closed Corporate Community." In *Articulating Hidden Histories: Exploring the Influence of Eric R. Wolf,* ed. J. Schneider and R. Rapp, 67–81. Berkeley: University of California Press.

Greenberg, Russell, Peter Bichier, and John Sterling
1997   "Bird Populations in Rustic and Planted Shade Grown Coffee Plantations of Eastern Chiapas, Mexico." *Biotropica* 29(4): 501–514.

Guthman, Julie
2003   "Fast Food / Organic Food: Reflexive Tastes and the Making of 'Yuppie Chow.'" *Social and Cultural Geography* 41(1): 45–58.
2004   "The 'Organic Commodity' and Other Anomalies in the Politics of Consumption." In *Geographies of Commodity Chains,* ed. A. Hughes and S. Reimer, 233–249. New York: Routledge.
2007   "The Polanyian Way? Voluntary Food Labels as Neoliberal Governance." *Antipode* 39(3): 456–478.

Hacker, Sally L., and Clara Elcorobairutia
1987   "Women Workers in the Mondragon System of Industrial Cooperatives." *Gender and Society* 1(4): 358–379.

Haenn, Nora
2005   *Fields of Power, Forests of Discontent: Culture, Conservation, and the State in Mexico.* Tucson: University of Arizona Press.

Hale, Charles R.
2006   *Más que un Indio: Racial Ambivalence and Neoliberal Multiculturalism in Guatemala.* Santa Fe, NM: School of American Research.

Hamilton, Sarah
2000   "The Myth of the Masculine Market: Gender and Agricultural Commercialization in the Ecuadorian Andes." In *Women Farmers and Commercial Ventures: Increasing Food Security in Developing Countries,* ed. A. Spring, 65–87. Boulder: Lynne Rienner.

Handelman, Don
1973   "Gossip in Encounters: The Transmission of Information in a Bounded Social Setting." *Man* 8(2): 210–227.

Works Cited

Handy, Jim
  1984   *Gift of the Devil: A History of Guatemala*. Boston: South End Press.

Hansen, Knud
  1981   "'Black' Exchange and Its System of Control." In *Networks, Exchange and Coercion*, ed. D. Willer and B. Anders, 71–83. New York: Elsevier.

Hartford, Tim
  2007   *The Undercover Economist: Exposing Why the Rich Are Rich, the Poor Are Poor—and Why You Can Never Buy a Decent Used Car!* New York: Random House Publishing.

Harvey, David
  1989   *The Condition of Postmodernity: An Enquiry into the Origins of Cultural Change*. New York: Blackwell Publishers.

Held, David, Anthony McGrew, David Goldblatt, and Jonathan Perraton
  1999   *Global Transformations: Politics, Economics, and Culture*. Stanford, CA: Stanford University Press.

Hendrickson, Carol
  1995   *Weaving Identities: Construction of Dress and Self in a Highland Guatemalan Town*. Austin: University of Texas Press.

Hernandez Castillo, Rosalva Aida, and Ronald Nigh
  1998   "Global Processes and Local Identity among Mayan Coffee Growers in Chiapas, Mexico." *American Anthropologist* 100(1): 136–147.

Holmes, Douglas
  1989   *Cultural Disenchantments: Worker Peasantries in Northeast Italy*. Princeton, NJ: Princeton University Press.

Holmes, Douglas R., and George E. Marcus
  2005   "Cultures of Expertise and the Management of Globalization: Toward the Re-functioning of Ethnography." In *Global Assemblages*, ed. A. Ong and S. J. Collier, 235–252. London: Blackwell.

Holt-Gimenez, Eric
  1996   *The Campesino a Campesino Movement: Farmer-Led Sustainable Agriculture in Central America and Mexico*. Oakland, CA: Institute for Food and Development Policy.

Hudson, Ian, and Mark Hudson
  2003   "Removing the Veil? Commodity Fetishism, Fair Trade, and the Environment." *Organization and Environment* 16(4): 413–431.

IMC (Instituto de Mujer y Comunidad)
  2009   "Diagnostico Participativo de Género en Organizaciones Certificadas por FLO Centroamérica en Nicaragua." IMC/FLO International/Irish Aid. Estelí, Nicaragua: ISNAYA.

Infopress
2006   "Environmental Negligence: Government Spending to Fight Contamination and Deforestation Remains Low." *Latinamerica Press* 2(8): 8–9.

James, Deborah
2000   "Justice and Java: Coffee in a Fair Trade Market." *NACLA* (September/October): 11–15. www.globalexchange.org/campaigns/fairtrade/coffee/nacla1000.html (accessed 10/14/10).

Jameson, Fredric
1991   *Postmodernism: The Cultural Logic of Late Capitalism*. Durham, NC: Duke University Press.

Jenkins, Rhys
2002   "The Political Economy of Codes of Conduct." In *Corporate Responsibility and Labour Rights: Codes of Conduct in the Global Economy*, ed. R. Jenkins, R. Pearson, and G. Seyfant, 13–30. Sterling, VA: Earthscan Publications Ltd.

Jha, Nitish
2004   "Gender and Decision Making in Balinese Agriculture." *American Ethnologist* 31(4): 552–572.

Johnson, P.
2006   "Situación Actual de los Mercados Justos en Guatemala." Guatemala: Programa de las Naciones Unidas para el Desarrollo.

Johnston, Josee
2002   "Global Justice: Fair Trade Shopping and Alternative Development." In *Protest and Globalisation: Projects for Transnational Solidarity*, ed. J. Goodman, 38–56. Annadale, NSW: Pluto Press.

Jonas, Susanne
1991   *The Battle for Guatemala: Rebels, Death Squads and U.S. Power*. Boulder, CO: Westview.
2000   *Of Centaurs and Doves: Guatemala's Peace Process*. Boulder, CO: Westview.

Jordan, Mary
2004   "The Cappuccino Effect: Quality Beans Revive Guatemala's Coffee Industry." *Washington* [DC] *Post*. October 17, p. 1.

Joseph, Miranda
2002   *Against the Romance of Community*. Minneapolis: University of Minnesota Press.

Kaplinsky, Raphael
2000   "Globalisation and Unequalisation: What Can Be Learned from Value Chain Analysis." *Journal of Development Studies* 37(2): 117–147.

Keck, Margaret E., and Kathryn Sikkink
1998   *Activists beyond Borders: Advocacy Networks in International Politics*. Ithaca, NY: Cornell University Press.

Works Cited

Kovic, Christine
    2005   *Mayan Voices for Human Rights: Displaced Catholics in Highland Chiapas.* Austin: University of Texas Press.

LaFeber, Walter
    1983   *Inevitable Revolutions: The United States in Central America.* New York: W. W. Norton.

Larner, Wendy
    2000   "Neo-Liberalism: Policy, Ideology, Governmentality." *Studies in Political Economy* 63: 5–25.

Levi, Jerome M., and Bartholomew Dean
    2003   "Introduction." In *At the Risk of Being Heard: Identity, Indigenous Rights, and Postcolonial States,* ed. Bartholomew Dean and Jerome Levi, 1–33. Ann Arbor: University of Michigan Press.

Lewin, Bryan, Daniele Giovannucci, and Panos Varangis
    2004   *Coffee Markets: New Paradigms in Global Supply and Demand.* Washington, DC: World Bank.

Li, Victor
    2000   "What's in a Name? Questioning 'Globalization.'" *Cultural Critique* 45: 1–39.

Lindsey, Brink
    2004   *Grounds for Complaint? Fair Trade and the Coffee Crisis.* London: Adam Smith Institute.

Little, Walter
    2004   *Mayas in the Marketplace: Tourism, Globalization and Cultural Identity.* Austin: University of Texas Press.
    2008   "A Visual Political Economy of Maya Representations in Guatemala, 1931–1944." *Ethnohistory* 55(4): 633–663.

Lobdell, William
    2004   "A House Blend Featuring Social, Economic Justice: Religious Groups Sell 'Fair-Trade' Coffee at Above-Market Prices to Assist Small Farmers in Developing Nations." *Los Angeles Times.* October 2, p. 2. http://articles.latimes.com/2004/oct/02/local/me-beliefs2 (accessed 10/14/10).

Lockie, Stewart, and Michael Goodman
    2006   "Neoliberalism and the Problem of Space: Competing Rationalities of Governance in Fair Trade and Mainstream Agri-Environmental Networks." In *Between the Local and the Global: Confronting Complexity in the Contemporary Agri-Food Sector,* ed. T. Marsden and J. Murdoch, 95–120. New York: Elsevier.

Lorenzetti, Linda Rice
    1999   "Grounds for Giving: Innovative Programs for People in Coffee Producing Countries." *Tea and Coffee Trade Journal* (April).

Luetchford, Peter
 2007 *Fair Trade and a Global Commodity: Coffee in Costa Rica*. London: Pluto Press.
 2008 "The Hands that Pick Fair Trade Coffee: Beyond the Charms of the Family Farm." *Research in Economic Anthropology* 28: 143–169.

Lukacs, Georg
 1971 *History and Class Consciousness: Studies in Marxist Dialects*. Cambridge, MA: MIT Press.

Lyon, Sarah
 2006 "Evaluating Fair Trade Consumption: Politics, Defetishization and Producer Participation." *International Journal of Consumer Studies* 30(5): 452–464.
 2007 "Maya Coffee Farmers and Fair Trade: Assessing the Benefits and Limitations of Alternative Markets." *Culture and Agriculture* 29(2): 100–112.

Lyon, Sarah, Josefina Aranda Bezaury, and Tad Mutersbaugh
 2010 "Gender Equity in Fairtrade-Organic Coffee Producer Organizations: Cases from Mesoamerica." *Geoforum* 41(1): 93–103.

Malkki, Lisa
 1990 "Context and Consciousness." In *Nationalist Ideologies and the Production of National Cultures*, ed. R. Fox, 2: 32–62. American Ethnological Society Monograph Series. Washington, DC: American Anthropological Association.

Mayoux, L.
 2001 "Impact Assessment of Fair Trade and Ethical Enterprise Development." http://www.enterprise-impact.org.uk/pdf/IAofFairTrade.pdf.

M'Closkey, Kathy
 2010 "NOVICA, Navajo Knock-offs and the 'Net: A Critique of Fair Trade Marketing Practices." In *Fair Trade and Social Justice: Global Ethnographies*, ed. S. Lyon and M. Moberg, 258–282. New York: New York University Press.

McCreery, David
 1986 "An Odious Feudalism: Mandamiento Labor and Commercial Agriculture in Guatemala, 1858–1920." *Latin American Perspectives* 31(1): 99–117.
 1994 *Rural Guatemala, 1760–1940*. Stanford, CA: Stanford University Press.
 1995 "Wage Labor, Free Labor, and Vagrancy Laws: The Transition to Capitalism in Guatemala, 1920–1945." In *Coffee, Society and Power in Latin America*, ed. W. Roseberry, L. Gudmundson, and M. S. Kutschbach, 206–231. Baltimore: Johns Hopkins University Press.
 2003 "Coffee and Indigenous Labor in Guatemala, 1871–1980." In *The Global Coffee Economy in Africa, Asia and Latin America 1500–1989*, ed. W. G.

Clarence-Smith and S. Topik, 191–208. Cambridge: Cambridge University Press.

McDonald, James H.

1999   "The Neoliberal Project and Governmentality in Rural Mexico: Emergent Farmer Organizations in the Michoacan Highlands." *Human Organization* 58(3): 274–284.

McEwan, Patrick J., and Marisol Trowbridge

2007   "The Achievement of Indigenous Students in Guatemalan Primary Schools." *International Journal of Educational Development* 27: 61–76.

Mehan, G. Tracy

2005   "Birds on the Brain." *The American Spectator*. October 1. http://www.high beam.com/doc/1P3-910266831.html (accessed 10/14/10).

Menchu, Rigoberta

1983   *I, Rigoberta Menchu: An Indian Woman in Guatemala*. London: Verso.

Méndez, V. Ernesto, Stephen R. Gliessman, and Gregory S. Gilbert

2007   "Tree Biodiversity in Farmer Cooperatives of a Shade Coffee Landscape in Western El Salvador." *Agriculture, Ecosystems and Environment* 119: 145–159.

Mendoza, R., and J. Bastiaensen

2003   "Fair Trade and the Coffee Crisis in the Nicaraguan Segovias." *Small Enterprise Development* 14(2): 36–46.

Merry, Sally Engle

1984   "Rethinking Gossip and Scandal." In *Reputation: Studies in the Voluntary Elicitation of Good Conduct*, ed. Daniel Klein, 47–74. Ann Arbor: University of Michigan Press.

Micheletti, Michelle

2003   *Political Virtue and Shopping: Individuals, Consumerism and Collective Action*. New York: Palgrave Macmillan.

Milford, Anna

2004   "Coffee, Cooperatives and Competition: The Impact of Fair Trade." Bergen: Chr. Micheleson Institute. http://www.cmi.no/publications/2004%5Crep%5Cr2004-6.pdf.

Miller, Daniel

1998   "Conclusion: A Theory of Virtualism." In *Virtualism: A New Political Economy*, ed. J. G. Carrier and D. Miller, 187–216. New York: Berg.

Mintz, Sidney

1985   *Sweetness and Power: The Place of Sugar in Modern History*. New York: Penguin Books.

Moberg, Mark
  2005   "Fair Trade and Eastern Caribbean Banana Farmers: Rhetoric and Re-
          ality in the Anti-Globalization Movement." *Human Organization* 64(1):
          4–16.

Moguel, Patricia, and Victor M. Toledo
  1999   "Review: Biodiversity Conservation in Traditional Coffee Systems of
          Mexico." *Conservation Biology* 13(1): 11–21.

Molyneux, Maxine
  2002   "Gender and the Silences of Social Capital: Lessons from Latin Ameri-
          ca." *Development and Change* 33(2): 167–188.

Moore, Geoff
  2004   "The Fair Trade Movement: Parameters, Issues and Future Research."
          Journal of Business Ethics 53: 73–86.

Moors, Marilyn M.
  1988   "Indian Labor and the Guatemalan Crisis: Evidence from History and
          Anthropology." In *Central America: Historical Perspectives on the Contem-
          porary Crisis*, ed. Ralph Lee Woodward Jr., 67–83. New York: Green-
          wood Press.

Morgan, Kevin, and Jonathan Murdoch
  2000   "Organic vs. Conventional Agriculture: Knowledge, Power and Innova-
          tion in the Food Chain." *Geoforum* 31: 159–173.

Municipalidad
  2005   "Diagnóstico de la Situación ante el Desastre del 5 de Octubre del 2005."
          Municipalidad de San Juan La Laguna, Departamento Solota, Guatema-
          la, C.A.

Muradian, Roldan, and Wlim Pelupessy
  2005   "Governing the Coffee Chain: The Role of Voluntary Regulatory Sys-
          tems." *World Development* 33(12): 2029–2044.

Murray, Douglas L., Laura T. Raynolds, and Peter L. Taylor
  2003   "One Cup at a Time: Poverty Alleviation and Fair Trade Coffee in Latin
          America." Fort Collins, CO: Fair Trade Research Working Group.
  2006   "The Future of Fair Trade Coffee: Dilemmas Facing Latin America's
          Small-Scale Producers." *Development in Practice* 16(2): 179–192.

Mutersbaugh, Tad
  2002   "The Number Is the Beast: A Political Economy of Organic Coffee Cer-
          tification and Producer Unionism." *Environment and Planning* A 34: 1165–
          1184.
  2003   "Ethical Trade and Certified Organic Coffee: Implications of Rules-
          Based Agricultural Product Certification for Mexican Producer House-
          holds and Villages." *Transnational Law and Contemporary Problems* 12:
          89–107.

2004 "Serve and Certify: Paradoxes of Service Work in Organic-Coffee Certification." *Environment and Planning D: Society and Space* 22: 533–552.

Nash, June
1993a "Introduction: Traditional Arts and Changing Markets in Middle America." In *Crafts in the World Market: The Impact of Global Exchange on Middle American Artisans*, ed. J. Nash, 1–24. Albany: State University of New York Press.

1993b "Maya Household Production in the World Market: The Potters of Amatenango del Valle, Chiapas, Mexico." In *Crafts in the World Market: The Impact of Global Exchange on Middle American Artisans*, ed. J. Nash, 127–154. Albany: State University of New York Press.

2005 "Introduction: Social Movements and Global Processes." In *Social Movement: An Anthropological Reader*, ed. June Nash, 1–26. Malden, MA: Blackwell Press.

Nash, June, Jorge Dandler, and Nicholas Hopkins, eds.
1976 *Popular Participation in Social Change*. The Hague: Moulton.

Nash, Manning
1958 *Machine Age Maya: The Industrialization of a Guatemalan Community*. Chicago: University of Chicago Press.

Nelson, Diane
1999 *A Finger in the Wound: Body Politics in Quincentennial Guatemala*. Berkeley: University of California Press.

2001 "Stumped Identities: Body Image, Bodies Politic, and the Mujer Maya as Prosthetic." *Cultural Anthropology* 16(3): 314–354.

2004 "Anthropologist Discovers Legendary Two-Faced Indian! Margin, the State, and Duplicity in Postwar Guatemala." In *Anthropology in the Margins of the State*, ed. V. Das and D. Poole, 117–140. Santa Fe, NM: School of American Research.

New York Times
2003 Small Town Life—The Village and the Nation. *New York Times*. February 25, A3.

Nicholls, Alex, and Charlotte Opal
2005 *Fair Trade: Market-Driven Ethical Consumption*. Thousand Oaks, CA: Sage Publications.

Nigh, Ronald
1976 "Evolutionary Ecology of Maya Agriculture in Highland Chiapas, Mexico." PhD diss., Stanford University. Ann Arbor: University Microfilms.

1997 "Organic Agriculture and Globalization: A Maya Associative Corporation in Chiapas, Mexico." *Human Organization* 56(4): 427–436.

2002 "Poverty Alleviation through Participation in Fair Trade Coffee Networks: Comments on the Implications of the Mexico Reports." Fort

Collins, CO: Fair Trade Research Working Group. http://welcome2
.libarts.colostate.edu/centers/cfat/wp-content/uploads/2009/09/
Commentary-on-Mexico-findings.pdf (accessed 10/14/10).

OCIA
2004   "Organic Crop Improvement Association International, Inc." Interna-
          tional Certification Standards, Vol. 2004. Effective July 6, 2004. Lincoln,
          NE: OCIA.

O'Connor, Mike
2005   "Geeks of a Feather." *New Scientist*. May 7, p. 21.

O'Neil, Brendan
2007   "How Fair Is Fairtrade?" BBC News, March 7. http://news.bbc.co.uk/2
          /hi/uk_news/magazine/6426417.stm.

Ortiz, Sutti
1973   *Uncertainties in Peasant Farming: A Colombian Case.* London: Athlone Press.

Oxfam
2004   *Trading away Our Rights: Women Working in the Global Supply Chain.* Lon-
          don: Oxfam International.

Paige, Jeffrey M.
1997   *Coffee and Power: Revolution and the Rise of Democracy in Central America.*
          Cambridge, MA: Harvard University Press.

Patrinos, Harry Anthony, and Eduardo Velez
2009   "Costs and Benefits of Bilingual Education in Guatemala: A Partial
          Analysis." *International Journal of Educational Development* 29: 594–598.

Paul, Benjamin
1999   "Education Changes in San Pedro La Laguna." Conference paper pre-
          sented at American Anthropology Association annual meeting, Chicago.

Paul, Benjamin, and William Demarest
1988   "The Operation of a Death Squad in San Pedro La Laguna." In *Harvest
          of Violence: The Maya Indians and the Guatemalan Crisis*, ed. R. Carmack,
          119–154. Norman: University of Oklahoma Press.

Paul, Elisabeth
2005   "Evaluating Fair Trade as a Development Project." *Development in Prac-
          tice* 15(2): 134–150.

Pearce, Jenny
1998   "From Civil War to 'Civil Society': Has the End of the Cold War Brought
          Peace to Central America." *International Affairs* 74(3): 587–615.

Pels, Peter
2000   "The Trickster's Dilemma: Ethics and the Technologies of the An-
          thropological Self." In *Audit Cultures: Anthropological Studies in Account-*

ability, Ethics and the Academy, ed. M. Strathern, 135–172. New York: Routledge.

Pendergrast, Mark
1999   *Uncommon Grounds: The History of Coffee and How It Transformed Our World*. New York: Basic Books.
2004   "Green Mountain Coffee Roasters: Doing Well by Doing Good." *Tea and Coffee Trade Journal Online* 178(3). http://www.teaandcoffee.net/0404/retail.htm (accessed 11/23/09).

Perezgrovas Garza, Victor Cervantes Trejo, and Edith Cervantes Trejo
2002   "Poverty Alleviation through Participation in Fair Trade Coffee Networks: The Case of Union Majomut, Chiapas, Mexico." Fort Collins, CO: Fair Trade Research Working Group. http://welcome2.libarts.colostate.edu/centers/cfat/wp-content/uploads/2009/09/Case-Study-Unión-Majomut-Chiapas-Mexico.pdf (accessed 10/14/10).

Perfecto, Ivette, Robert A. Rice, Russell Greenberg, and Martha E. van der Voort
1996   "Shade Coffee: A Disappearing Refuge for Biodiversity." *BioScience* 46(8): 598–608.

Petkova, Iva
2006   "Shifting Regimes of Governance in the Coffee Market: From Secular Crisis to a New Equilibrium?" *Review of International Political Economy* 13(2): 313–339.

Pigg, Stacy
1993   "Unintended Consequences: The Ideological Impact of Development in Nepal." *South Asia Bulletin* 13(1/2): 45–58.

Pimentel, David, Ulrich Stachow, David A. Takacs, Hans W. Brubaker, Amy R. Dumas, John J. Meaney, John A.S. O'Neil, Douglas E. Onsi, and David B. Corzilius
1992   "Conserving Biological Diversity in Agricultural/Forestry Systems." *BioScience* 42(5): 354–362.

Pine, B Joseph, II, and James H. Gilmore
1998   "Welcome to the Experience Economy." *Harvard Business Review* (July/August): 97–105.

Plattner, Stuart
1985   "Equilibrating Market Relationships." In *Markets and Marketing: Monographs in Economic Anthropology*, ed. S. Plattner, 133–152. New York: University Press of America.

Plaza Sanchez, Jose Luis
1998   "Organic Coffee Production and the Conservation of Natural Resources in Las Margaritas, Chiapas." In *Timber, Tourists and Temples: Conservation and Development in the Maya Forest of Belize, Guatemala and Mexico*, ed. R. B. Primack, D. B. Bray, H. A. Galletti, and I. Ponciano, 299–315. Washington, DC: Island Press.

Polanyi, Karl
    1985   *The Great Transformation.* Boston: Beacon Press.

Ponte, Stefano
    2002   "The 'Latte Revolution'? Regulation, Markets and Consumption in the Global Coffee Chain." *World Development* 30(7): 1099–1307.

Postero, Nancy, and Leon Zamosc
    2004   "Indigenous Movements and the Indian Questions in Latin America." In *The Struggle for Indigenous Rights in Latin America*, ed. N. Postero and L. Zamosc, 1–31. Portland, OR: Sussex Academic Press.

Power, Michael
    1996   "Making Things Auditable." *Accounting, Organizations and Society* 21: 289–315.
    2003   "Accounting." *Accounting, Organizations and Society* (28): 379–394.

Pratt, Jeffrey
    2008   "Food Values: The Local and the Authentic." *Research in Economic Anthropology* 28: 53–70.

Prechtel, Martin, and Robert S. Carlsen
    1988   "Weaving and Cosmos amongst the Tzutujil Maya." *Res* 15: 122–132.

Putnam, Robert D.
    2000   *Bowling Alone: The Collapse and Revival of American Community.* New York: Simon and Schuster.

Querna, Elizabeth
    2004   "Become a Birder." *U.S. News and World Report* 137: 78.

Rabinow, Paul
    1997   *Reflections on Fieldwork in Morocco.* Berkeley: University of California Press.

Raikes, P., M. F. Jensen, and S. Ponte
    2000   "Global Commodity Chain Analysis and the French Filière Approach: Comparison and Critique." *Economy and Society* 29(3): 390–417.

Raynolds, Laura T.
    2000   "Re-embedding Global Agriculture: The International Organic and Fair Trade Movements." *Agriculture and Human Values* 17: 297–309.
    2002   "Consumer/Producer Links in Fair Trade Coffee Networks. *Sociologia Ruralis* 42(4): 404–424.
    2004   The Globalization of Organic Agro-Food Networks." *World Development* 32(5): 725–743.
    2008   "The Organic Agro-Export Boon in the Dominican Republic: Maintaining Tradition or Fostering Transformation?" *Latin American Research Review* 43(1): 161–184.

Works Cited

Raynolds, Laura T., Douglas Murray, and Andrew Heller
   2007   "Regulating Sustainability in the coffee Sector: A Comparative Analysis
           of Third-Party Environmental and Social Certification Initiatives." *Agri-
           culture and Human Values* 24(2): 147–163.

Raynolds, Laura T., Douglas Murray, and Peter Taylor
   2004   "Fair Trade Coffee: Building Producer Capacity via Global Networks."
           Journal of International Development 16(8): 1109–1121.

Redfern, Andy, and Paul Snedker
   2002   "Creating Market Opportunities for Small Enterprises: Experiences of
           the Fair Trade Movement." Seed Working Paper No. 30. Geneva: ILO.
           http://www.bdsknowledge.org/dyn/bds/docs/220/wp30-2002.pdf
           (accessed 10/14/10).

Redfield, Robert, and Alfonso Villa Rojas
   1934   *Chan Kom*. Washington, DC: Carnegie Institute.

REMHI
   1999   *Guatemala Never Again!* Maryknoll, NY: Orbis Books for the Recovery of
           Historical Memory Project.

Restrepo, Jairo
   1996   *Abonos Organicos: Experiencias de Agricultores en Centroamerica y Brasil.*
           San Jose, Costa Rica: CEDECO Corporacion Educativa del Desarrollo
           Costarricense.

Rice, Robert A., and Jennifer McLean
   1999   "Sustainable Coffee at the Crossroads." Washington, DC: Consumers
           Choice Council.

Rice, Robert A., and Justin R. Ward
   1996   *Coffee, Conservation and Commerce in the Western Hemisphere: How Indi-
           viduals and Institutions Can Promote Ecologically Sound Farming and Forest
           Management in Northern Latin America.* Washington, DC: Natural Re-
           sources Defense Council and Smithsonian Migratory Bird Center.

Rodas, N., O. Flavio, C. Rodas, and L. F. Hawkins
   1940   *Chichicastenango: The Kiche Indians, Their History and Culture.* Guatemala
           City: Union Typografica.

Rodriguez, George
   2004   "Less Education Means More Child Labor." *Latin America Press* 26:7
           (December 29): 7.

Ronchi, Lisa
   2002   *The Impact of Fair Trade Producers and their Organizations: A Case Study
           with Coocafe in Costa Rica*, vol. 2006. Brighton, UK: University of Sussex.

Roper, J. Montgomery, Thomas Perreault, and Patrick C. Wilson
   2003   "Introduction." *Latin American Perspectives* 39(1): 5–22.

Roseberry, William
1995   "Introduction." In *Coffee, Society and Power in Latin America*, ed. W. Rose-
        berry, L. Gudmundson, and M. Kutschbach, 1–37. Baltimore: Johns
        Hopkins University Press.
1996   "The Rise of Yuppie Coffees and the Reimagination of Class in the
        United States." *American Anthropologist* 98(4): 762–775.

Roseberry, William, Lowell Gudmundson, and Mario Semper Kutschbach, eds.
1995   *Coffee, Society and Power in Latin America*. Baltimore: Johns Hopkins Uni-
        versity Press.

Routledge, P.
1997   "Imagineering of Resistance: Pollok Free State and the Practice of Post-
        modern Politics." *Transactions of the Institute of British Geographers* 22:
        359–376.

Sanford, Victoria
2003   *Buried Secrets: Truth and Human Rights in Guatemala*. New York: Palgrave
        Macmillan.

Schirmer, Jennifer
1998   *The Guatemalan Military Project: A Violence Called Democracy*. Philadel-
        phia: University of Pennsylvania Press.

Schmitz, Hubert
2000   "Global Competition and Local Cooperation: Success and Failure in the
        Sinos Valley Brazil." *World Development* 27(9): 1627–1650.

Scott, James C.
1972   *Comparative Political Corruption*. Englewood Cliffs, NJ: Prentice-Hall.
1976   *The Moral Economy of the Peasant: Rebellion and Subsistence in Southeast
        Asia*. New Haven, CT: Yale University Press.
1985   *Weapons of the Weak: Everyday Forms of Peasant Resistance*. New Haven,
        CT: Yale University Press.

Sexton, James
1972   *Education and Innovation in a Guatemalan Community: San Juan La Lagu-
        na*. Los Angeles: Latin American Center University of California Los
        Angeles.
1985   *Campesino: The Diary of a Guatemalan Indian*. Tucson: University of Ari-
        zona Press.

Shore, C., and S. Wright
2004   "Whose Accountability? Governmentality and the Auditing of Univer-
        sities." *Parallax* 10(2): 100–117.

Shreck, Aimee
2002   "Just Bananas? Fair Trade Banana Production in the Dominican Re-
        public." *International Journal of Sociology of Agriculture and Food* 10(2):
        25–52.

Works Cited

Sick, Deborah

1997   "Coping with Crisis: Costa Rica Households and the International Coffee Market." *Ethnology* 36(3): 255–275.

1999   *Farmers of the Golden Bean: Costa Rican Households and the Global Coffee Economy.* DeKalb: Northern Illinois University Press.

Sidwell, Mark

2008   *Unfair Trade.* London: Adam Smith Institute. http://www.adamsmith.org/images/pdf/unfair_trade.pdf (accessed 10/28/09).

Silver, Sara

2003   "Coffee's Crisis Stirs Traders to Take Action." *Financial Times*, May 14.

Simpson, Charles, and Anita Rapone

2000   "Community Development from the Ground Up: Social Justice Coffee." *Human Ecology Review* 7(1): 46–57.

Smart, Alan

1993   "Gifts, Bribes, and Guanxi: A Reconstruction of Bourdieu's Social Capital." *Cultural Anthropology* 8(3): 388–408.

Smith, Carol

1978   "Beyond Dependency Theory: National and Regional Patterns of Underdevelopment in Guatemala." *American Ethnologist* 5: 574–617.

1984   "Local History in Global Contexts: Social and Economic Transformations in Western Guatemala." *Comparative Studies in Society and History* 26: 193–228.

1990   "Class Position and Class Consciousness in an Indian Community: Totonicapan in the 1970s." In *Guatemalan Indians and the State, 1540–1988*, ed. C. Smith and M. Moors, 205–229. Austin: University of Texas Press.

Smith, Julia

2010   "Fair Trade and the Specialty Coffee Market: Growing Alliances, Shifting Rivalries." In *Fair Trade and Social Justice: Global Ethnographies*, ed. S. Lyon and M. Moberg, 28–46. New York: New York University Press.

Smith, Sally, and Catherine Dolan

2006   "Ethical Trade: What Does It Mean for Women Workers in African Horticulture." In *Ethical Sourcing in the Global Food System*, ed. S. Barrientos and C. Dolan, 79–95. London: Earthscan Press.

Starbucks

N.d.   http://www.starbucks.ch/en-US/_Worlds+Best+Coffee/Geography+is+a+flavour.htm (accessed 9/10/10).

Starr, Amory, and Jason Adams

2003   "Anti-globalization: The Global Fight for Local Autonomy." *New Political Science* 25(1): 19–42.

Stecklow, Steve, and Erin White
  2004   "How Fair Is Fair Trade? That's Tough to Figure." *Wall Street Journal*, June
          8. http://www.globalexchange.org/campaigns/fairtrade/coffee/2066
          .html (accessed 10/14/10).

Stephen, Lynn
  1993   "Weaving in the Fast Lane: Class, Ethnicity, and Gender in Zapotec
          Craft Commercialization." In *Crafts in the World Market*, ed. J. Nash,
          25–57. Albany: State University of New York Press.
  2005   *Zapotec Women: Gender, Class and Ethnicity in Globalized Oaxaca*. Dur-
          ham, NC: Duke University Press.

Stepputat, Finn
  2001   "Urbanizing the Countryside: Armed Conflict, State Formation, and
          the Politics of Place in Contemporary Guatemala." In *States of Imagina-
          tion: Ethnographic Explorations of the Postcolonial State*, ed. T. B. Hansen
          and F. Stepputat, 284–313. Durham, NC: Duke University Press.

Stoll, David
  1999   *Rigoberta Menchu and the Story of All Poor Guatemalans*. Boulder, CO:
          Westview Press.

Stonich, Susan C.
  1994   "Producing Food for Export: Environmental Quality and Social Jus-
          tice Implications of Shrimp Mariculture in Honduras." In *Who Pays the
          Price?* ed. B. R. Johnston, 110–120. Washington, DC: Island Press.

Strathern, Marilyn
  2005   "Robust Knowledge and Fragile Futures." In *Global Assemblages: Tech-
          nology, Politics and Ethics as Anthropological Problems*, ed. A. Ong and S. J.
          Collier, 464–481. Malden, MA: Blackwell Publishing.

Talbot, John
  2002   "Tropical Commodity Chains, Forward Integration Strategies and In-
          ternational Inequality: Coffee, Cocoa and Tea." *Review of International
          Political Economy* 9(4): 701–734.
  2004   *Grounds for Agreement: The Political Economy of the Coffee Commodity
          Chain*. Lanham, MD: Rowman and Littlefield.

Tallontire, Anne
  2000   "Partnerships in Fair Trade: Reflections from a Case Study of Cafedi-
          rect." *Development in Practice* 10(2): 166–177.

Taussig, Michael
  1980   *The Devil and Commodity Fetishism in South America*. Chapel Hill: Univer-
          sity of North Carolina Press.

Tax, Sol
  1937   "The Municipios of the Midwestern Highlands of Guatemala." *Ameri-
          can Anthropologist* 39: 423–444.

1953   *Penny Capitalism: A Guatemalan Indian Economy*. Washington, DC: Smithsonian Institution, Institute of Social Anthropology.

Taylor, Peter

2002   *Poverty Alleviation through Participation in Fair Trade Coffee Networks: Synthesis of Case Study Research Question Findings*. New York: Community and Resource Development Program, The Ford Foundation.

2004   "In the Market But Not of It: Fair Trade Coffee and Forest Stewardship; Council Certification as Market-Based Social Change." *World Development* 33(1): 129–147.

Tea and Coffee Trade Journal

1994   "The Plight of Coffee's Children." *Tea and Coffee Trade Journal* 174(1): 20.

Tendler, Judith

1983   *What to Think about Cooperatives: A Guide from Bolivia*. Rosslyn, VA: Inter-American Foundation.

Tendler, Judith, and Monica Alves Amorim

1996   "Small Firms and Their Helpers: Lessons on Demand." *World Development* 24(3): 407–426.

Topik, Steven, and William Gervase Clarence-Smith

2003a   "Conclusion: New Propositions and a Research Agenda." In *The Global Coffee Economy in Africa, Asia, and Latin America 1500–1989*, ed. W. G. Clarence-Smith and S. Topik, 385–410. Cambridge: Cambridge University Press.

2003b   "Introduction: Coffee and Global Development." In *The Global Coffee Economy in Africa, Asia, and Latin America 1500–1989*, ed. W. G. Clarence-Smith and S. Topik, 1–17. Cambridge: Cambridge University Press.

Topik, Steven, Carlos Marichal, and Zephyr Frank

2006   "Commodity Chains in Theory and in Latin American History." In *From Silver to Cocaine: Latin American Commodity Chains and the Building of the World Economy, 1500–2000*, ed. S. Topik, C. Marichal, and Z. Frank, 1–24. Durham, NC: Duke University Press.

TransFair

2009   "Fair Trade Almanac 2008." http://transfairusa.org/pdfs/almanac_2008.pdf (accessed 1/29/10).

N.d.   TransFair website http://transfairus.org (accessed 6/05).

Tsing, Anna

1993   *In the Realm of the Diamond Queen: Marginality in an Out-of-the-Way Place*. Princeton, NJ: Princeton University Press.

2005   *Friction: An Ethnography of Global Connections*. Princeton, NJ: Princeton University Press.

UN
    2007   "Crime and Development in Central America: Caught in the Cross
            Fire." New York: United Nations Office on Drugs and Crime.

UNDP
    2002   *Informe 2002 Guatemala: Desarrollo Humano, Mujeres y Salud*. Guatemala
            City: UNDP.

Utting-Chamorro, Karla
    2005   "Does Fair Trade Make a Difference? The Case of Small Coffee Produc-
            ers in Nicaragua." *Development in Practice* 15(3–4): 584–599.

Vander Hoff Boersma, Franz
    2002   "Poverty Alleviation through Participation in Fair Trade Coffee Net-
            works: The Case of UCIRI, Oaxaca, Mexico." Fort Collins, CO: Fair Trade
            Research Working Group. http://welcome2.libarts.colostate.edu/
            centers/cfat/wp-content/uploads/2009/09/Case-Study-UCIRI-Oaxaca-
            Mexico.pdf (accessed 10/14/10).

Varangis, Panos
    2003   "Dealing with the Coffee Crisis in Central America: Impacts and Strate-
            gies." In World Bank Policy Research Working Paper: Washington, DC:
            World Bank. http://ideas.repec.org/p/wbk/wbrwps/2993.html (accessed
            10/14/10).

Wagley, Charles
    1941   *Economics of a Guatemalan Village*. Menasha, WI: American Anthropo-
            logical Association.

Wagner, Regina
    2001   *The History of Coffee in Guatemala*. Bogota: Villegas Editores.

Wallengren, Maja
    2000   "Mexico's Organic Coffee: More than Caffeine!" *Tea and Coffee Trade
            Journal* 172(8): 40.

Wallerstein, Immanuel
    1974   *The Modern World System*. New York: Academic Press.

Walsh, Andrew
    2004   "In the Wake of Things: Speculating in and about Sapphires in North-
            ern Madagascar." *American Anthropologist* 106(2): 225–237.

Warner, K.
    1991   *Shifting Cultivators: Local Technical Knowledge and Natural Resource Man-
            agement in the Humid Tropics*. Rome: Food and Agriculture Organization
            of the United States.

Warren, Kay B.
    1978   *The Symbolism of Subordination: Maya Identity in a Guatemalan Town*.
            Austin: University of Texas Press.

1998   *Indigenous Movements and Their Critics: Pan-Maya Activism in Guatemala.* Princeton, NJ: Princeton University Press.

Wasserstrom, Robert
1975   "Revolution in Guatemala: Peasants and Politics under the Arbenz Government." *Comparative Studies in Society and History* 17(4): 443–478.

Watanabe, John M.
1992   *Maya Saints and Souls in a Changing World.* Austin: University of Texas Press.
1995   "Unimagining the Maya: Anthropologists, Others and the Inescapable Hubris of Authorship." *Bulletin of Latin American Research* 14(1): 25–45.

Waterbury, Ronald
1989   "Embroidery for Tourists: A Contemporary Putting-Out System in Oaxaca, Mexico." In *Cloth and Human Experience*, ed. A. B. Weiner and J. Schneider, 243–271. Washington, DC: Smithsonian Institution Press.

Weiss, Brad
2003   *Sacred Trees, Bitter Harvests: Globalizing Coffee in Northwest Tanzania.* Portsmouth, NH: Heinmann.

Werner, Cynthia
2000   "Gifts, Bribes and Development in Post-Soviet Kazakstan." *Human Organization* 59(1): 11–22.

West, Harry, and Todd Sanders
2003   *Transparency and Conspiracy: Ethnographies of Suspicion in the New World Order.* Durham, NC: Duke University Press.

West, Paige
2006   *Conservation Is Our Government Now.* Durham, NC: Duke University Press.

Whatmore, Sarah, and Lorraine Thorne
1997   "Nourishing Networks: Alternative Geographies of Food." In *Globalising Food: Agrarian Questions and Global Restructuring*, ed. D. Goodman and M. Watts, 287–304. London: Routledge.

Wilk, Richard
1991   *Household Ecology: Economic Change and Domestic Life among the Kekchi Maya in Belize.* Tucson: University of Arizona Press.
1995   "Learning to be Local in Belize: Global Systems of Common Difference." In *Worlds Apart: Modernity through the Prism of the Local*, ed. D. Miller, 110–133. London: Routledge.
1997   "Emerging Linkages in the World System and Challenge to Economic Anthropology." In *From Local to Global*, ed. T. Hall and R. Banton, 97–105. Lanham, MD: University Press of America.

2006 "The Ecology of Global Consumer Culture." In *The Environment in Anthropology: A Reader in Ecology, Culture and Sustainable Living*, ed. N. Haenn and R. Wilk, 418–426. New York: New York University Press.

Wilkinson, John
2006 *Fair Trade Moves Centre Stage*. Rio de Janeiro: The Edelstein Center for Social Research.

Williams, Robert G.
1994 *States and Social Evolution: Coffee and the Rise of National Governments in Central America*. Chapel Hill: University of North Carolina Press.

Wilson, Patrick J.
1974 "Filcher of Good Names: An Enquiry into Anthropology and Gossip." *Man* 9(1): 93–102.

Wolf, Eric
1966 *Peasants*. Englewood Cliffs, NJ: Prentice-Hall.
1982 *Europe and the People without History*. Berkeley: University of California Press.

Woodward, Ralph Lee, Jr.
1990 "Changes in the Nineteenth-Century Guatemalan State and Its Indian Policies." In *Guatemalan Indians and the State: 1540–1988*, ed. Carol Smith and Marilyn Moors, 52–71. Austin: University of Texas Press.
1999 *Central America: A Nation Divided*, 3rd ed. New York: Oxford University Press.

World Conservation Union and Future Harvest
2001 *Common Ground, Common Future: How Eco-Agriculture Can Help Feed the World and Save Wild Biodiversity*. Washington, DC: Future Harvest.

WFP (World Food Programme)
2009 "Guatemala Overview." http://www.wfp.org/countries/guatemala (accessed 10/27/2009).

Zorn, Elayne
2004 *Weaving a Future: Tourism, Cloth and Culture on an Andean Island*. Iowa City: University of Iowa Press.

Index

Page numbers in italics indicate illustrations.

Index